THE POLICING OF TRANSNATIONAL PROTEST

Advances in Criminology
Series Editor: David Nelken

Titles in the Series

University of Hertfordshire

College Lane, Hatfield, Herts AL10 9AB

Learning and Information Services

For renewal of Standard and One Week Loans,
please visit the website: **http://www.voyager.herts.ac.uk**

This item must be returned or the loan renewed by the due date.
The University reserves the right to recall items from loan at any time.
A fine will be charged for the late return of items.

The Policing of
Transnational Protest

Edited by

DONATELLA DELLA PORTA
European University Institute, Italy

ABBY PETERSON
University of Gothenburg, Sweden

HERBERT REITER
European University Institute, Italy

ASHGATE

Published by
Ashgate Publishing Limited
Gower House
Croft Road
Aldershot
Hampshire GU11 3HR
England

Ashgate Publishing Company
Suite 420
101 Cherry Street
Burlington, VT 05401-4405
USA

Ashgate website: http://www.ashgate.com

British Library Cataloguing in Publication Data
The policing of transnational protest. - (Advances in criminology)
   1. Riot control 2.Demonstrations 2.Protest movements
   I.Della Porta, Donatella, 1956- II.Peterson, Abby
   III.Reiter, Herbert
   363.3'2

Library of Congress Cataloging-in-Publication Data
The policing of transnational protest / edited by Donatella della Porta, Abby Peterson and Herbert Reiter.
     p. cm. -- (Advances in criminology)
   Includes bibliographical references and index.
   ISBN-13: 978-0-7546-2676-3
   ISBN-10: 0-7546-2676-8
  1. Police. 2. Demonstrations. 3. Riot control. 4. Protest movements. I. Della Porta, Donatella, 1956- II. Peterson, Abby. III. Reiter, Herbert.

   HV7921.P587 2006
   363.32'3--dc22

2006018468

ISBN-13: 978-0-7546-2676-3
ISBN-10: 0 7546 2676 8

Printed and bound in Great Britain by Antony Rowe Ltd, Chippenham, Wiltshire.

Contents

List of Figures and Tables

Figures

Tables

List of Contributors

Donatella della Porta, professor of Sociology, Department of Political and Social Sciences, European University Institute, Florence, Italy. Currently she is involved in several comparative projects on citizenship and social movements. Among her recent publications on transnational protest and protest policing are: with Massimiliano Andretta, Lorenzo Mosca and Herbert Reiter, *Globalization from Below* (Minneapolis, University of Minnesota Press, 2006); with Olivier Fillieule (eds), *Police et manifestants* (Paris, Presses de Science Po, 2006); with Sidney Tarrow (eds), *Transnational Protest and Global Activism* (New York, Rowman and Littlefield, 2004); and with Herbert Reiter, *Polizia e protesta* (Bologna, Il Mulino, 2003) and (eds) *Policing Protest. The Control of Mass Demonstration in Western Democracies* (Minneapolis, University of Minnesota Press, 1998).

Olivier Fillieule, professor of Political Sociology, Institut d'Etudes Politiques et Internationales, University of Lausanne. He is co-editor, with Donatella della Porta, of *Police et manifestants* (Paris, Presses de Science Po, 2006); editor of *Le désengagement militant* (Paris, Belin, 2005); co-author, with Eric Agrikoliansky and Nonna Mayer, of *L'altermondialisme en France* (Paris, Flammarion, 2005); and co-author, with Mounia Bennani-Chraïbi, of *Résistances et protestations dans les sociétés musulmanes* (Paris, Presses de Sciences Po, 2002). He is also the author of *Stratégies de la rue. Les manifestations en France* (Paris, Presses de Sciences Po, 1997).

Patrick F. Gillham, assistant professor in Sociology, Department of Sociology, Anthropology, and Justice Studies, University of Idaho. His research focuses on social movements, the policing of protest, and globalization. Recent work includes his PhD dissertation on 'Mobilizing for Global Justice: Social Movement Organization Involvement in Three Contentious Episodes, 1999–2001' (2003); with Gary T. Marx, 'Complexity and Irony in Policing and Protesting: The World Trade Organization in Seattle' (*Social Justice,* 2000); and with John Noakes and Brian Klocke, 'Whose Streets? Police and Protester Struggles Over Space in Washington, D.C., September 29–30, 2001' (*Policing and Society*, 2005).

Mike King, professor of Criminal Justice, Centre for Criminal Justice Policy and Research, School of Social Sciences, UCE Birmingham. He is an expert on police and policing. He has published widely on national and international policing issues and his works on policing public order include (with Nigel Brearley) *Public Order Policing: Contemporary Perspectives on Strategy and Tactics* (Leicester, Perpetuity Press, 1996).

John Noakes, Department of Sociology, Anthropology and Criminal Justice, Arcadia University. He teaches Criminal Justice and Sociology courses at Arcadia University, where he is the coordinator of the Criminal Justice major. His research focus is on social movements and the policing of protest. He is co-editor with Hank Johnston of *Frames of Protest* (Lanham, MD, Rowman and Littlefield, 2005), author of 'Official Frames in Social Movement Theory: The FBI, HUAC, and the Communist Threat in Hollywood' (*Sociological Quarterly,* 2000), and co-author of 'Whose Streets? Police and Protester Struggles Over Space in Washington, DC, September 29–30, 2001' (*Policing and Society*, 2005).

Mikael Oskarsson, Department of Criminology, Stockholm University. He is a police inspector and currently holds a position as an advisor at the Ministry of Justice in Sweden. He recently received his PhD from the University of Stockholm on the police handling of the EU Summit meeting in Gothenburg in 2001.

Abby Peterson, professor of Sociology, Department of Sociology, Gothenburg University, Sweden. She has worked extensively on social movements and police issues. She is the author of *Neo-Sectarianism and Rainbow Coalitions: Youth and the Drama of Immigration in Contemporary Sweden* (Aldershot and Brookfield, VT, Ashgate, 1997) and *Contemporary Political Protest: Essays on Political Militancy* (Aldershot and Brookfield, VT, Ashgate, 2001). She also edited, together with Micael Björk, *Policing Contentious Politics in Sweden and Denmark* (Maastricht, Shaker Verlag, 2006).

Herbert Reiter, historian and researcher, European University Institute, Florence, Italy. He has published extensively on the policing of protest, including, with Donatella della Porta, *La protesta e il controllo. Movimenti e forze dell'ordine nell'era della globalizzazione* (Milan, Berti/Altreconomia, 2004); *Polizia e protesta* (Bologna, Il Mulino, 2003); and (eds), *Policing Protest. The Control of Mass Demonstration in Western Democracies* (Minneapolis, University of Minnesota Press, 1998). He has also published, with Donatella della Porta, Massimiliano Andretta and Lorenzo Mosca, *Globalization from Below* (Minneapolis, University of Minnesota Press, 2006).

David Waddington, Cultural Studies, Department of Communication Studies, Sheffield Hallam University. He teaches Sociology with a strong focus on police and public order. He is the author of *Contemporary Issues in Public Disorder: A Comparative and Theoretical Approach* (London, Routledge, 1992); co-author (with Chas Critcher and Karen Jones) of *Flashpoints: Studies in Public Disorder* (London, Routledge, 1989); and co-editor (with Chas Critcher) of *Policing Public Order* (Aldershot, Avebury, 1996). His latest book, *Public Order Policing – Theory and Practice*, is due to be published by Willan in 2007.

Mattias Wahlström, researcher, Department of Sociology, Gothenburg University, Sweden. He is writing his PhD on learning processes in connection with the policing of protest.

Acknowledgements

This book is the result of a workshop held on the west coast of Sweden in May 2004, which brought the authors together with colleagues for four days of lively discussions. We wish to extend our appreciation to our colleagues who used this time to comment upon and generally mangle our texts – James Sheptycki, Janne Flyghed, John D. McCarthy, Andrew Martin, Clark McPhail, Micael Björk, P.A.J. (Tank) Waddington, and Anneli Bergholm-Söder. The workshop was made possible by generous funding from the Swedish Academy of Sciences. Last, we wish to extend our heartfelt thanks to Sarah Tarrow, who has had the thankless job of making our texts readable.

Chapter 1

Policing Transnational Protest: An Introduction

Donatella della Porta, Abby Peterson and Herbert Reiter

Policing transnational protest: New strategies for managing public order?

The 1999 protest events in Seattle made the American and global publics aware of the existence of a mass movement which, after years of social and political tranquillity, was again challenging not only specific policy choices, but also the dominant model of societal development. If in the 1980s social movements had been described as increasingly institutionalized, preferring lobbying to protest, at the turn of the millennium street politics again became visible – and concurrently, so did the interactions between protesters and police forces.

As in earlier cycles of protest, social movements are again testing the limits of demonstration rights and civil liberties within national states, but also with a new transnational quality. A specific characteristic of this wave of protest is, in fact, a high degree of transnationalism: the global justice movement not only appeals to cosmopolitan identities, but also organizes more and more transnationally. If the movement's capacity to be truly global is still an open question, there is no doubt that the cycle of protest that became visible in Seattle developed intense interactions within transnational networks.

In particular – and this is one of the topics at the heart of this volume – protest increasingly tended to target international institutions. The most visible forms of protest are organized around (or against) summits of international governmental organizations (IGOs), from the (more criticized) financial institutions such as the World Trade Organization (WTO), the International Monetary Fund (IMF), and the World Bank to 'elite' informal networks like the G8 or the World Economic Forum; from macro-regional organizations such as the European Union (EU) or the North American Free Trade Agreement (NAFTA) to global ones like the United Nations (UN). Large demonstrations are organized during *counter-summits*, defined as arenas of 'international-level initiatives during official summits and on the same issues but from a critical standpoint, heightening awareness through protest and information with or without contacts with the official version' (Pianta 2002, 35). After some preliminary experiences in the 1980s, especially on the occasion of large-scale UN conferences, counter-summits multiplied over the succeeding decade, supported by frenetic activity of NGOs claiming to represent not only their hundreds of thousands of members, but, more generally, the interests of millions of citizens without a public voice in transnational arenas.

Even before the emergence of the global justice movement, protest had been increasingly directed against IGOs. Especially in the case of the EU, recent research has debated the existence of a Europeanization of conflict (Imig and Tarrow 2002; Rucht 2002). However, the farmers' organizations and trade unions (and also environmental organizations) did not initially question the decision making practised within the EU (Ruzza 2004). For the global justice movement, on the other hand, one of the major objectives is denouncing the lack of democratic legitimacy in this supranational process (della Porta et al. 2006; della Porta 2004).

Elaborating on older traditions, in particular civil disobedience, the activists of the global justice movement also developed innovative action repertoires that set them apart from established social movement organizations. Attempting to penetrate 'red zones' during counter-summits, demonstrators in Prague, Gothenburg and Genoa were perfecting what in Great Britain is called 'pushing and shoving' – that is, shoulder-to-shoulder confrontations between police and strikers at picket lines. Also crucial in the revival of civil disobedience in demonstrations against neoliberal globalization is symbolic provocation: 'Confrontations are staged at the fence – but not only the ones involving sticks and bricks: tear-gas canisters have been flicked back with hockey sticks, water cannon have been irreverently challenged with toy water pistols and buzzing helicopters, mocked with swarms of paper airplanes' (Klein 2002, XXV).

If the counter-summits represent strategic adaptation by social movements to the perceived shift of decision-making power from nation states to supranational institutions, police counterstrategies to control this form of protest have also adapted to the (perceived) nature of the challenge: 'red zones' were established as part of larger efforts to remove the targets of the protests in time or space from demonstrators; individual police officers are more commonly equipped with 'less-lethal' arms; databanks of 'travelling troublemakers' have been constructed; special anti-insurgent units have been created; and in some cases the military has also been deployed for public order tasks. These new strategies challenge social scientists' approaches to protest policing.

For many years a neglected issue in the social science literature, the policing of protest did attract attention in the 1980s and 1990s. Quantitative research, based mainly upon large-scale cross-national designs, addressed the issue of the causes (Poe, Tate and Camp Keith 1999; Davenport 1995; Poe and Tate 1994) and effects (Moore 1998; Francisco 1996; Gupta, Singh and Sprague 1993; Opp and Roehl 1990; Lichbach 1987) of repression. At the same time, ethnographic approaches and case studies contributed to the analysis of police behaviour in public order intervention (Waddington and Critcher 2000; Critcher and Waddington 1996; P.A.J. Waddington 1994; D. Waddington 1992; D. Waddington, Jones and Critcher 1989). The collection on *Policing Protest: The Control of Mass Demonstration in Western Democracies*, edited by Donatella della Porta and Herbert Reiter (1998a), introduced the concept of *protest policing*. Social movements have been seen as challengers directing their demands to institutions chiefly through forms of protest. Their very use of unconventional forms of action involves the State, not just as a counterpart in negotiating the movement's objectives, but also as the guarantor of public order. Accordingly, one important aspect of the institutional response to protest is the strategies for controlling it.

Although the policing of protest is much more brutal in authoritarian regimes, where challenges to public order not infrequently end in massacres (see, among others, Sheptycky 2005 on Latin America; Uysal 2005 on Turkey), encounters between demonstrators are a very delicate issue in democratic regimes as well. For police in modern democratic societies, indeed, *protest policing*, that is, the control of protest, requires a difficult balance between the protection of legal order and the defence not only of individual freedom, but also of citizens' rights to political participation, and thus the very essence of the democratic system. The public order strategies employed by police are in fact reflected in citizens' perceptions of the respect the State shows toward their rights and freedoms. In this sense, the way in which a police officer intervenes in order to control protest is perceived as an indicator of the quality of democracy in the political system (della Porta and Reiter 1998b).

Empirical research has indicated that the policing of protest not only functions as an indicator of the willingness of the political authority to listen to the voices of protesters, but also affects the evolution of protest. Repression might indeed thwart protest, by increasing the costs of challenging authorities; when, however, the protest is widespread and well supported, repression can backfire due to outrage about police disrespect for citizens' rights at the national as well as the transnational level (Davenport 2005b; Francisco 2005). Different effects of repressive behaviours have been related to the timing of police intervention as well as to the characteristics of the affected social and political groups. However, it is also true that protest has an impact on police forces and strategies. The policing of protest is a key feature for the development and the self-definition of the police as an institution and as a profession. Its gradual affirmation as the main agency specializing in this task was of fundamental importance to the process of modernization and professionalization of the European police forces in the nineteenth and twentieth centuries. Moreover, waves of protest have had important effects on both police strategies and the organization of the police – observed, for instance, by Jane Morgan (1987) in her research on the police in Britain. In contemporary democratic societies, the way in which the police address protest seems to be a significant aspect of its self-image (Winter 1998a).

According to many studies, the 1968 protest wave had a profound impact on protest policing. A by-product of the increasing legitimacy of (once) unconventional forms of political participation has been an increasing tolerance of protest by the police. From the 1970s onwards, modes of controlling protest in Western democracies became generally more tolerant and the traditional strategy of 'escalated force' (based on harsh repression of even minor forms of transgression) more rare with the development of a strategy of 'negotiated management' (della Porta and Fillieule

2004; McPhail, Schweingruber and McCarthy 1998). Police forces implemented new public order strategies based on the search for dialogue with the new social movements, marked by less frequent recourse to force and growing tolerance towards new forms of protest, even formally unlawful ones such as civil disobedience. Over the same period, students of social movements wondered if they were becoming institutionalized, or at least 'civilized', with a reduction in more radical forms of action.

After decades of apparent 'normalization' of the confrontation between police and protest, what had been considered by many as a generally accepted 'post-1968 standard' proved fragile when confronted by the mass demonstrations of an emerging transnational movement. Indeed, in the history of what came to be known as the global justice movement (or the movement for a 'globalization from below' or a 'globalization of rights'), clashes between police and demonstrators have been frequent. Authorities have typically attributed responsibility for those clashes to the extreme fringes of the movement – whom they allege to have used urban guerrilla tactics – but also to the movement as a whole, accusing it of ambiguous positions on the question of violence. The police, on the other hand, have been criticized by the movement and a sizeable part of public opinion for disproportionate actions infringing upon the civil rights of the majority of peaceful demonstrators. In its 'Report on the Situation of Fundamental Rights in the European Union and its Member States in 2002' (2003a, 58), the EU Network of Independent Experts in Fundamental Rights (CFR–CDF), set up by the European Commission in September 2002, emphasized that 'Police conduct at demonstrations organized on the occasion of big international summit meetings constitutes a source of particular concern.' Even the movement's more moderate sections have seen the clashes 'on the street' as part of a broader strategy of repression against the movement: not coincidentally, Naomi Klein titled a section of her book *Fences and Windows* (2002) 'Fencing in the Movement. Criminalizing Dissent'. After Seattle, Jackie Smith (2001, 16) warned: 'The repression faced by protesters should raise warning flags for scholars of social movements about how globalization affects democracy.'

Criticism of the police is not limited to their intervention 'in the streets', but extends to operations during the preparatory phase of demonstrations. They have been accused of trying to impede demonstrations, either by an outright ban[1] or by obstructing access to the demonstration site;[2] of suspending the free movement of people inside the EU by reintroducing border controls; of dubious intelligence activities and intrusive Internet surveillance; of indiscriminate searches of private homes and organizations' offices, on a weak legal basis; and of various acts of

---

1   For example, in Davos in 2001 or in Munich in February 2002; on other occasions, as in Prague in September 2000, an initial ban was lifted by court order.

2   At the World Economic Forum in Davos in January 2003, or the peace rally in New York City in February 2003, where the police had refused to grant a parade permit.

intimidation, either directly[3] or indirectly, by making protest seem so scary that potential participants are discouraged from attending (Klein 2002, 133ff.).

It was, however, media images of police intervention during demonstrations that focused the world's attention on the conflict between police and protest. In Seattle, on the occasion of the protests against the WTO meeting in November 1999 and at numerous subsequent demonstrations, the police were accused of excessive use of force, directed also against peaceful demonstrators and innocent bystanders. Criticism was directed specifically against the indiscriminate use of tear gas and other less lethal weapons, including protesters not involved in violent behaviour or posing any threat to property or police. The use of firearms at Gothenburg (EU Summit, June 2001) – which would repeat itself just a month later at Genoa with more tragic consequences – led to the recommendation by the UN Human Rights Committee (in its concluding observations on the fifth periodic report on Sweden) that the State ensure that no equipment that could endanger human life be used during demonstrations. Reports of unjustified arrests and, above all, disrespect for the rights of people in police custody, from verbal abuse to physical maltreatment, accompanied numerous demonstrations, among them Seattle, Prague, Gothenburg, Genoa, Barcelona (in June 2001 and in March 2002) and New York City (15 February 2003).

What human rights activists refer to as the 'criminalization' of protest includes the massive use of intelligence,[4] often legitimized as an alternative to brutal intervention on the street. Especially in the wave of increasing investigative power granted to the police by recent antiterrorist laws, restrictions on individual freedoms and individual rights have been presented as necessary in order to defend democracy. Emergency laws and regulations have extended the potential for legally tapping individual communications and monitoring the Internet, violating individual privacy and restricting freedom of expression (EU Network 2003b; *New York Times*, 23 November 2003).

Criticism was also raised with regard to the judicial proceedings: some have talked of 'judicial repression' for the trials of demonstrators; in connection with judicial proceedings against members of the police forces, various human rights organizations and institutions have warned of a climate of impunity. Police fabrication of evidence against demonstrators was alleged in connection with proceedings concerning the events in Gothenburg, Genoa and Saloniki (EU Summit, June 2003).

One of the main sets of questions addressed by the contributions collected in this volume is: are we witnessing the re-emergence of the escalated force model, or the development of a new repressive protest policing style? Can we observe a definite break with the de-escalating, negotiated model of protest policing that dominated

---

3   For example, in Munich in February 2002, associations involved in the preparation of the demonstration against the NATO security meeting were threatened with a cut-off of public funding.

4   Davenport (2005) defined this as domestic intelligence techniques such as electronic and physical surveillance, mail opening and the use of informants and *agents provocateurs*.

in the 1980s and well into the 1990s? Or is the control of transnational counter-summits an exception in a policing of protest that remains mainly negotiated? Or is the escalation in Seattle and afterwards proof that the de-escalating strategies were only applied in some spaces (for instance, in Washington, DC) and to some political groups (for example, the more 'civilized' new social movements), while more repressive strategies dominated elsewhere (see McPhail and McCarthy 2005)? Although our contributors do not aim to provide a definitive answer on these issues, they will stress the presence of some continuities and innovations in the policing of counter-summits, with a mix of (often incoherently carried out) negotiations and use of (more or less restrained) coercive force, the construction of no-go areas and increasing intolerance for minor violations and the massive use of intelligence and legal repression. Additionally, our research indicates that the policing of counter-summits can be interpreted as a continuum, in which assessments of the policing of previous counter-summits are exchanged and discussed among the different police forces, resulting in both similarities and variations in the strategies chosen (see in particular the chapters by della Porta and Reiter; Peterson; and King and Waddington).

Explaining the policing of transnational protest: Where to look

A further set of questions addressed by the chapters collected in this volume refers to how this evolution in protest policing can be explained: to what extent do transnational events present special challenges for police as well as for protesters? What specific threats does the movement improperly termed 'no-global' present to police forces and governments? What internal features of police forces, or external factors that influence them, have facilitated the escalation?

In this context, the volume's empirical studies do in fact have theoretical relevance. Is the explanatory model developed in *Policing Protest* (della Porta and Reiter 1998a), which emphasized a processual, relational interpretation of protest policing styles, still useful in understanding these recent changes in public order policing? Several hypotheses presented in that model, but also in the more recent research on protest policing, will be discussed in the various contributions: the new challenge re/presented by transnational protest (from the heterogeneous social and political characteristics of protesters and their weak capacity (or willingness) for self-policing, to the need to protect foreign dignitaries); the shift in the political opportunities for challengers, related, among other factors, to the development of multilevel governance; the strength of civil rights versus law-and-order coalitions in 'postdemocracies' (Crouch 2004); and the ongoing reorganization of police structures as well as innovations in public order tactics and equipment. As suggested in *Policing Protest*, the impact of these variables on protest policing styles is filtered through 'police knowledge', that is, how the police perceive their role and the surrounding society. Of particular relevance in this context are the images of protesters developed by the police, especially their views of the new actors emerging during the recent protest waves. How do police perceive social movements characterized by 'tolerant' identities and plural repertoires of action (della Porta et al. 2006)?

The contributions collected in this volume address some of the main hypotheses developed in the social sciences to explain police behaviour, focusing on the specific challenges presented by transnational protest and the global justice movement. First, police have been said to be sensitive to their environment, to the characteristics of the perceived threat but also to the expected demands from authorities and public opinion. Research on the police has stressed that the organizational imperative is keeping control over situations, rather than enforcing the law (Rubinstein 1980; Bittner 1967; Skolnick 1966). Police officers indeed enjoy a high degree of discretion in their encounters with citizens. However, they must also maintain (to different extents) the support of authorities and the public. Research on the policing of social movements has identified a tendency to use harsher styles of protest policing against social and political groups that are perceived as larger threats to political elites, as being more ideologically driven or more radical in their aims (see della Porta and Fillieule 2004; Earl 2003; Davenport 2000, 1995). Additionally, police repression is more likely to be directed against groups that are poorer in material resources as well as in political connections (Earl, Soule and McCarthy 2003; della Porta 1998).

In our case studies, we shall stress that the policing of counter-summits addresses situations and groups that are considered particularly threatening by political authorities and the police. On the one hand, the presence of foreign personalities imposes the defence of their security as a priority (see chapter by King and Waddington); and on the other hand, any challenge to the guests or the summit will be seen as internationally delegitimizing by the host governments. But, even more, some of the very characteristics of the global justice movement – such as its heterogeneity, use of direct action, multi-issue identity, and presumed 'anti-politics' – correspond to police and political authorities' definition of high threat (see chapters by della Porta and Reiter, Noakes and Gillham, and Peterson). A history of escalation at counter-summits increases mutual mistrust and discourages negotiations (see in particular Wahlström and Oskarsson as well as chapters by della Porta and Reiter).

Beyond the external factors, internal characteristics of the police forces – their organizational resources and professional culture – are also considered as important explanations behind different protest policing styles. Degree of militarization, legal competences, and degree of professionalization all play a role in the definition of police styles; there is more country variation in federal states where police training and organization are decentralized (see McPhail and McCarthy 2005; Winter 1998a; Wisler and Kriesi 1998) and a more important role for the national leadership in more centralized institutions (see, for instance, Cunningham 2004 on the FBI). As for the policing in and after Seattle, our contributors stress the importance of the trend towards militarization in police training and equipment (see McPhail and McCarthy 2005 on the development of SWAT (Special Weapons and Tactics) police units during the war on drugs, and their increasing use in public order policing; see also Kraska and Kaeppler 1997). With an original insight with respect to previous research, Noakes and Gillham underline the importance of shifts in the dominant visions of the causes of crime and in the corresponding conceptual principles underlying police intervention for protest policing, in particular the implications of the 'new penology' with its emphasis on protection and risk management. Zero-tolerance doctrines, as well as militaristic training and equipment, are imported into the field of protest policing from other forms of public order control addressing micro-criminality or football hooliganism. Special units constructed for the fight against organized crime and terrorism also have been frequently deployed at counter-summits. These developments and circumstances may have lowered the cost of repression through what has been defined as 'coercive habituation' (Davenport 2005b, xii; see also Gurr 1986, 60).

There is, however, one further explanation for the weak defence of demonstration rights observed in the policing of counter-summits. As Reiter and Fillieule's chapter argues in depth, while protest is becoming more and more transnational, protest rights remain state-centred. States maintain the right to reduce freedom of movement to non-nationals. Additionally, the policing of transnational events tends to involve international policing, characterized by a very low level of democratic accountability (Sheptycki 2002, 1994). The involvement of multiple law enforcement agencies, as well as secret services, further reduces internal coordination and external controls on police intervention. A supranational public sphere capable of keeping a critical eye on the defence of citizens' rights is emerging (as, for instance, the wave of international protest against police brutality at the Genoa counter-summit indicates); but it is still weak and surfaces only occasionally.

These are some of the questions discussed in the contributions to this volume, via a systematic analysis covering a large set of cases of transnational protest, from the US (WTO protest in Seattle and IMF/WB protest in Washington), Canada (among others, the protest against the Organization of the American States (OAS) Summit in Ontario and the Summit of the Americas in Quebec City) and Europe (anti-EU counter-summits in Gothenburg and Copenhagen, anti G8 protests in Genoa and the European Social Forum in Florence). Research methods used for the in-depth analysis of the policing of transnational protests include interviews with activists and police officers, focus groups, participant observation and content analysis of judicial procedures and the press.

Beyond describing and explaining the styles developed for the control of transnational protest events, the dense narratives collected in this volume address the normative issues involved in transnational protest policing (especially in the development of a supranational level of control of protest and demonstration rights). The protection of a public space for political deliberations, which extends to the squares and streets of democratic societies, is crucial for the enhancement of democratic discourses in a globalizing world.

The content of this volume

In order to address these questions, the first chapters of the book bring the reader's attention to the policing of transnational protest in Western Europe, presenting case studies of specific protest events that focus in depth upon the interactions between protesters and police. In their contribution, 'The Policing of Global Protest: The G8 at Genoa and its Aftermath', Donatella della Porta and Herbert Reiter analyse the special challenges that new forms of protest associated with the global justice movement presented for the police forces committed to containing them; factors internal to the Italian police forces (organizational structure, public order strategies, dominant images of demonstrators, democratic accountability) that influenced police intervention; and intervening external factors, above all the institutional political responses to this new wave of protest. The authors weigh these three different sets of variables in their analysis of the violent events that played out in conjunction with the G8 Summit meeting in Genoa in 2001. While della Porta and Reiter find explanatory power for understanding the brutality of the police action in Genoa in factors related to the new forms of protest as well as to internal aspects of the Italian police forces, they argue that this hardening of the police response to the global justice movement finds its main explanation in the relative closure of domestic as well as transnational political opportunities to the claims presented by this new collective actor(s). What we witnessed in Genoa, they argue, can be seen as a partial reaffirmation of the traditional response to new 'challengers' in Italy; that is, an overall strategy of exclusion that lies behind the subsequent heavy-handedness of the police response to these new challengers. The Genoa case is then contrasted with the policing of the first European Social Forum in Florence, where learning processes on both sides contributed to the peaceful outcome of the gathering and the concluding mass demonstration.

In the third chapter, 'Policing Contentious Politics at Transnational Summits: Darth Vader or the Keystone Cops?', Abby Peterson examines and compares police responses to the political protest events staged in conjunction with European Union summit meetings in two Scandinavian countries: in Sweden (Gothenburg) in 2001, and in Denmark (Copenhagen) in 2002. In contrast with the Italian case, both countries represent state institutional structures that are relatively open to challenges posed by new political actors. Nevertheless, police forces in both countries responded to these new challengers with different degrees of repression, which jeopardized, also to different extents and in different ways, constitutionally guaranteed political and civil liberties. For Gothenburg, Peterson describes an overall police strategy wedded to the occupation of territorial spaces, with an excessive use of coercive force and non-selective forms of mass arrest. She argues that the dysfunctional police strategy, the breakdown of the command and communication structure, and a police culture that readily demonized the protesters gathered in the city, together with poorly trained and poorly equipped officers, led to what is best described as police riots. The protests against the European Summit in neighbouring Copenhagen a year later, which were largely peaceful and orderly, were a dramatic contrast to these violent events. The policing of protest in this case is characterized as a textbook example of the new (in the Scandinavian context) strategy developed by police chief Kai Vittrup: on the one hand assigning considerable importance to negotiation, on the other hand based on a paramilitary operation and command structure and characterized by an offensive propensity aimed at keeping control of situations, both expected and unexpected, by always maintaining the initiative. While the spaces for democratic protest were less significantly threatened in this case, encroachments upon civil liberties occurred nonetheless, and both direct and indirect threats to the rights of protesters took place, albeit in more subtle ways than in Gothenburg or Genoa.

The following two chapters map and evaluate changing trends in public order policing in North America. Mike King and David Waddington's chapter, 'The Policing of Transnational Protest in Canada', examines seven major public order events that occurred in Canada between 1997 and 2002, leading up to and including the 2002 G8 Summit in Kananaskis. The authors maintain that the policing of 'national' protest events in the mid-1990s had gelled into a recognizable 'two pronged' model characterized by conciliatory and consultative processes on the one hand, and an increasingly militarized and *potentially* overtly offensive and escalatory public order strategy on the other. Following Ericson and Doyle (1999), they argue that where 'international protected persons' (IPPs) were present and economic and trade interests were at stake, the policing was openly coercive. However, also at transnational events where IPPs were not present, policing was covertly coercive even while police consulted and negotiated with protesters in some respects. They refer to this latter trend as a 'superficially soft-hat' policing mode. This new form of covertly coercive protest policing identified by King and Waddington in Canada dovetails with the 'smart' mode of policing Peterson observed in the Danish case.

In 'Aspects of the "New Penology" in the Police Response to Global Justice Protests in the United States, 1999–2000', John Noakes and Patrick F. Gillham study the 'strategic and tactical chess match between global justice protesters and police' on the basis of three recent events in the US: the WTO protests in Seattle; the 2000 IMF/World Bank meetings in Washington, DC; and the Republican National Convention in Philadelphia. Despite differences in the cases studied, the authors contend that a new mode of policing has surfaced, and new strategies and innovative tactics have been developed to respond to global justice protests. It was the increase in the numbers of 'transgressive' protesters rejecting contained forms of action that led to a crisis of negotiated management. Focusing on police philosophy, Noakes and Gillham argue that the development of negotiated management had drawn heavily on penal modernism, the paradigmatic philosophy in criminal justice in the US after World War II. In dealing with the most recent waves of transnational protests, officials now drew heavily on new penology, the current dominant philosophy. The authors maintain that these new public order strategies, while not a return to the escalated force style, privilege control and protection against the disruption caused by transgressive demonstrators, with recourse to coercive preventive intervention aimed at selectively incapacitating these demonstrators. Negotiated management strategies, intended to diffuse tension and guarantee demonstrator rights through detailed negotiations regarding the planned protest event, find application only with contained demonstrators (which are the clear majority).

The role played by negotiations between protesters and police in connection with transnational protest events in two Scandinavian cities is analysed by Mattias Wahlström and Mikael Oskarsson in their chapter on 'Negotiating Political Protest in Gothenburg and Copenhagen'. Negotiations, both prior to and during protest events, open channels for a de-escalation of violence and, as such, can play an important role in the maintenance and protection of democratic spaces for political contention. The authors found evidence in both of the cases studied that negotiations played a role, while limited, for defusing potentially violent situations. However, negotiations and the forging of mutual agreements are carried out under considerable constraints – for example, asymmetric relations between the parties based on their respective legal powers and access to intelligence, as well as the lack of authority that both police and protester negotiators may have in their own groups and organizations. Past experiences are an important element underlying reactions on both sides. Prior interactions with protesters are brought to bear on how the police respond to future protests. Like other factors influencing police response, these experiences are filtered through what della Porta and Reiter (1998b) have called police knowledge, that is, police images about their role and the external reality. Wahlström (2004) has developed the concomitant notion of 'activist knowledge'. Just as the police filter internal and external factors for policing, together with past experiences of interactions with activists, activists filter attendant factors and experiences through a similar body of knowledge. In their chapter, Wahlström and Oskarsson analyse activist knowledge as it manifested itself in Gothenburg and Copenhagen. They also map the 'transnational' learning processes of activists who brought their (direct and indirect) experiences from the confrontations in Gothenburg to bear upon their experiences of negotiations with police in Copenhagen.

In their chapter 'Formalizing the Informal: The EU Approach to Transnational Protest Policing', Herbert Reiter and Olivier Fillieule argue that the transnational nature of contentious politics today, highlighted in this volume, necessitates an understanding of the increasingly transnational response to it, in terms of both politics and public order. Reiter and Fillieule look at the ways in which the European Union is beginning to come to terms with transnational protest within its borders. The European Council reacted, in fact with specific measures to the rise of the global justice movement. These measures aimed at furthering information exchange and cooperation among the national police forces of the Member States within the institutional framework of the EU – repeatedly criticized for shortcomings in transparency of decision making, involvement of parliaments and democratic accountability. As Reiter and Fillieule argue, the movement challenges European institutions' openness to participation from below and the limits of protest rights, formalized at the EU level in human rights conventions, but until recently rarely tested in their concrete forms and boundaries beyond the national level.

Donatella della Porta and Herbert Reiter conclude this volume discussing if and how new protest policing styles are developing in the face of transnational protest.

Enriching the empirical material presented in this volume with a comparative overview of police responses to major political protest events since the 'battle of Seattle', the authors single out the new elements in public order policing in an era of global political contention. They emphasize as common elements the tendency to control demonstrations by (if need be, forceful) preventive exclusion of certain activists and action repertoires and extensive protection of protest targets, often making protest invisible. In these instances of protest policing, the element of protection of demonstration rights has definitely moved into the background, while 'control' has taken on a new quality due to the possibilities of 'information-led' policing and communication technologies. While policing styles are selective and changing, with new reciprocal adaptations of police and demonstrators strategies in each new wave of protest, the model developed for the explanation of policing protest (della Porta and Reiter 1998a) still seems valid. Indeed, protest policing still depends on internal (police organizations and police culture/philosophy) and external (political opportunities as well as civil rights and law-and-order coalitions) factors, as filtered through police knowledge of protesters and other political and social actors. At this explanatory level, the cases collected in this volume help to focus on some relevant elements that had remained under-theorized in previous research – first and foremost, transnational political opportunities and the characteristics of transnational policing. The transnational level of protest and policing presents new challenges for the development of a commonly accepted definition of demonstration rights in democracies.

Chapter 2

The Policing of Global Protest:
The G8 at Genoa and its Aftermath[1]

Donatella della Porta and Herbert Reiter

Public order and international summits: An introduction

Research has singled out three main interrelated strategic areas for protest control
that the police have favoured differently in various historical periods (della Porta
and Reiter 1997): *coercive strategies*, that is, the use of weapons and physical
force to control or disperse demonstrations; *persuasive strategies*, meaning all
attempts to control protest through discursive contacts with activists and organizers;
and *information strategies*, consisting of widespread information gathering as a
preventive feature in protest control, as well as the targeted collection of information
(sometimes using modern audiovisual technologies) to identify law-breakers without
having to intervene directly.

Police actions can vary in terms of force used ('brutal' or 'soft'), the extent
of conduct regarded as illegitimate (ranging between repression and tolerance),
strategies for controlling the various actors (generalized or selective), police respect
for the law (illegal or legal), the moment when police act (pre-emptive or reactive),
degree of communication with demonstrators (confrontation or consensus), capacity
to adjust to emerging situations (rigid or flexible), degree of formalization of the
rules of the game (formal or informal) and the degree of training (professional or
improvised) (della Porta and Reiter 1998b, 4). It has been noted that the combination
of these dimensions tends to define two different internally consistent protest policing
styles (see Table 2.1). The first (*escalated force*) gives low priority to the right
to demonstrate: innovative forms of protest are poorly tolerated, communication
between police and demonstrators is reduced to essentials and there is frequent
use of coercive or even illegal methods (such as *agents provocateurs*). The second
(*negotiated management*), by contrast, prioritizes the right to demonstrate peacefully:
even disruptive forms of protest are tolerated, communication between demonstrators
and police is considered basic to the peaceful conduct of protest, and coercive means
are avoided as much as possible, emphasizing selectivity of operations (della Porta
and Fillieule 2004; McPhail, Schweingruber and McCarthy 1998, 51–4). To these

---

1 A first version of this chapter was translated by Iain L. Fraser.

Table 2.1   Protest control strategies

	Escalated force	Negotiated management	Italy in the 1980s and 1990s	Demonstrations against the G8 in Genoa
Coercive strategies	Massive use of force to deter even minor violations	Tolerance of minor breaches	Selective toleration	Massive use of force even against peaceful demonstrators
Strategies of negotiation	Intimidating use of relations with organizers	Partnership aimed at ensuring the right to demonstrate	Informal negotiations	Low trust in negotiation
Information strategies	Generalized information gathering	Information gathering focused on punishing offences	Generalized information gathering	Generalized information gathering, and alarmist use of information

dimensions one might add the type of information strategy that police forces employ in controlling protest, with a distinction between generalized control and control focusing on those possibly guilty of an offence.

In Western democracies, we can note a radical transformation in strategies for controlling public order and the associated operational practices and techniques: particularly following the great protest wave that culminated in the late 1960s, there was a trend from *escalated force* to *negotiated management*. While the widespread conception of the right to demonstrate dissent has tended to become more inclusive, intervention strategies have moved away from the coercive model predominant until then. During the 1970s and 1980s, although there were pauses and temporary reversals, we may note a trend towards growing tolerance of 'minor' breaches of the law. Among the changes apparent in strategies for controlling public order is a reduction in the use of force, greater emphasis on 'dialogue' and the investment of significant resources in gathering information (della Porta and Reiter 1998a).

These strategies, called de-escalation (or also, in the Italian case, prevention), are based on a number of specific pathways and assumptions. Prior to demonstrations, demonstrator representatives and police meet and negotiate in detail as to routes and conduct to be observed during demonstrations (including the more or less symbolic violations permitted to demonstrators). Police charges are never aimed at peaceful groups, agreements reached with demonstration representatives are respected and lines of communication between demonstration organizers and police are held open throughout the demonstration. The police must, first and foremost, guarantee the right to demonstrate peacefully: violent groups are separated from the rest of the march and stopped without endangering the security of the peaceful demonstrators (della Porta 1998; Fillieule and Jobard 1998; McPhail, Schweingruber and McCarthy 1998; Winter 1998a; P.A.J. Waddington 1994).

Though these are developments common to Western democracies, differences remain among the various national models in State responses to the new 'challengers'. In postwar Italy, in the special climate of 'Cold Civil War', a particularly marked form of the *escalated force* style developed.[2] While the early 1960s, with centre-left governments in power, were typified by *détente*, elements of traditional strategies re-emerged in connection with 1968, which in Italy was particularly long and conflict ridden. During the 1980s and 1990s we can identify a shift from the *escalated force* style to *negotiated management*, albeit with some peculiarities. This change was promoted not so much by the political institutions as by the movement for democratization and demilitarization of the police that developed within the state police force, basic to the 1981 reform that led to the demilitarization and unionization of the state police (della Porta and Reiter 2003).

In *coercive strategies*, there was less and less recourse to force, although a harsher control repertoire survived, particularly against the social centres[3] but also in controlling hooliganism on football grounds. *Persuasive strategies* evolved from the use of various forms of intimidation to negotiation toward the common end of the peaceful holding of demonstrations. By contrast with other countries, however, negotiating practices were not formalized, nor did police officers specializing in dialogue with organizers emerge, with a possible 'opportunistic' use of negotiation. Smaller changes came in the use of *information strategies*, consistent with the all-pervading traditional Italian conception of the police as chief intelligence gatherer of the State (della Porta 1998).

Even 'policing by consent' (P.A.J. Waddington 1998) is a police strategy to *control* protest, albeit one that respects demonstrators' rights and freedoms as far as possible. What was seen by many as the consolidated 'post-68' standard, no longer in question, proved fragile when faced with the new challenge of a transnational protest movement. The Genoa G8 Summit re-ignited an almost forgotten debate on the fundamental rights of citizens and the question of how much power the State is allowed in protecting the rule of law (*Der Spiegel* 31/2001, 22ff.). Police forces that had, in a period of demand for greater security by citizens, seen themselves legitimized – in the Italian case first by the fight against terrorism and later regarding organized crime – were again being associated with the image of the brutal truncheon wielder. Signs of warning had emerged, however. Amnesty International, for instance, has expressed concern in recent years at police conduct in the great majority of current

---

2   According to a recent stocktaking, not aspiring to completeness, 109 demonstrators were killed in clashes with the police between 1947 and 1954 (Marino 1995, 169). According to Interior Ministry statistics, from 1 January 1948 to 30 June 1950, workers killed 'on the occasion of public-order duties' numbered 34 (28 of them Communists), with 695 injured (572 Communists) and 13,609 arrested (10,728 Communists) (Caredda 1995, 94f.).

3   The *centri sociali* are self-organized youth centres in buildings occupied by squatters, close to the ideology of 'class autonomy' (in which the working class must organize itself independently from the socialist or communist parties).

EU Member States. The EU Network of Independent Experts in Fundamental Rights has affirmed that 'Violence committed by the police remains a source of concern in all the member States of the European Union' (EU Network 2003a, 57).

Police conduct in various countries in Europe and North America has been strongly criticized in the preparatory stage of movement demonstrations as well as for their actions on the streets and their treatment of persons detained, focusing on coercive as well as preventive and information strategies. The *negotiated management* style seems in fact to have been applied inconsistently in many demonstrations organized by the movement for globalization from below, in particular those against the international summits, in the course of which a long escalation has come about. In particular, the administrators of public order at the summits often seem to have been unable to defend peaceful demonstrators' right to demonstrate.

In the following we shall describe, in a first section, the specific features of police action at Genoa. We shall go on to seek to explain protest control at Genoa by discussing some of the characteristics of police knowledge – that is, how the police perceive their role in society as well as external demands and challenges. In a third section we shall analyse the characteristics of the Italian police forces' organizational structure that may have influenced police response at Genoa. A concluding section will aim to understand, by considering the European Social Forum (ESF) in Florence in November 2002, what lessons have been drawn from the Genoa experience by the political authorities, the police and the movement.

Escalating police strategies in Genoa

The control of the Genoa anti-G8 protest has to be located within a series of interactions between protesters and the police during counter-summits. First, there was a confirmation of *persuasive* strategies fundamentally based upon the physical isolation of the locations for the summit (what King and Waddington call exclusionary fortress oriented policing and Noakes and Gillham see as part of a selective incapacitation; see Chapters 4 and 5): access roads to the city were partially closed, a buffer zone (the yellow zone) with restrictions on freedom to demonstrate was set up, and the site of the summit was fortified. In mid July, tall barriers were set up to isolate the 'red zone' barred to demonstrators, and the closure of railway stations, the airport and motorway tollbooths was announced. The red zone, with 13 access portals and an eight-kilometre perimeter (at Prague it had been barely two km, and at Quebec it reached 6.1 km), enclosed not just the areas for the summit but also several city streets, among them Via XX settembre, the location of major commercial centres. The government also concentrated considerable energies on trying to keep 'dangerous' foreign activists out of Italy through massive frontier controls. On 11 July, the Schengen agreement abolishing internal border controls within the EU was suspended until midnight on 21 July. One hundred and forty thousand border checks were carried out and 2,093 people rejected, only 298 of them alleged members of the black bloc (Hearing 28 August 2001, 139).[4] Particularly in these endeavours to keep violent activists (or those so presumed) far from the city hosting the summit, a transnational level of *protest policing* was manifest (see Chapter 7).

Previous experience with movement demonstrations in their own and other countries influenced the strategies of the police forces. In Italy, with the centre-left government still in office, the 17 March demonstrations against the Global Forum on *e-government* in Naples had ended in violent clashes. After some attempts by the more radical fringes to force police cordons, peaceful groups were caught in charges as the procession was breaking up. In contrast with the Swedish reaction after the clashes during the Malmö ECOFIN Summit in April 2001 (see Chapter 3), it does not seem that the Naples precedent led to efforts to strengthen the search for dialogue with the movement or to enhance the *accountability* of police personnel in Genoa. To the contrary, the persuasive strategies pursued by the Italian police in the preparatory stages of the Genoa G8 did not favour the element of negotiation, even though police leadership repeatedly claimed attempts to establish a relationship and open lines of communication with protest movements.

Again with the centre-left government in office, authorities long sought to persuade the movement to drop any demonstration in conjunction with the summit in Genoa, an attitude that in itself provoked protest actions.[5] An interlocutor, Margherita Paolini, was mandated by the government for dialogue with the Genoa Social Forum (GSF), organizer of the anti-G8 protest, and held in high regard by a part of the movement for her great experience in seeking to smooth out relations between institutions and civil society (Hearing 6 September 2001, 83ff.). However, the *questore* (local police chief), charged with arranging the public order services, claims to have seen her only once, and not to have regarded her as a valid interlocutor (Hearing 28 August 2001, 43) – thus confirming the impression of low trust in negotiations. It was only after the violent events in Gothenburg (see Chapter 3; also Peterson and Oskarsson 2002) that the new centre-right government announced its decision to follow a 'line of dialogue'. The negotiations with the movement, until then conducted at the local level, were entrusted to the national coordination of police forces.[6] As in Gothenburg, the negotiations on hosting demonstrators and on the execution of protest actions

---

4   Among the 1,795 rejected for other reasons, there were cases like the translator for the Council of the European Union, who reached Milan by air but was rejected at the border with the written explanation 'Because he arrogantly declared he was going to Genoa to demonstrate' (in *Diario*, Speciale Genova, supplement to no. 31/2001, 13).

5   A proposal to hold the demonstrations between 27 June and 15 July, a week before the summit, was formalized on 8 February and communicated to the GSF, which rejected it (Report III, 111). On 4 April the movement organized 'telegram day' – with thousands of telegrams, emails and faxes sent to the president of the republic and government figures asking for meetings to define the details of the protest – a day after sit-ins in front of the Ministry of the Interior in Rome and dozens of Prefectures throughout the country (Hearing 6 September 2001, 20).

6   After 'telegram day', the prefect was mandated to negotiate with the GSF, but without new instructions. His attempts ended on 20 April, when he told the government that

began only very late: the first meeting between the GSF and the national police chief was on 24 June.

Again, as in Gothenburg, not just at the preparatory stages of the protest event but also later 'on the street', the lines of communication between protesters and police officers were often interrupted. Organizers were unable to contact the police on more than one occasion: for instance, the Lilliput pacifists assembled in Piazza Manin were informed by telephone by a GSF spokesperson three-quarters of an hour ahead that a black bloc group was probably moving towards the square. All efforts to contact the police failed, and it was the non-violent activists that managed to defend the square from the black bloc, only to fall victim to a police charge (Hearing 6 September 2001, 34ss, 59, 125s.). For their part, police officers complained that various GSF spokespersons had, even during the course of the demonstrations, given contradictory indications and requests.

Incoherent with the negotiated management strategy are also measures such as the expulsion notice (used to keep some Italian social-centre militants away from Genoa, with a three-year ban on returning; see Pepino 2001, 895) and the searches of private houses and social centres, often carried out on the basis of Article 41 of the Penal Code, which allows searches without authorization by a magistrate – although only to search for weapons, and in exceptional cases of necessity and urgency. That the police were aware of sending non-verbal signals through certain preventive measures is evident from the statement by the former head of UCIGOS (central political police), Arnaldo La Barbera, who stated that systematic activities of preventive pressure were abandoned in order to avoid adversely affecting attempts at dialogue (Hearing 28 August 2001, 61).[7]

The *information* strategies employed at Genoa, as later in Florence, were characterized chiefly by the indiscriminate and generalized collection of information, but also by the spreading of alarmist and false news. The collection of information aimed at rejecting presumed violent activists at the borders, partly through collaboration with other European police forces, proved of little use. Just under 300 people were refused entry as black bloc members, with the total number of arrivals estimated at 2,000; the Italian police had compiled a list of 1,439 names (Hearing 28 August 2001, 134ff.). There also seems to have been a lack of use of specific information by the police: for instance, the SISDE (civil secret service) had informed police headquarters that on 20 July a black bloc group would assemble in the Piazza da Novi, allocated to the Network for Global Rights as its theme square; but no police action followed, and the Network felt compelled to abandon the square (Gubitosa 2003, 170ff.).

---

the movement was insisting on its demands: demonstrations during the summit days, and premises and infrastructure to host demonstrators (Hearing 9 August 2001, 101s.).

7   In addition to searches, many telephone taps were carried out, along with computer monitoring and a census of the most extremist social centres (Hearing 28 August 2001, 64s.).

The most visible policing strategies in Genoa were *coercive*. The brutality and non-selectivity of many police operations, and the elements of downright illegality that are apparently emerging from inquiries by the magistrates, have led a police officer to assert: 'We "saw" ourselves and found we were different from what we thought we were, what we believed we were.'[8] The police made massive use of tear gas and irritants (with over 6,200 grenades launched between Friday and Saturday), ignoring a February 2001 circular from the national police chief recommending maximum caution and care in using truncheons or teargas.[9] Members of the police forces fired at least 20 pistol rounds, one of which killed the young demonstrator Carlo Giuliani (Report III, 145). On both Friday and Saturday, repeated violent charges massively involved the great bulk of peaceful demonstrators as well. On the initiative of some of the most senior police officers present, armoured vehicles were launched at high speed against the crowd (Gubitosa 2003, 219ff.). There was no provision to protect demonstrators with a police cordon opening the procession (Report III, 164; Gubitosa 2003, 505); as at Gothenburg, no serious attempt was made to react against black bloc provocations (all far from the red zone).

With its brutal coercive strategies, Genoa seems to mark the culmination of the escalation of coercive strategies employed against the movement. At Gothenburg, too, individual officers resorted to firearms, wounding three demonstrators, one seriously (see Chapter 3); but the Swedish police did not use tear gas, and public demonstrations organized by the movement could take place without police charges. While at Prague there were 600 injured, including 150 police; for Genoa estimates of the injured reach over 1,000 (Gubitosa 2003, 177f.). As in Prague and Gothenburg, the large number of detentions was reflected only minimally in arrest warrants (mostly against foreigners),[10] pointing at the inability to detain violent individuals (who, according to figures supplied by the police themselves, were much more numerous) or to supply the magistracy with sufficient proof to validate detentions.

---

8   In Zinola 2003, 73. For a detailed reconstruction of the three days at Genoa, see Gubitosa 2003.

9   Police chief De Gennaro stated that teargas 'was to be regarded as an ultimate remedy for tackling particularly serious situations that cannot be handled otherwise, given also the heavy impact it has on the crowd [...] We hear in the reports I have cited that officers were saying: "Then I also used teargas". I think that these are pointers to the thinking – on my part too – so as to improve, and correct if necessary' (Hearing 8 August 2001, 51).

10 Twenty-eight arrestees were freed directly by the prosecution service, which did not apply for confirmation of their arrests; 76 arrests were not confirmed. 'Against 225 applications for preventive detention, only 20 people remained in prison, and 29 bans on residing in Genoa were applied. [...] Failure to confirm arrests is an outcome a lawyer hardly ever sees, since the judge has to assess whether the arrest was legitimate on the basis solely of what appears on the arrest report, plus the accused's statements. In this position it is rather hard for the judge to reach the point of saying that there were no elements justifying arrests, essentially disowning the police action; the greatest success is usually to see the accused freed on the grounds that while having committed an offence they are not dangerous' (Genoa Legal Forum 2002, 114).

On Friday, the *carabinieri* charge against the 'disobedients'[11] parade, still on an authorized route and still peaceful, represented a clear move away from a *negotiated management* strategy.[12] The official version from the police that the attack started from the demonstrators is refuted by a large amount of evidence and video material.[13] No effort by the police forces to communicate with the contact group, which (as always) was at the head of the 'disobedient' march, is known. There are worrying implications in the version supplied in an interview with the officer leading the *carabinieri* squad, who claimed that the charge was necessary since, with the red zone at their backs, they could not let the disobedients advance as far as Piazza Verdi – that is, the point up to which police headquarters had itself given authorization.[14] While the 'disobedients' claimed there was a premeditated trap, it seems no less serious if the order to charge was simply the outcome of incompetence, confusion or a collapse in lines of communication and command.[15]

The charge against the disobedients had dramatic consequences. While until then – except for episodes of vandalism by black bloc people not on the march – there had been no incidents, 'disorder was', according to *La Stampa* newspaper correspondent Giulietto Chiesa (2001, 44), 'from that moment the direct, unambiguous outcome of a choice by the carabinieri'. In fact, self-defence and solidarity reactions, including violent ones, were triggered: 'the carabinieri advance accordingly met with resistance which, apart from being active, was inevitable: either you wait for the truncheon to hit you, or you defend yourself. Thus, before my very eyes, the two or three thousand

---

11　The 'disobedients' emerged from the 'tute bianche' (white overalls), a coordination of social centres (see note 3 above) that towards the end of the 1990s abandoned a classical revolutionary vision and moderated their action repertoires. One of the main lines of differentiation between the White Overalls and the other more radical social centres concerns their relationship with institutions. Some of the social centres that mobilized in the White Overalls have gradually become 'legalized' and established and maintained good relations with such parties as the Greens and RC. In their action repertoires, the 'disobedients' privilege civil disobedience actions that they define as nonviolent but protected, collective and self-organized. The action consists in reaching police lines and attempting to move into the out-of-bounds 'red areas' by 'pushing and shoving'. The activists wear protective materials for their physical safety, but objects of aggression are banned.

12　Before the parliamentary investigative commission, police spokesmen long maintained that the demonstrations on 20 July had not been authorized. It was, however, to emerge that due notice had been given, and that police headquarters had taken note by denying the use of particular squares and barring the 'disobedients' parade from going further than Piazza Verdi.

13　The official version was watered down even in the report of the parliamentary investigative commission drafted by the centre-right majority. For the differences between the first draft of the majority report and the final version, see Gubitosa 2003, 304ff.

14　See Gubitosa 2003, 214f. The 'disobedients' were the only GSF group that did not manage to enter even the yellow zone.

15　Audio recordings capturing the conversations inside the police command room, which recently emerged during the trials concerning the Genoa events, reveal surprise and disbelief as reactions to the *carabinieri* attack on the march of the disobedients.

young people heading the march were converted into active, angry combatants' (Chiesa 2001, 45). During these clashes a *carabinieri* Land Rover was trapped and its occupants attacked by the demonstrators; one of the *carabinieri* on board fired, killing 23-year-old Genoese demonstrator Carlo Giuliani.

The violation of the negotiated management strategy is even more evident in the beating of protesters after the demonstration was over, or at any rate off the streets – police conduct that even spokespersons for the centre-right majority have deemed particularly serious, and that seems to display a punitive imprint.[16] The break-in at the Pertini-Diaz school, which the GSF was being allowed to use as a dormitory, was carried out on the basis of Article 41 of the Penal Code: no authorization by the magistrates was requested, though they were informed of the impending action, even though the search (aimed at finding not just weapons but also material useful for reconstructing the facts) was decided with enough time to allow meetings at police headquarters and communication with the national police chief (Pepino 2001, 895, n. 44). Sixty-two of the 93 demonstrators arrested inside the school were hospitalized, with prognoses ranging from five days to indeterminate. Only one of those arrested remained in custody; one residence ban was decided by the judges. The police report of an attempt to stab an officer inside the school was denied by a subsequent *carabinieri* investigation. The list of objects confiscated contains, *inter alia*, 10 Swiss knives, various gas masks and swimming goggles, one wig, various greaves and other physical protections, six films and three audio tapes, two walkmans, three cell phones, 17 cameras, 60 black t-shirts and other clothes the same colour, and one red flag (Gubitosa 2003, 386ff.). It now seems clear that the two Molotov cocktails, presented as the most serious evidence of the dangerousness of the people inside Diaz-Pertini, had been brought and deposited in the school by the police themselves (Gubitosa 2003, 389ff.). In another part of the school complex, the police broke into the headquarters of the Genoa Legal Forum and Indymedia, destroying the lawyers' computers and removing video and paper material, including the denunciations collected against the police.

Brutalities were also reported by the hundreds of men and women detained by the police at the Bolzaneto barracks, who stated they were repeatedly beaten, forced to sing songs against Communists, Jews and gays, and threatened with sexual abuse. Talks with lawyers were delayed based on a previous agreement with the prosecution service, postponing exercise of the arrestee's right to confer with a defender (Pepino 2001, 902). Foreign detainees (mostly EU citizens) were given expulsion orders without going before a magistrate. Many expulsions, accompanied by a ban on returning to Italy without special authorization from the Ministry of the Interior, were based on police detentions that the magistracy had already, by not confirming them, pronounced illegitimate. There was an attempt to expel an Italian citizen with dual

---

16 The assault at Gothenburg on the night after the hardest clashes seem to have had similar features, though with much less severe consequences to demonstrators. It was conducted by a special paramilitary unit on a school being used as a dormitory by demonstrators, and justified by the search for an armed German terrorist.

nationality (Swiss and Italian), and to expel to her homeland a Turkish girl who was a political refugee in Switzerland under the 1951 Geneva Conventions. Subsequently, the magistracy accepted all the appeals against expulsion orders by EU citizens (and 10 of the 12 by non-EU citizens) (Genoa Legal Forum 2002, 157ff.).

Police knowledge and the Genoa escalation

The brutal intervention by the police in Genoa opened a harsh political debate on the possible explanations for the escalation, ranging from a police riot – facilitated by not-yet-overcome authoritarian traditions – to the orders of a (post-fascist) right-wing government. In what follows we shall focus on some characteristics of police knowledge, that is, how the Italian police perceive their role in society as well as external demands and challenges, discussing how these may have facilitated the move away from *détente* strategies of public order control.

In explaining police conduct, the literature has stressed the importance of their professional culture, particularly the fact that many police actions are provoked by situational moments and not by well-defined rules or orders. The need to make on-the-spot decisions about whether or not to intervene leads police to develop stereotypes of people and situations perceived as possible sources of difficulty or danger. These stereotypes, filtered through police knowledge, become a sort of guideline for the actions of individual police and the force as a whole, with distinctions, for instance, between 'good' demonstrators (peaceful, pragmatic, with a direct interest in the conflict and a clear aim, etc.) and 'bad' demonstrators (predominantly young, misinformed, destructive, professional troublemakers with no direct interest in the conflict, and so on) (della Porta 1998; della Porta and Reiter 1998b).

The police often claim to be simply responding to the external challenges, and demonstrators' attitudes have clearly been stigmatized as responsible for the escalation. In the majority report of the parliamentary investigative commission we read, for instance, that:

> on both July 20th and 21st the intention for soft control of public order clashed with the mass provocations brought by the intermingling – unopposed by the organizers – of a crowd of some 10,000 violent individuals in the peaceful demonstration; this intermingling made it impossible to separate the violent from the non-violent. (Report I, 221)

Again, the parliamentary majority, accusing the GSF of playing a double game, claims that 'throughout the G8, the violent, subversive sector of demonstrators took advantage of tolerance by the peaceful demonstrators. These took no specific actions aimed at identifying, isolating or excluding violent and subversive individuals' (Report I, 243). The day after the searches at the Diaz school, Prime Minister Berlusconi declared that it was impossible to distinguish between the GSF and the black bloc.

However, our research points to a widespread rejection of violence, whether from support for the ideology of non-violence or as a politically opportune strategic choice. Ninety per cent of the demonstrators we interviewed at Genoa stated they had never used violent tactics. For 40 per cent of those interviewed, recourse to violence was always to be condemned; 53 per cent regarded it as undesirable even if justifiable, and only 6.7 per cent as necessary. Still clearer is the non-violent orientation emerging from the data collected at the Florence ESF: for 51.7 per cent of the participants interviewed, even violence against symbols of neoliberalism is always to be condemned; only 5.5 per cent considered it necessary.[17]

While the movement is mainly peaceful, some of its features do resonate with police stereotypes about 'bad demonstrators'. In the first place, the movement's novelty tests police capacity to assess properly its numerical strength, cohesion and the objectives of protest actions. Already after Seattle, and later after Gothenburg and Genoa, the police claimed they had to face a totally unheard-of phenomenon. While these assertions seem exaggerated, particularly in the Italian case, the fact remains that, after there had been a long period of relative social and political peace, the new millennium began with large street demonstrations. Research has also pointed at the fact that repression tends to increase against movements that are considered as ideologically driven (see della Porta and Fillieule 2004; Earl 2003; Davenport 2000, 1995; as well as the introduction to this volume). The transnational counter-summits challenge not only particular political decisions but also a model of development for society, expressing the desire for 'another world'.

In addition, the movement's loose structure, with its rejection of a leadership as well as of a marshal body, meets police mistrust of crowds that are not able to 'police themselves'. Traditionally, organizational fluidity and the inability for self-administration of order on marches is interpreted by those in control of public order as risky, potentially multiplying the number of groups for negotiation and reducing the capacity for control over participants.[18] Police spokesmen heard by the parliamentary investigative commission in fact repeatedly stressed the difficulties of dialogue with an entity like the GSF, made up of 800 components and unable to guarantee any real representativeness in relation to the totality of demonstrators.

The police professional culture also tends to perceive as particularly challenging protest in which peaceful forms mix with acts of civil disobedience or even violence. While the movement for globalization from below presents itself as nonviolent – an option which at Genoa was formalized by the signing of an agreement of understanding – there is nonetheless an acceptance of the diversity of the repertoires of action adopted by the various groups, in the name of tolerance for different lines taken, and also perhaps of the tactical advantages that might arise from

---

17 During the European Social Forum, the Gruppo di Ricerca sull'Azione Collettiva in Europa (GRACE) interviewed 2,384 activists, randomly selected at various meetings during the Forum, using a semi-structured questionnaire (1,668 Italians, 124 French, 77 Germans, 88 Spanish, 118 British, and 309 from other countries) (see della Porta et al. 2006 for more details). At the Genoa anti-G8 protests, GRACE had interviewed 763 Italian activists, using the same methods (see Andretta et al. 2002 for more details).

18 See, for example, P.A.J. Waddington 1994, on the control of public order in London.

complementarity between symbolic provocations and nonviolence, play and civil disobedience. While the actions planned for Genoa were apparently confined to ritualized, symbolic confrontation with the police at the entrance to the red zone, civil disobedience strategies carry the risk of misunderstanding and disproportionate response, especially if, partly because of lack of dialogue between the movement and authorities, there is uncertainty or lack of understanding of the objectives pursued. Hence the need for prior clarification of the objectives of disobedience actions on the one hand, and of the limits beyond which coercive intervention will be triggered on the other.[19]

While there was no lack of individual episodes following the model of tolerance for formally illicit forms of protest, before the parliamentary investigative commission *questore* Colucci (the police officer responsible for the public order services) defined as illegitimate the ranges of actions not only of the 'disobedients' but also of the 'pacifists'. In connection with the announcement by the 'disobedients' that they wished to prevent the summit peacefully by blocking entry, he stated: 'You have to tell me if an intention like that can be called peaceful; at that point what was being rather clearly stated was a no longer verbal but also physical challenge' (Hearing 28 August 2001, 52). Citing the pacifists' attempt to create a human buffer between the violent activists and the police, Colucci declared: 'I ask: does "creating a human buffer between the black bloc and the police" not perhaps mean putting oneself in between in order to prevent the police from acting?' (Hearing 28 August 2001, 15).

Also, the strategy of movement mobilizations in conjunction with major international summits poses special problems for the police (Ericson and Doyle 1999). International summit meetings are traditionally particularly delicate situations for the maintenance of public order, as they also involve the protection of foreign dignitaries. Defence of the right to demonstrate comes into conflict with the objective of guaranteeing the safety of guest heads of State or government. Symbolically, the host nation State has a need to assert itself before international public opinion as able to display a monopoly of force on its own territory, an indispensable corollary of its sovereignty in international interactions. But the fortification of the summits produces effects that tend to be dangerous, by concentrating police efforts on defending it, restricting the possibilities of protest that can be peaceful but visible, and increasing the distance between the rulers and the population. The perceived risks of invasion reduce the room for dialogue and encounters between demonstrators and the institutions, as well as between demonstrators and the press.

From Seattle to Genoa, conflict around breaches of the red zone became ritualized, with an escalation of police strategies to defend summit sites, but also with a multiplication of tactics tried by demonstrators aiming at penetrating them: some threw paint balls (or garlic in the Genoa case); the non-violent contingent lay

---

19 A general reference to the law is not enough, since it is a common practice to tolerate minor infractions; nor is a statement like that by the police chief to the GSF that the police would suit the deterrent response to the conduct of those who had broken the law (Gubitosa 2003, 58).

down in front of the entries; the civil disobedient people attempted physical pressure on the gates. In some cases (though not in Genoa), anarchist groups seek to force the blockades. As with the workers' movement's pickets, the student movement's occupations, the peace movement's sit-ins around Cruise and Pershing II missile installation sites, and the anti-nuclear movement's blockades on nuclear power stations or radioactive waste transports, so for the movement for globalization from below: the loci of summits are becoming the terrain of direct interaction with police forces.

The information strategies used for the Genoa G8, with the indiscriminate, widespread collection of information, led the police to an undifferentiated image of the 'no-globals' as 'bad demonstrators'. Ex-head of UCIGOS La Barbera said, in connection with the documentation of the secret services on the G8 (364 documents), that there was a:

> multitude of information, in the bulk of cases without any basis [...] For instance, the SISDE [civil secret service] note of 20 March 2001 foresaw the use of bladders full of blood, at least in part human, collected with the complicity of doctors, veterinarians and nurses, to be thrown during the demonstrations. SISDE note of 5 April: the antagonists had gathered a sizeable number of old tires to set on fire and roll down the descending streets leading to the sea, where the police forces were to be stationed. SISDE note of 30 March: the antagonists were allegedly intending to rent a satellite channel in order to disseminate protest world wide [...] SISDE note of 19 July: the 'white overalls', to break into the red zone, were alleged to have planned two human 'testudos' of 80 militants each. (Hearing 28 August 2001, 66)

Another SISDE note even says that Casarini's 'right-hand man' had the task of giving military-style training young people from the Rivolta social centre 'with the strategic aim of teaching the most sophisticated techniques of the most modern urban guerrilla warfare [...] At Genoa, all have been ordered to carry slings for launching ball-bearings so as to make holes in the security shields' (*La Repubblica* 23 June 2001). Information from the secret services filtered through the press alleged that the demonstrators planned to take police hostage to use as human shields. There was also talk of Forza Nuova neo-fascists armed with knives, and of extreme self-injuring gestures by PKK Kurds (*La Repubblica* 3 September 2001).

The negative image of the 'no-globals' as 'troublemakers' also dominates the analysis of the individual organizational sectors of the movement that was prepared before the G8: the 'pink' block of pacifists, who would seek visibility in actions pursuing the goal of obstructing, boycotting and delaying the work of the summit; the 'yellows' of the 'white overalls' (the so-called 'disobedients') and other social centres, ready for civil disobedience and direct action not excluding recourse to violence; the 'blues' of the autonomous groups and anarchists, committed to direct, violent action against the police, even by way of provocation; and the 'black bloc', the element of greatest risk to public order (Hearing 28 August 2001, 60). This assessment of the blue and yellow blocks seems to take little account of the evolution of a great part of these two groups – which had in recent times abandoned more direct, violent types of action in favour of 'protected civil disobedience'. Recognizing the development of their strategies would have facilitated opening a constructive dialogue that could eventually lead to mutual trust. Still clearer were assessments of the movement given after Genoa: in retrospect, the whole GSF was portrayed as untrustworthy, and a great proportion of the demonstrators as sharing responsibility for the violence.

The dominant image of the 'no-global' demonstrator seems based not so much on analysis of the new movement as on a reprocessing of experiences and images from the foregoing decade, which had become part of the police knowledge mentioned above (della Porta and Reiter 2003, 287ff.). During the 1990s the public order discourse in Italy had become depolarized and de-ideologized, accompanied by a clear dominance of 'soft policing', but at the same time hard approaches survived towards small antagonistic groups. Foremost among these were the social centres, perceived as detached from a larger movement, or from a 'political family', and hence as isolated and with no cover. Furthermore, in the absence of mass demonstrations, football hooliganism emerged as the biggest public order problem. Indeed, the image of the 'no-globals' as 'summit hooligans' emerges most insistently in the Italian and also the European media, especially after the Gothenburg clashes. The experience of hooliganism, with repercussions on the operational level, is emphasized by Alessandro Pilotto, of one of the police's public order units:

> It seems incredible, but did anybody ask if someone accustomed on an everyday basis for years now to hold thousands of enraged fans from the most diverse sporting backgrounds at bay can manage to recognize, understand and peacefully confront those parading in front of them with shields and helmets. Will there not be a conditioned reflex that after months of a publicity barrage will trigger every self-defence mechanism in your possession? (Zinola 2003, 135)

The alarmist notions underlying the image of the 'no-globals' as 'bad demonstrators' – although subsequently regarded as 'absolutely at the limit of the ridiculous' (Forza Italia MP Cicchito, Hearing 28 August 2001, 69) – had noteworthy effects on the attitudes of individual police officers in Genoa. As one policeman said: 'The tension among us was sky high: for the whole foregoing week we had been told that the demonstrators would have pistols, and would be throwing infected blood and ball bearings covered in acid at us. On the Friday evening after that lad's death they told us that a carabiniere had died too' (in *Diario* 32–33/2001, 18). More important still, the alarming information influenced police tactics and personnel deployment, confirmed by ex-*questore* Colucci in relation to the indication that police personnel might be attacked and kidnapped. Accordingly, 'the initial option to use few men in order to fight and move more easily over the territory (groups of 40, 50 or 60 people) was perforce overcome by the idea of setting up bigger squads' (Hearing 28 August 2001, 23).

Finally, research on the policing of protest has also indicated that repression tends especially to target groups of protesters that are perceived as socially and politically isolated (Earl, Soule and McCarthy 2003; della Porta 1998). It has often been stressed that police actions are sensitive to political institutions' behaviour and attitudes towards specific movements. A historically consolidated feature of the Italian police is in fact the continuation of the model of the 'King's police', or police of the monarch, traditionally present on the European continent – by contrast with the 'citizens' police' of the English-speaking world. The Italian police were built up and legitimized as above all a political instrument, formed and utilized chiefly for public order tasks, with close links to central government. This tradition, criticized by the police reform movement, nonetheless seems to have survived, both in the still-militarized police organization structures and in a type of police 'knowledge' extremely sensitive to the political attitudes of the majority. In these circumstances, the public order response is heavily influenced by the political response to the movement, at both the supranational and the national levels.

The conduct and attitudes of institutional political actors before, during and after Genoa indicate a closure not just towards the issues presented by the various currents in the movement but to its very identity, finding difficulty in recognizing it as a political subject. The movements' questioning of the legitimacy of the 'Big 8' to decide for everyone – 'You G8, we six billion' – was met by the government with a refusal to recognize it as an interlocutor, instead interpreting and presenting it as primarily a public order problem.

Several months after the Genoa demonstrations, among many denials, Minister of the Interior Scajola claimed to have given, after Giuliani's death, an order to fire on anyone seeking to enter the red zone, justifying himself by the presence in Genoa of '200,000 hotheads whose ranks may have been infiltrated, and pointers to terrorist attacks from all the intelligence services' (*La Repubblica*, 16 February 2002). The majority report of the parliamentary investigative commission tirelessly defended the police operations in Genoa. Criticism is confined to a reference to 'a few excesses by individual members of the police forces', with a refusal to discuss them in order to avoid interfering with judicial authorities (*La Repubblica*, 16 February 2002, 245). Recommendations for the future go no further than a call for greater coordination among the police forces and more effective cooperation in the sphere of information and prevention among individual European countries.

As far as the centre-left coalition is concerned, scepticism and uncertainties as to the attitude to adopt towards the emerging movement started when it was in government but continued even when it went into opposition. As regards the Saturday demonstration, on 19 July it was still divided on whether or not to take part; after Carlo Giuliani's death, the Democrats of the Left (DS), the main centre-left party, withdrew their support. The centre-left opposition has explained the Genoa events as a political option if not of the whole government at least of a part of it – in particular, of the most right-wing part of the coalition, Alleanza Nazionale (AN). The main responsibility for the errors in controlling public order is assigned to the instrumentalization of the police forces by the right, most visibly expressed in the presence of Deputy Prime Minister Gianfranco Fini and three MPs from his party in the *carabinieri* operational command room at Genoa.[20] According to the Ulivo (centre-left coalition) proposal for a concluding document to the work of the investigative commission, the presence of the AN MPs was not just an attempt to exercise an illegitimate influence but also an indication of attempts by the more extreme wing of the majority coalition to 'force the issue' on public order. The Ulivo in fact denounced 'the attempt by the most extremist component of the majority to open up a laceration between the forces of order and civil society' (Report II, 95). Declarations by AN speakers, including Fini, even before the summit are said to have dwelt on the confrontational atmosphere, informing the public and the police forces that every street demonstration was by violent and subversive groups, and guaranteeing that in the event of clashes on no account would responsibility be allotted by the government to the forces of order (Report II, 103ff.). At the same time, though, the Ulivo did not reflect on responsibilities of the centre-left, for instance in the policing of the Global Forum on e-government in Naples in March 2001 or during the preparatory phase of the Genoa G8, and insisted that ambiguous conduct by a part of the movement supplied the pretext for assigning a violent image to the whole of it.

The Italian police organizational model

While the prevailing image of the demonstrators among police forces did not favour de-escalation strategies, organizational features may also have enhanced aspects of a 'tough' approach to controlling public order. In general, certain features of police organizational structures, particularly degree of militarization, accountability vis-à-vis citizens, and politicization (as compared to professionalism), are central for the quality of a democracy. In particular, a high degree of police militarization may, through the type of weaponry and training, predetermine certain types of action and preclude others, as well as creating a climate of separateness and mistrust in relations between police and citizens. Particularly important is the extent to which police, both as an institution and as individuals, are responsible for their decisions in action, in particular through the ability to identify individual officers (through visible identification numbers or badges), the possibility of independent review of police decisions, and the presence of procedures facilitating submission of formal complaints by citizens.

From the organizational viewpoint, the traditional model of the Italian police forces seems remote from the democratic ideal. Both the State police and the *carabinieri* have been highly militarized bodies with particularly marked centralization, reflected in their strong political dependence on the government. The national police reform law of 1981 was only partially successful in meeting the objective of demilitarization,

---

20 Because of the disorder around the barracks, all four were allegedly forced to remain there until the march dispersed (Report I, 225). Colonel Graci, commander of the *carabinieri* operational division, stated that this was the first time in his five years in Genoa that MPs had come into the operational command room (Hearing 29 August 2001, 52).

a condition regarded even within European police forces as essential to a democratic police force. Most significantly, only the State police took on features of a non-military body, while the *carabinieri* and financial police, also employed in public order, remain military in nature. Law 78/2000 on the reordering and coordination of police forces (passed under a centre-left government) further aggravated the difficulties traditionally associated with the presence of a large number of police forces: unclear definition of the division of competences, in particular between the State police and the *carabinieri* force; limitations on the civilian public security authorities; and wide margins of autonomy for the *carabinieri* and financial police. A further difficulty is the limited accountability and low professionalism of the Italian police, also in the sphere of public order, already criticized by the movement for police democratization in the 1970s. The failure of the control of public order in Genoa confirms the persistence of shortcomings in the organizational structure of the Italian police forces.

In Gothenburg, the breakdown of the police communication system and command and coordination structure has been identified as one of the causes of situations usually defined as 'police riots' (Peterson 2003a, 7ff.; see also Chapter 3 of this volume) – that is, forms of rebellion by police officers disobeying the orders of their own hierarchical superiors – which seem also to have marked the Genoa Summit. In Italy, in fact, the joint presence of various national police forces, with a historical rivalry and poor coordination, holds particular complications for the organization of police operations – already difficult for big events and often involving serious problems for the police – and at Genoa seems to have had severe effects on the lines of communication.[21]

During the Genoa days, communication between the inter-force operations room at police headquarters and the *carabinieri* units came about not directly but through the provincial *carabinieri* operations room, or in the field in the form of direct communication between state police officers and commanders of the individual *carabinieri* groups. Direction of public order services is actually always assigned to state police officers (*funzionari*); but when these officers have to lead *carabinieri* units, they cannot give orders directly to the men under them, but are forced to go through *carabinieri* officers. At Genoa the *carabinieri* were all in direct contact with each other and with their provincial operations room through throat microphones; however, neither the officers leading the services nor the operations room at police

---

21 For an account of the organizational confusion during massive personnel transfers, especially those involving *carabinieri* and financial police, see the interview with a SIULP leader in Gubitosa (2003, 512). For the burdensome work situation of the policemen deployed in Genoa, see Gubitosa (2003, 501f., 512; Report II, 109s). Problems range from long shifts, often assigned at the last moment, to the unsuitability of accommodation structures. These, too, have operational repercussions, since officers often see demonstrators as responsible for the situation. The confusion in police organization for major events is not, however, a purely Italian problem. The Swedish police union has published its own inquiry into Gothenburg based on responses from 900 officers in service during the summit days, with the significant title 'Kaos'.

headquarters were included in this network, but were in turn linked through a separate radio network. These coordination and communication difficulties seem to have had an impact on specific episodes, including the events leading to the death of Carlo Giuliani. Vice *questore* Adriano Lauro, in charge of about a hundred *carabinieri*, explains the dynamics of his group's retreat, which left the *carabinieri* Land Rover isolated in Piazza Alimonda, as follows:

> I was in charge of public order, but had to give orders to the captain materially in command of the men. Thus at that moment, in that situation, it was impossible to find the captain among a hundred carabinieri all dressed the same! Moreover, they were linked by throat mikes, but I wasn't linked with them. Consequently I was unable to give the captain orders. A disordered withdrawal is not controllable at moments like that. (Hearing 5 September 2001, 72)

It should be added that, according to the police officers' association, the two radio links between police headquarters and the *carabinieri* had already failed on Friday, 20 July (*La Repubblica* 17 August 2001).

The lack of coordination seems greatest during the break-in and search operation at the Diaz-Pertini school, conducted by state police and *carabinieri* public order units, the DIGOS (local political police), and anti-crime squads. The contrasting versions of the event draw attention to a situation of great confusion in the lines of command, emphasized also by the centre-right (Report I, 233). The break-in, furthermore, brought out a problem that seems to typify the whole police operation in Genoa: the local police chief, responsible for deployment of public order services, and the other local officers were flanked by top leaders of the national level, with no clear identification of specific competences, resulting in further confusion in lines of command and possible removal of responsibility.

An additional element of the police organization, in line with changes mentioned for other countries, is a trend towards the militarization of equipment as well as training (McCarthy, Martin and McPhail 2004; Kraska and Kaeppler 1997; Kraska 1996). The police responsible for the anti-G8 demonstrations in Genoa were going through a period of restructuring: on 16 June 1999 a working group had been set up to bring the mobile squads of the state police in line with the changed requirements of public order duties. At the hearing before the parliamentary investigative commission (5 September 2001, 29ff.), Valerio Donnini (in charge of this reorganization) explained how over the years the tasks of the mobile units had been steadily diversified, as they were increasingly used as reservoirs of personnel and less as public order units. Incidents of wounds and injuries among personnel had increased, both at football events and at big street demonstrations, indicating a certain lack of training (Hearing 5 September 2001, 31). Plans had been made to set up specialized multi-task units among the mobile divisions for deployment on more challenging public order duties, redefine the equipment of the mobile divisions, focus on training, develop operational methodologies appropriate to the various types of demonstration, identify a specific training ground for nationwide use and create unitary control and guidance structures for the units from different police forces.

The imminence of the G8 Summit made available the financial resources to achieve the almost complete modernization of equipment for the public order divisions (not just of the State police but also of the *carabinieri* and financial police), regarded as necessary for the new requirements. As regards weaponry, all components of the mobile divisions used at Genoa had been authorized to use spray cans with irritant CS gas to immobilize possible 'antagonists' at close range (Hearing 5 September 2001, 75), whereas use of the *tonfa* truncheon, already allotted to *carabinieri* mobile battalions, had been limited to a single specialized unit of the first Rome mobile division.[22] As a first step towards setting up special mobile division units for deployment on the most challenging public order duties, a volunteer-based experimental squad had been formed within that division, a decision that after Genoa – where the squad had taken part *inter alia* in searching the Diaz-Pertini school – was criticized even within the police. Gigi Notari, from the secretariat of the police union SIULP, stated: 'I think the NOA [the experimental squad] should be dissolved, since we have seen the results. The union opposes the trend to creeping militarisation of the police' (*Gente*, 14 August 2001, 22).[23]

The assessment of the dangers the movement presented, based on the reports of the secret services, seems to have strongly influenced the specific training of the police divisions for the G8. Giuseppe Bocuzzi, an officer of the seventh Bologna mobile division, describes the training at Ponte Galeria as follows:

> The course began in the run-up to the G8 emergency, and I felt that it was improvised. [...] They taught us only to repress, not to prevent; the no-global movement was presented to us as the enemy, there was no training about the various components of the movement, no distinction between violent and peaceful groups. We were prepared for much throwing of Molotovs, for walking through flames, for hitting the deck running. (*Diario* 18/2002)

For Angela Burlando, vice *questore* (retired in spring 2002), the courses did not tend to construct a serene atmosphere: 'When they did the course at Ponte Galeria the officers were bludgeoned about these risks. When we desk officers went there for a day, I saw that risks were being presented, with specific, proper forms of defence.

---

22 Use of the new truncheons (clubs made of polycarbonate) had been authorized by the Amato government (Report III, 136). Taken up by the *carabinieri* – who at Naples were still using the butts of their guns – even before Genoa, these truncheons are in fairly widespread use among other police forces. The accusation raised after Genoa that the *tonfa* caused much more serious injuries than the traditional type was rejected by Valerio Donnino, who did, however, admit the risks associated with improper use of the weapon, documented in some episodes: namely with the handle the other way around (like a hammer), and used vertically (Hearing 5 September 2001, 35, 45).

23 Specialized units, with the task *inter alia* of intervening against violent fringes at demonstrations, exist in most European police forces. They are fundamental to the strategy of *de-escalating force*, which combines commitment to dialogue with targeted action against the violent, to isolate and arrest them without involving peaceful demonstrators. For the polemics accompanying their creation and deployment in Germany, see Sturm and Ellinghaus 2002, 26ff.

But the emphases were perhaps unnecessary …' (Zinola 2003, 81). Among the issues allegedly underestimated were the physical and mental state of the personnel and their possible responses in a situation of tension and physical stress (Zinola 2003, 124). The main instrument of coercive action by the police – the baton charge – in fact sparks off a cocktail of psychological conditions that reduce self-control.[24]

In addition to personnel safety, the biggest concern in the training during the run-up to the Genoa G8 seems to have been challenging the direct, violent attacks against police forces previously identified as a new feature in street incidents (Hearing 5 September 2001, 31; Hearing 8 August 2001, 67), whereas the problem of separating the small violent groups from the great bulk of peaceful demonstrators was neglected. Indeed, *carabinieri* commanding general Siracusa asserted: 'We shall certainly have to reconsider a number of aspects, especially as regards isolating the troublemakers from those who are by contrast peaceful' (Hearing 8 August 2001, 94).

For the G8, all police personnel had received a manual inviting police officers to keep to cautious, measured rules of conduct and to avoid regarding the demonstrators as enemies (see the citations in Gubitosa 2003, 70). However, as Filippo Saltamartini, general secretary of the police union SAP, states, the pamphlet would ultimately be an attempt to offload responsibilities: 'The booklet did not go to any teaching institutions or the police stations, no discussion meetings were organized; that is, its contents did not become part of the common stock' (*Micromega* 4/2001, 83). Even had these discussion meetings been held, it should be stressed that convinced application of a negotiating, dialogue strategy requires more intense, more specific information and education work within the police. As experience teaches, strong mistrust of the strategy among policemen must be overcome, and margins for action in specific situations must be brought out (Driller 2001, 36f., 46f.).

A direct connection between the survival of militarized features in the organization of the mobile divisions, more than in other sections of the Italian police, and the insufficient attention to professionalism, further emerges from the utilization for public order of auxiliary personnel on military national service or substitute service for national service. The *carabinieri* mobile battalions, normally earmarked for public order deployment, are 70 per cent made up of draftees on voluntary service (Hearing 8 August 2001, 67). According to the *carabinieri* commanding general, of 6,300 *carabinieri* at Genoa, 1,700 were auxiliaries (young draftees) (*La Repubblica* 27 July 2001), including the one who killed Carlo Giuliani. The State police mobile divisions until 2000 were 70–80 per cent auxiliary draftees or retained draftees, with an extremely high turnover (an almost total turnover every two years); it was only

---

24 It requires officers to act aggressively in conditions of relative anonymity: protective armour is worn; a helmet at least partly covers the face; and especially, one acts not as an individual but as part of a group. The target of the action is not other individuals, but an equally anonymous collective – the crowd, 'them' – which is perhaps insulting and physically attacking 'us' – the police. If officers' resentment and frustration is stimulated by demonstrator actions perceived as aggressive, the charges permit retaliation in conditions that minimize individual responsibility (P.A.J. Waddington 1991, 177–8).

after that date, with a reduction in the proportion of auxiliaries, that the percentage of full-time officers rose at all significantly (Colomba 2003, 194). A police trade union complained that over 50 per cent of personnel in the 13 mobile divisions deployed in Genoa consisted of auxiliaries on draft service (*Liberazione* 21 August 2001). The recruitment mechanisms brought in for the period after abolition of the draft, scheduled for January 2005, with 60 per cent of places in the competitions reserved for those coming from the armed forces, will in all probability enhance the militarized features of the personnel.

Failing recent relevant experience of coercive public order associated with political demonstrations, the tactics used in Genoa frequently seem borrowed from those tried in other 'emergencies'. We have already mentioned the directly operational repercussions that the complete predominance of hooligan control in the work experience of the mobile divisions may have had. Strategies used for isolating and protecting specific areas at football grounds seem to have been applied in concentrating control on the red zone, and in part in the yellow zone. Testimony from many detainees cites the fact that the penitentiary officers in the special units (GOM) apply the same techniques to demonstrators – 'stand up and face the wall' – as those used to prevent recognition by Mafia members; the same seems true of the *carabinieri* NOCS, who acted with covered faces.[25] The presence at Genoa of special units set up chiefly to fight organized crime – like the GOM and the NOCS – indicates how the personnel deployed make control strategies developed to fight the Mafia or control football violence spill over into control of political demonstrations.

Moreover, also the policing of protest in Italy has been influenced by general conceptions of public order developed to face assumed emergencies (see also Chapter 5 in this volume). The terrorism, mafia and football hooliganism emergencies have given the police ambiguous powers – on top of the considerable powers guaranteed by the consolidated text of the public security laws adopted during the Fascist period and never completely reformed. A broad conception of public order as a criterion of a higher order than civil and political rights, the possibility of carrying out searches without warrants when looking for weapons, and conspiracy offences with generic definitions (at Genoa many arrestees were initially accused of association to commit crimes of devastation and plunder) are all features enhancing the potential for arbitrary actions by the police authorities.[26]

On top of this is the problem, not solved by the 1981 reform, of the limited transparency of the police forces in interactions with citizens: identification numbers

---

25 The mobile operational groups (GOM) of the prison police were set up in 1997 (and then regulated by Ministerial Decree of 19 February 1999), with the task of controlling the most dangerous prisoners, transfers of mafia-collaborators and intervention in cases of revolt. They were involved in episodes of jail violence – in Milan in 1998 and in Sassari in 2000.

26 In this context it should also be noted that one of the features of protest policing in the 1980s and 1990s was its selectivity: certain 'hard' methods survived in opposing small groups, especially the 'social centres'. Among precedents recalled for certain features of the search at the Diaz school were the searches of two social centres, the Leoncavallo in Milan in 1995 and the Askatasuna in Turin in 1999 (Pepino 2001, 892).

are concealed, complaint procedures are tortuous and powers of review exclusively internal. The uncertain definition of the powers of the DIGOS, the replacement for the old political offices of police – authorized to collect information on all political and social actors with no constitutional limits or checks by judicial authorities – is one of the most glaring examples of the maintenance of severe limits on democratic accountability of the police forces. These limits are still more marked for the *carabinieri* (who have always been closed to outside eyes, as shown *inter alia* by the absence of academic research on them) and for the special divisions.

The EU Network of Independent experts in fundamental rights recently underlined that, in general, the complaint procedures in most Member States are not satisfactory because they do not provide for an independent investigative structure (EU Network 2003, 57f.).[27] In specific cases connected with the movement, the problem of internal police investigative procedures has been raised in connection with Sweden and the Czech Republic.[28] After the Naples incidents, Amnesty International had already asked in a letter to the Italian Ministry of the Interior for an independent commission to analyse police tactics and conduct and examine the accusations of violence and mistreatment, both 'on the street' and in police barracks (*AI Index* 30/001/2001).[29] After Genoa, the government and the parliamentary majority displayed little desire to favour an independent review of police operations.

In parliament, the majority rejected the setting up of a commission of inquiry (which would have had the powers of a court of justice), conceding an investigative commission only after intervention by the president of the republic, with the consequence that the contrasting versions given by various police officials about individual episodes could not be clarified. Various centre-right figures attacked the magistracy when it opened inquires into police conduct for the Naples and Genoa

---

27 The requirement for an independent investigative structure cannot be met by the magistracy investigating only facts of criminal relevance. Moreover, the practical conduct of judicial inquiries always remains a task for the police forces.

28 In July 2001, the UN Human Rights Committee underlined that the current system of investigating complaints against the police in the Czech Republic 'lacks objectivity and credibility and would seem to facilitate impunity for police involved in human rights violations' (*AI index EUR* 71/001/2001; POL 10/001/2002). In its concluding remarks in the fifth periodic report on Sweden, the same committee expressed concern about cases of excessive use of force by the police, for instance during the Gothenburg summit, and recommended: 'The state party should ensure the completion of investigations into such use of force, in conditions of total transparency and through a mechanism independent of the law enforcement authorities' (http://www.humanrights.se/svenska/Concluding%20observ%20MP0204.pdf). The 188 charges filed against the police after Gothenburg did not result in any convictions (Alternative Report, 61s.).

29 In his deposition to the parliamentary commission on the Genoa events, ex-Minister of the Interior Bianco reports on an internal inquiry into the Naples actions that had found 'some excessive initiatives by uniformed personnel, not yet identified since they were wearing the protective helmet' (Hearing 7 September 2001, 54). Depositions of some detained demonstrators about brutality and harassment would lead over a year later to a judicial inquiry, accompanied by heavy polemics.

events. The three senior officials removed from their posts after Genoa were all reassigned to new prestigious posts within the police (Gubitosa 2003, 419ff.). No other disciplinary measures were made public following the inspections ordered by the Ministry of the Interior. The commission of inspection on Bolzaneto appointed by the Ministry of Justice included the very person in charge of coordinating the activities of the Genoa penitentiary administration (Report I, 246).

The climate within the police forces is, moreover, unfavourable to independent review, as demonstrated by the stances of the police unions, at least initially all or almost all concerned with fiercely defending the actions of the police forces. Already on 22 July 2001, the SIULP (the most representative police union, and a protagonist in past years in the political struggle to demilitarize the force) expressed 'sincere, heartfelt thanks to the government representatives' for having indicated their solidarity with the policemen deployed at Genoa (Pepino 2001, 894). On 22 August, SAP, the second largest trade union, protested the decision by the magistracy to investigate the 140 policemen present at the Diaz school, accusing them of 'shooting at sitting ducks', while on the day when some officers were being interrogated a picket was organized at the prosecution offices by the Coordination for Trade Union Independence of the Police Forces (COISP). On 5 September, the police union COSAP demonstrated under the windows of the ministry where the committee for public order and security was meeting. The small right-wing union LISIPO talked of the 'steady rain of warrants raising demotivation almost to the point of psychological disarmament' (*La Repubblica* 23 August 2001). In a communiqué in Naples, SIULP dictated the 'sole, necessary' conditions for guaranteeing public order at the NATO Summit scheduled for September 2001: 'The police will guarantee security only on definite conditions: single command, adequate deployment of men, the essential logistics, but above all an end to the campaign of hatred, delegitimation and criminalization of the police forces.'[30] Scoppa of the COCER (the *carabinieri* trade-union-type organization) called for 'a climate of serenity. Continuation of the attacks is causing severe loss of motivation among people who do not feel at all guilty.' 'We have to see the protection of our personnel guaranteed, who should not be risking, in addition to their personal safety, criminal and administrative proceedings or even only suffering condemnation from a part of public opinion' (*Micromega* 4/2001, 70, 72). The autonomous unions and many police circles reject the proposal for a code of ethics for conduct as recently introduced in Portugal, calling it insulting (Zinola 2003, 187).

However, there has also emerged from within the police a move to return to a path of reform, with a call to start a dialogue with the movement, specifically to avoid the risk of delegitimizing the police in at least part of public opinion. The SIULP (SIULP/CS) stated: 'It is wrong to shut ourselves up in ourselves. We have to

---

30 According to the communiqué, among the enemies are 'The Genoa fire-hydrant thrower, the Agnolettos, Casarinis and our very own Carusos, in no way peaceful little lambs but fomenters of disorder, culprits or promoters of attempted lynching' (*La Repubblica*, 21 August 2001).

open up dialogue with the anti-globals. Not start an attack: woe betide us were we to go back to the repressive structures.' The more leftist SILP–CGIL (8,000 members) criticized the 'purely military conditions of the public order seen at Genoa', warning against 'favouring the break between police and civil society, who must instead attain a dialectical relation of mutual control and vigilance' (*Il Manifesto*, 21 August 2001). The capacity of the police unions to play a role in learning and innovation seems, however, limited by a corporatism enhanced by the two decades of delays in implementing police reform, particularly as regards careers, with a consequent explosion in the number of unions, accused on several quarters of becoming clientele-based. In a situation of polarization around public order issues, while some trade unionists reaffirm the need to repair the break with part of the citizenry, nonetheless the threatening tones against those who 'delegitimize' the police forces have grown within the police, creating the potential for further escalation.

The lessons of Genoa and protest policing at the Florence ESF

In summary: at Genoa, as on other previous occasions, the security of the summit was the chief objective, to which the right to demonstrate peacefully was subordinated. While the movement – the novelty of which severely tries the police's capacity to properly assess its objectives and strategies – is largely peaceful, widespread mistrust of the police, the conflict around the red zones, the simultaneous presence of socially and politically heterogeneous groups and sometimes of tiny but vigorous violent fringes, enhance the public order maintenance problems. Above all, though, these features make it easy for the police to categorize demonstrators as dangerous by attributing credibility to the most dramatic information on their intentions. Police knowledge that is suspicious of emergent, diverse collective actors, moreover, was interwoven with an organizational structure still marked by incomplete democratic reform – in part militarized, with poor accountability, uncertain professionalization and poor coordination. The hypothesis that the brutality of police action at Genoa derives from a political order requires as a corollary the existence of police forces willing to follow those political orders – that is, of police forces endowed with an organizational structure and professional culture that predispose them to follow indications for actions which are not just 'tough' but go beyond the limits of legality.

This does not alter the fact that the hardening of the police response to the movement for globalization from below in fact finds its main explanation in the (lack of) political response to the protest. Particularly the government and the centre-right majority have refused to recognize the movement as an interlocutor, instead interpreting and presenting it as a public order problem. 'Recognition' of the movement as a legitimate political actor seems, however, uncertain even by the centre-left opposition, which in the case of the protest against the Genoa G8 did not line up so decisively in defence of dissent as the parties of the Italian left had traditionally done. The movement's apparent isolation from the institutional political forces and its prevalent presentation as a public order problem was combined with the historically consolidated 'King's police' model, with a police 'knowledge' extremely sensitive to the political orientations of the majority.

While the Gothenburg and Genoa events underline the transnational nature not just of the movement but also of the response to it, in both political and public order terms, the national styles of policing do nonetheless remain highly identifiable.[31] Many of the elements that emerged at Genoa can in fact be explained as a partial reaffirmation of the traditional response to new 'challengers' in Italy: an overall strategy tending to exclusion instead of inclusion; as regards political power, a mistrust of more direct forms of political participation and a tendency to see in public demonstrations an attempt to overthrow the parliamentary majority; as regards the police, organizational gaps such as the lack of coordination among the various forces, low accountability, inadequate public order professionalism and a public order culture that does not favour the right to demonstrate (della Porta and Reiter 2003).

It must be stressed, however, that one cannot talk of a return in Italy to the period of the 'cold civil war' of the 1950s in relation to public order strategies, as shown by the many peacefully held demonstrations since the autumn of 2001. A decisive factor was the staying power of the civil rights coalition, which although it did not seem consistently supported by the parties of the institutional left nonetheless seems more extended and rooted in Italian and international civil society. Other factors have also contributed to a correction of the Genoa line: criticisms by other states as well as European and international institutions, the manifest lack of success of the police operations and the downright illegalities that emerged from inquiries by the magistracy.[32]

Reflection in institutional terms on the Genoa errors is expressed *inter alia* in the conclusions of an Interior Ministry committee on reorganization of the mobile divisions, made public in October 2002. The committee stresses, among other things, the need for training and practice courses for all (not just for special squads) and especially for the mobile divisions, with the aim of training officers in relationships and contact with demonstrators in emergency situations. There are also calls for the institutionalization of 'contact groups' to guarantee the right of assembly and to isolate and challenge the violent contingents. Finally, there are recommendations to strengthen the lines of command and abolish the *tonfa*. The CS tear gas remains as

---

31 As regards the EU, the decision to hold *all* European summits in Brussels rather than in the country holding the presidency will very likely lead to a strengthening of the 'international police'.

32 For the break-in to the Diaz school, the Genoa prosecution service made official the request to try 29 officials and officers, while 39 are being investigated for the Bolzaneto violence (*La Repubblica*, 4 March 2004). 26 demonstrators were tried for devastation and sacking, with a minimum penalty in the Civil Code of eight years (*La Repubblica*, 2 March 2004).

an extreme resort in tackling particularly serious situations that cannot be handled otherwise (*La Repubblica* 10 October 2002).[33]

The committee's conclusions seem to make official a return to the negotiated management strategies that had been abandoned in Genoa. Considering particularly the occasion of the Florence ESF in November 2002 – where a huge demonstration against the war in Iraq (500,000 participants) remained strictly peaceful, refuting the highly alarmist rumours coming particularly from the centre-right on the eve of the event – we shall seek to understand what has specifically changed in handling the street, and what lessons have been drawn from the Genoa experience by the political authorities, the police and the movement itself.

A first feature to stress is that, as in Copenhagen on the occasion of the EU Summit in December 2002, negotiations between authorities and organizers started months ahead and were conducted with the prefect as constant interlocutor, thus permitting a reduction in mutual mistrust. Despite the movement's heterogeneity and a climate of high tension fed by many centre-right figures and sections of the press with a virulent campaign against the event, the verdict of both authorities and movement spokespersons on the dialogue was positive. To counterbalance the effect of the alarmist reports coming from the secret services, which were widely disseminated in the press, a one-month course held by sociologists and psychologists was organized for the police deployed in Florence (*Il Manifesto*, 1 November 2002).

The positive outcome of the Florence negotiations was also helped by the process of self-critical reflection within the movement after the Genoa experience (emerging in part from the focus groups conducted by our research team), which *inter alia* brought a commitment to contribute to the peaceful holding of the demonstration with a marshal body of their own.[34] Apart from the different nature of the occasion, one should also bear in mind that the organizers for the ESF included part of the institutional left and major European and Italian trade union organizations.

The self-critical reflection after Genoa seems to bring out the point that the movement, while on the one hand seeking to moderate its forms of action (an indication of which might be seen in the fact that in Florence and at other demonstrations immediately after Genoa the disobedients did not wear their usual protection), on the other hand feared a tendency to designate as 'violent' certain effective, high-profile forms of direct action it internally accepts as legitimate. Police

---

33 The special anti-riot squad of the Roman public order police unit is to be dissolved (*La Repubblica*, 20 June 2002); its commander, vice-chief of police Canterini, is under investigation by the Genoa magistracy.

34 Rejection of militarization and organizational fluidity made the movement reluctant to set up a marshal body. On the role of such services in the escalation of the 1970s which led to terrorism, see della Porta 1995, 90–4, 153–8. At the 30 June meeting with the police chief, the GSF was informed that the black bloc would seek to infiltrate its demonstrations and was asked if it would be able to avoid that. The answer was no, since the GSF did not intend to stand in for the forces of order. The police chief stated at that point that it was in any case a task for the forces of order to deter or isolate violent demonstrators, and thus not a matter for the movement (Hearing 6 September 2001, 54).

attempts (for instance on the occasion of the European Summit in Copenhagen in December 2002) to exclude these forms of action in principle and block them even by questionable preventive measures may bring about radicalization of clashes, especially if combined with a trend, noted in challenges to President Bush's policies in the US, to limit protest visibility by confining it to peripheral, isolated areas.[35]

Coming back to the Florence ESF: as had been the case for the G8 Day in July in Genoa commemorating the events of the previous year, police operations were run by a unified operations room for the State police and the *carabinieri*. They were directed by the local police chief, who in Genoa in 2001 had been flanked by national vice-chief of police Andreassi (Zinola 2003, 139). The police – who indicated to lawyers on the demonstrators' legal team their intention to wipe out the image of Genoa (*Il Manifesto*, 6 November 2002) – accompanied the march but kept a distance, remaining 'invisible' as far as possible, a strategy recalling the one often used in the 1980s and 1990s with the social centres (della Porta 1998).[36] A special telephone number was activated for communication between prefect and organizers.[37] While border checks remained – the Schengen agreement was once again suspended from 1 to 11 November – with people turned back on the basis of the questionable expulsion measures taken at Genoa (*Il Manifesto*, 7 November 2004), no restrictions were imposed on the sites of ESF initiatives, many of which took place in the centre.

If these features seem to confirm a return to negotiated-control strategies by the Italian police, that does not mean that Genoa can be classified as an incident along the way. The chosen tactic of remaining invisible as far as possible, as well as the specific training concentrated on prevention, also met with criticism from within the police, with the SIULP in favour and the SAP, by contrast, opposing. It was also

---

35 Prior to the Copenhagen summit, Danish police chief Kai Vittrup had declared that under no circumstances would the police accept the anticipated symbolic actions of occupation of multinational concerns and public spaces, and that such actions would be regarded as an invitation to voluntary arrest. The Danish police tactics to throw the activists out of balance by preventive detentions (e.g. of Luca Casarini, leader of the Italian disobedients) and impounding of material (even purely propaganda) for use in such actions are problematic from not just a political and legal but even from a technical viewpoint: they seem ill suited to bigger demonstrations (Peterson 2003a; Wahlström 2003b). In the United States, the ACLU started a lawsuit against the Secret Service for the continuing practice of allowing pro-Bush demonstrators to remain visible to cameras during presidential appearances while corralling anti-Bush protesters into pens or designated areas far from the media.

36 Also without incident were the demonstrations on the occasion of the EU summit in Copenhagen in December 2002, where police action followed a partly different line: dialogue with the movement, actively sought a full year before the event, and a mobile, flexible strategy not statically concentrated on defending certain places as in Gothenburg or Genoa, but seeking to take and keep the offensive to control all situations regarded as dangerous or wrongful developments (Peterson 2003a).

37 At the demonstrations against the EU summit in Copenhagen, situations of tension during demonstrations were successfully defused by direct contact between police and movement figures (Wahlström 2003b).

claimed from within the police that the peaceful holding of the Florence ESF did depend – apart from the police preventive services – not on dialogue but on the fact that by contrast with Genoa, there was neither an opposing party to challenge nor a red zone. The presence of a marshal body organized by the CGIL (a national left-wing trade union) alongside that of the movement had given the necessary security guarantees (Colomba 2003, 204f., 212; Zinola 2003, 173ff.). There seems, therefore, a persisting mistrust of the movement as a credible interlocutor for dialogue on the carrying out of demonstrations. As regards police organization, the Genoa events did not lead to a full debate on structural problems but to specific adjustments on the occasion of individual events.

As regards politics, the centre-right temptation especially after September 11 to portray the movement as a public order problem – even ranking it alongside terrorism – and to denounce public demonstrations as attempts to overthrow the democratically elected majority seems to remain high.[38] For its part, the institutional left continues to be divided on its attitude towards the movement, some seeing it as a disturbing, dangerous element. Above all, though, political forces have not proved interested or ready, at a national or a European level, for open discussion on public order strategies and on democratic control over the nascent EU internal security apparatus.

It thus becomes clear that the development of strategies for maintaining public order is not following an unambiguous trend towards de-escalation, but taking on an at least partly cyclical dynamic. It should be recalled that these strategies are not technical questions but reflect the quality of democratic systems. The Swedish Commission on the Gothenburg events stated: 'The events that took place in Göteborg cannot merely be regarded as public order issues to be dealt with by the police but also as political issues relating to democracy, influence, exclusion, etc.' The commission stresses 'the importance of political dialogue in the form of discussion and through other channels of influence and participation in democratic decision-making processes – at the international, national and local levels. It is crucial to find forms for such discussion between decision-makers and today's opinion movements.'[39]

---

38   In reference to the Genoa G8, we read in the report on information and security policy (second half of 2001) presented by the Italian government to the senate: 'The symbolic scope of the event as a potential catalyst for many vehicles of threat was confirmed, on the information level, by indications of possible convergence of activation of Islamic fundamentalism, ideological terrorism and the autonomous and anarchic area, and on the factual level by the violence employed by the squads of the so-called black bloc' *Per Aspera ad Veritatem – Rivista di intelligence e di cultura professionale*, 22 (January–April 2002).

39   Göteborg 2001, *Betänkande av Göteborgskommittén* (SOU 2002: 122), summary, available at www.justitie.regeringen.se/propositionermm/sou/Göteborg_2001_eng.pdf, last accessed 2004.

Primary Sources

Alternative Report: Swedish NGO Foundation for Human Rights and the Swedish Helsinki Committee for Human Rights, 'Alternative Report to the Human Rights Committee. With Respect to Sweden's Commitments under the International Covenant on Civil and Political Rights', Stockholm, 2002.

Hearing: Parlamento Italiano, 'Audizioni di fronte alla commissione d'indagine conoscitiva sui "fatti accaduti a Genoa nei giorni 19, 20, 21 e 22 luglio 2001 in occasione del vertice G8"', verbali delle sedute di 8, 9, 28, 29, 30 agosto e 4, 5, 7 settembre 2001 [Italian Parliament, 'Hearings in front of the investigative commission on the "events which occurred in Genoa on 19, 20, 21, and 22 July 2001 on the occasion of the G8 Summit"', minutes of the sessions on 8, 9, 28, 29, 30 August and 4, 5, 7 September 2001], available at www.camera.it.

Report I: Parlamento Italiano, 'Documento conclusivo approvato dalla commissione d'indagine conoscitiva sui "fatti accaduti a Genoa nei giorni 19, 20, 21 e 22 luglio 2001 in occasione del vertice G8"', allegato alla seduta del 20 settembre 2001 [Italian Parliament, 'Final document approved by the investigative commission on the "events which occurred in Genoa on 19, 20, 21, and 22 July 2001 on the occasion of the G8 Summit"', enclosure to the meeting on 20 September 2001], available at www.camera.it.

Report II: Parlamento Italiano, 'Proposta alternativa di documento conclusivo ai lavori della commissione d'indagine conoscitiva sui "fatti accaduti a Genoa nei giorni 19, 20, 21 e 22 luglio 2001 in occasione del vertice G8"', presentata dai deputati Luciano Violante et al., allegato alla seduta del 20 settembre 2001 [Italian Parliament, 'Alternative proposal of a final document to the proceedings of the investigative commission on the "events which occurred in Genoa on 19, 20, 21, and 22 July 2001 on the occasion of the G8 Summit"', presented by deputy Luciano Violante et al., enclosure to the meeting on 20 September 2001], available at www.camera.it.

Report III: Parlamento Italiano, 'Proposta alternativa di documento conclusivo ai lavori della commissione d'indagine conoscitiva sui "fatti accaduti a Genoa nei giorni 19, 20, 21 e 22 luglio 2001 in occasione del vertice G8"', presentata dal deputato Graziella Mascia, allegato alla seduta del 20 settembre 2001 [Italian Parliament, 'Alternative proposal of a final document to the proceedings of the investigative commission on the "events which occurred in Genoa on 19, 20, 21, and 22 July 2001 on the occasion of the G8 Summit"', presented by deputy Graziella Mascia, enclosure to the meeting on 20 September 2001], available at www.camera.it.

SIULS-CS: Press release of the police union SIULP, available at http://www.siulp. it/sez/flash.asp?TipoFunzione=ListaAnno&Anno=2001.

Chapter 3

Policing Contentious Politics at Transnational Summits: Darth Vader or the Keystone Cops?

Abby Peterson

Introduction

Political activists are increasingly confronting world leaders temporarily gathered in venues hosting transnational summits, for example at European Union summits, G8 and WTO meetings and others. The empirical focus in this chapter is a comparison between the two protest campaigns, and the police handling of them, at European Union Summit meetings in Gothenburg in June 2001 and Copenhagen in December 2002. The police campaigns mobilized to handle protest events in conjunction with these two meetings offer us radically different political policing approaches to dealing with contentious politics.

The analytical focus in this chapter revolves, first, around how territorial places, temporarily transformed into transnational political spaces in the advent of transnational summits, become the loci of contentious politics. In this chapter I will analyse the strategies and tactics used by activists to temporarily occupy and/or disrupt these territorial places, together with the police strategies and operational tactics employed to counteract those territorial strategies and tactics. These 'reconnaissance battles' (Bauman 2002) being fought out in specific territorial places are in turn battles to define and redefine the political spaces of transnational and national power. Second, the analytical focus revolves around the dimension of control, more specifically, how the police perceive and implement their mandate to control public order. Connected to the discussion of control is the notion of paramilitarism, which I will clarify in this section. The two police forces analysed here offer us two radically different strategies in their efforts to control public order in the frontier-lands.

The chapter poses two sets of questions that are at the heart of a working democratic system relying upon public political discussions among its citizenry. First, how are the alternative spaces for democratic deliberation more or less successively maintained and protected by public order policing? Second, in what ways are civil and political liberties – the rights to assemble, demonstrate and voice political protest – jeopardized by the police's quest for public order? In general, Scandinavian states are more hospitable to their contenders than many other countries. Denmark, and to an even greater degree Sweden, have historically employed strategies of inclusion or cooptation of the challenges posed by social movements (Wahlström and Peterson 2005). Despite this track record, activists assembled during the protest campaigns studied here were met with various degrees of police coercion. The new challengers emerging today are, even in a Scandinavian context, met with different strategies of political exclusion, and this is reflected in the policing measures taken.

Contentious politics in the frontier-lands

The general issues I will address are the ways in which public spaces for democratic deliberation are being revitalized, alternatively threatened, by the new faces of contemporary contentious politics, together with the state's responses to these mobilizations and actions. According to Zygmunt Bauman (2002), contemporary societies are under siege – under attack on two fronts: from the global frontier-land where old structures and rules do not hold and new ones are slow to take shape, and from the fluid, undefined domain of life politics. How are two Western European societies 'under siege' responding to these challenges to democratic spaces and institutions?

Bauman (2002) argues that we have left the era of space, when territory was the prime guarantee of security, and entered an era where global space has assumed the character of a 'frontier-land'. Territory can no longer offer us our sought-after security.

> In a frontier-land, agility and cunning count for more than a stack of guns. In frontier-lands, fences and stockades announce intentions rather than mark realities. In frontier-land, efforts to give conflicts a territorial dimension, to pin divisions to the ground, seldom bring results. Suspected from the start to be ultimately ineffective, those efforts tend to be half-hearted anyway: wooden stakes signal a lack of the self-assurance that stonewalls embody and manifest. In frontier-land warfare, trenches are seldom dug. The adversaries are known to be constantly on the move – their might and nuisance-making power lie in the speed, inconspicuousness and secrecy of their moves. For all practical intents and purposes, the adversaries are *extraterritorial*. (Bauman 2002, 90)

The global space opened in Gothenburg in conjunction with the 2001 EU Summit meeting, as with the global space that was opened during the 2002 EU Summit meeting in Copenhagen, bore the characteristics of Bauman's frontier-land: politically, these were spaces that were under-defined, under-determined and under-regulated (p. 91). And despite massive police presence and the erection of formidable police cordons, the policed territories of the two cities were nevertheless fractured, offering cracks and fissures for political contention. This under-definition, under-determination and under-regulation is a result of the progressive deterioration of structures of authority – in this case the structures of legitimate authority exercised by the European Union, together with the nation-state and its coercive arm, the police.

The global parameters of protest mobilizations today have encouraged disparate groups and individuals to participate in mass demonstrations. Diversity is a major characteristic of contemporary protests and demonstrations, often described as multigenerational, multiethnic, multiclass and multi-issue. These temporary action mobilizations represent a broad spectrum of causes and goals. Participants represent a variety of issues and a wide diversity of targeted adversaries. The combination of groups and participants coming together creates a powerful impression and an impact that is perhaps out of proportion with their individual strengths. The melding together of the various groups into one large body implies power and attracts attention and publicity, which, in turn, draws more and more participants. The new globalization-critical protest phenomenon has been characterized by the broad range of interests that have come together to conduct demonstrations with minimal dissension – a tactical innovation that protesters have adopted to promote their causes *en masse* (Cf. Klein 2000, 311).

The 'rainbow coalition' refers to a metaphorical notion well suited to an analysis of the contemporary forms of political alliances we have witnessed in conjunction with various summit meetings. Within the rainbow we can readily distinguish among the range of colours that constitute it, perhaps with the obvious exception of the so-called black bloc. An ephemeral natural phenomenon, the rainbow can disappear before our eyes as readily as it first appeared. Such is the case with the rainbow coalition. A rainbow coalition is a communication network among organizations, groups and persons, constructed to temporarily mobilize protest events in a specific place and time, across a broad political spectrum. The rainbow coalition is the transgression of the hegemonic form of political struggle and introduces the notion of a space for dialogue, for give and take between different political positions, which demands generosity and sacrifice in order to reach beyond the specificity of the narrow sense of belonging of one's own group and its specific interpretation of the political struggle (Peterson 2002; 1997, 168).

The various groups and organizations, which represented a broad range of causes and planned a broad range of activities for the EU Summits in Gothenburg and Copenhagen, formed various coalitions for the purpose of mobilizing participants. In contrast with those involved with expressly global events such as the World Bank Summit in Seattle or the G8 Summit meeting in Genoa, the coalitions in our case studies mobilized protest in cities hosting EU Summit meetings in countries with strong public opinion against the EU as well as highly organized anti-EU action networks and groups. Subsequently, the protest campaigns were explicitly divided: the action fields opened by these summit meetings included, on the one hand, new protesters who could be included in a notion of an emerging global justice movement, and on the other, protesters who specifically directed their challenges to the Swedish state, demanding a withdrawal from the Union. This reminds us that at what appears to be global events, the protest is not necessarily globally directed; rather the scales of protest are multilayered to include local, national and global issues and causes. What distinguishes this new political phenomenon is its *lack of an organization*, understood in its traditional sense. Rainbow coalitions join together a temporary and loosely knit array of organizations and action groups within particular countries, as well as like-minded groups and organizations across national borders, in a communication network coordinated through Internet channels. What distinguishes this communication network and its specific communication logic is the lack of controlling elements. While perhaps not 'headless', the coalition does bring into reciprocal communication a cacophony of 'heads'. Paradoxically, while the rainbow coalition is distinguished by its lack of formal organization, it is equally distinguished by the degree of its effective *coordination*, which relies largely on the Internet.

These new modes of political organizations and mobilizations that are emerging – under-defined, under-determined and under-regulated – pose new problems for political policing. Just as the organizers of the temporary rainbow coalitions in Gothenburg and Copenhagen had little control over all of the action groups participating in the summit events, so too was the police's control effectively diminished. This was particularly felt by the police in their efforts to negotiate with the activists prior to the summit (see Oskarsson 2002 and Wahlström and Oskarsson in this volume).

The protest events were in practice what Bauman (2002) calls 'reconnaissance battles' with one purpose: 'to sift the grain of the hopefully possible from the chaff of the impossible or hopeless' (2002, 291). In military practice, reconnaissance battles precede the setting of war objectives and the design of war strategy. In the practice of contentious politics, they explore adversaries' determination and endurance, the resources they can command and the speed with which those resources may be brought to the field of struggle. They help to clarify feasible goals and the range of realistic options at hand in the wider struggle, to gain information intended to lay bare the adversaries' strong points and weaknesses and subsequently expose the cracks in the facade of structures of authority, challenging the legitimacy of the power relations upon which they rest.

The territorialization strategies of contemporary contentious politics reflect this shift from the era of space to an era of the frontier-land. While mass actions, deploying what Routledge (1997) calls a swarm of protesters, are designed to occupy space, whether a street or a square, these are temporary occupations of territorial space in order to lend this space new meaning – to inscribe provisionally upon it a redefinition of the relations of power. They are temporary challenges to structures of authority, orderly and peaceful as well as violent, in order to reconnoitre the relations of power in a field of struggle. As ephemeral challenges, they are for all intents and purposes extraterritorial. The provisional occupation of a territory does not provide protesters with the security of a fortified geographical place; it only provides them with an under-regulated and under-defined space for their challenges.

The hit-and-run tactics of the pack, small groups of militant high-risk activists, are extraterritorial in another sense. These tactics are not designed to occupy spaces even temporarily; rather they are intended to disrupt them with quick forays, nonviolent acts of civil disobedience as well as violent direct actions, into adversaries' territories, initiating situations that disrupt the dominion of authorities (Peterson and Oskarsson

2002; Peterson 2001). In the under-determined, under-regulated and under-defined territory over which authorities attempt to exercise control, activists assume the initiative and create situations that lay bare the futility of those attempts. This brings our discussion to the second analytical focus of the study, that of control.

Controlling public order

As P.A.J. Waddington has pointed out, 'the desire of police officers to maintain control over their essentially precarious working environment is a persistent theme in the literature on routine policing' (1994, 127). This desire remains even in regards to political policing. Control over the working environment can take one of two strategic directions: control over places *or* control over situations. The analysis offered here contrasts these two distinctive approaches to controlling public order to investigate the ways in which each one protects or threatens the democratic spaces for political contention.

On the one hand, we have the Swedish approach, as illustrated during the summit meeting in Gothenburg, tied to maintaining order by protecting territorial spaces. This is a classic strategy of control that has its roots in times when territories could be readily defined, determined and regulated – 'the era of space'. The police's adversaries were easily identifiable and could be contained in their presubscribed roles and places. The 'rules of the game' of contentious politics had been practised for decades. Police and activists forged agreements as to which public spaces could be temporarily annexed for political protests; other spaces were 'off limits'. The boundaries for protest were fixed by the police and most often respected by protesters. Sometimes political manifestations led to violent confrontations, but most often demonstrations proceeded in an orderly, peaceful manner. Demonstrators stuck to their previously agreed upon routes and the police assumed their role in leading the marches and maintaining a wait-and-see defensive posture.

The foundation for political policing in Sweden was centred upon a strategy relying upon the protection and regulation of defined territorial spaces – an overall defensive territorial policing strategy built upon the occupation of space. Such a strategy was employed in Gothenburg in June 2001. The police doggedly attempted to control territories for protest with their deployment of personnel, riot fences and shipping containers. However, protest situations erupted outside the police cordons in territories over which they held no or sorely inadequate control. The rigidity of their territorial strategies made them ill-prepared to deal with the flexible and mobile extraterritorial tactics of the militant activists. While the police retained control over their occupied territories – the venues for the summit and for President Bush's visit – and eventually regained control over Hvitfeldska School, Vasa Park and the Avenue with new territorial occupations, they were often shown to be out of control of the situations that broke out during the three days of protest. A strategy designed for the era of space proved ineffectual to deal with protest in the frontier-land. The overall operative territorial strategy of the police command staff was a pivotal factor behind many rank-and-file police officers' repeated loss of personal control during the protest events in June, an issue to which I will return later in the chapter.

On the other hand, we have the Danish general concept for policing political protest, which has as its point of departure efforts to exert maximum control over events, in expected as well as unexpected situations. Their strategy is to keep situations under control: an offensive strategy to disrupt space. In his research on public order policing in London, P.A.J. Waddington goes so far as to say: 'it seems that it is loss of control by the police that prompts serious confrontation between police and others, not violence itself. Violence that can be contained is preferable to non-violent behaviour that threatens to "get out of hand"' (1994, 171; cf. Skolnick and Fyfe 1993, 94ff.).

A central element in the Danish offensive strategy is a high degree of mobility and flexibility, allowing a greater capability to control unexpected situations. They have implemented these elements with the introduction of small heavy- and light-armoured vehicles carrying specially trained squads of eight to 12 officers. The officers work close to their vehicles in the field, at a relatively close distance to the event being policed, so that they can effectively move in if a 'troublesome' situation arises. In order to remain on the offensive, police must be prepared to move in quickly either their tactical reserves or – in the last instance – their operational reserves, both in effect their coercive forces. During the summit, forces were assigned to stationary protective objects such as Bella Centre, the venue for the summit, Christianborg (the seat of government) and hotels housing key delegates; but the remaining Copenhagen uniformed police force were deployed in mobile positions.

Throughout Europe, public order police have developed tactical mobile units, an increasingly paramilitary operational capacity (della Porta 1998, 230; Wisler and Kriesi 1998, 98–9; P.A.J. Waddington 1998, 1994). Some tactical reserve units were available even in Sweden during the summit in Gothenburg, although they were not an integral part of the general policing strategy. However, these units have been formed and equipped in different ways and are deployed differently in the various national contexts. In Denmark they are part of routine public order policing and maintain high visibility at most larger protest events.

Control over events can be achieved through interventions on the part of the police, but it can also be achieved through controlling police forces in the field *not* to act. A retreat on the part of the police, a passive or 'wait-and-see' posture will often be the most effective means to maintain control over a situation. In exercising power, P.A.J. Waddington argues, 'what the police abstain from doing is as important as the actions they take' (1994, 199). Choosing not to invoke the law, not making arrests for minor offences and not confronting activists is simply another way of using police power in their best interests, essentially the overriding interest of control over the situation. Abstaining from action in certain situations during a protest event can be their most potent weapon for policing public order.

To assure that this 'weapon' is available to the police, it would seem that a paramilitary structure of command is necessary; in other words, the rank and file among the deployed police are under the control of senior officers and act in a disciplined manner. This internal sense of control, that is, senior officers in control over their officers in the field, is an aspect that is also highlighted in the analysis. It is argued that strong first-line supervision is an internal structure of control, particularly important when police officers are faced with chaotic and volatile situations in the field. Control over situations involves not only control over protesters but also over the rank-and-file officers in the field – in other words, that the hierarchical chain of command and order structure functions smoothly.

Fillieule and Jobard (1998) observed that senior officers in the public order police were often wary of their rank and file. They claim that an out-and-out gulf exists between the goals of officers in command and the way the rank and file think with regard to what constitutes good protest policing.[1] 'Non-intervention and a dispassionate approach are two criteria for excellence in the senior officers' view, but their men do not consider the operation a success without some kind of physical confrontation or without having evened the score with the demonstrators' (Fillieule and Jobard 1998, 82). In order to bridge this gap and assure that unnecessary force is not used against demonstrators, senior officers in the field must exert control. Internal control is thus vital for the protection of civil liberties and the protection of public spaces for contentious politics.

Most often, the offensive strategy of public order policing relies upon the control of space (P.A.J. Waddington 1994). However, within the controlled spaces of the frontier-lands, disruptions can occur, as these spaces can be, and often are, contested by protesters. The Danish offensive strategy does not depart from territorialization strategies, the control of spaces, as much as it departs from the capability of the disruption of spaces, which is even the preferred strategy of militant activists (Peterson and Oskarsson 2002; Peterson 2001). While the use of mobile units does relinquish the possibility of maximum control over spaces[2] where events take place, it also maximizes their capabilities to control the unexpected volatile situations that can arise during protest events through the strategy of disruption of spaces. In other

---

1 During an interview with a senior field officer (5 July 2002) this problem was ventilated. The officer claimed that in the restructuring of protest policing in Denmark, a transformation of the mentality of officers was more important than the addition of paramilitary hardware. This change in the software of policing, rank-and-file officers' attitudes and perceptions of activists was the most difficult to change and required long-term efforts. Further, he remarked that as most of their new recruits did not have military experience, they were unused to following orders in the field. This too required concerted efforts in their training. While he maintained that officers' attitudes and perceptions of activists/demonstrators had dramatically changed during these years of restructuring, a few 'rotten apples' remain; it is these officers in particular who must be controlled in the field by their senior officers.

2 Vittrup claims that police attempts to territorialize the spaces of events are largely doomed, as is impossible to control these spaces totally. First, the spaces will tend to grow, stretching the police forces to a point that containment is impossible. Secondly, these deployments do not only contain protesters, but also contain the police, locking them into static positions unsuitable to deal with unexpected situations (interview, Copenhagen May 2002).

words, what they lose in the control of spaces is won with the increased effectiveness of tactical manoeuvrability and the subsequent capability to control unexpected situations. While a police strategy to occupy territorial spaces would appear to be out of tune with contentious politics in the 'frontier-lands', one that is designed to control situations would appear to be in harmony with this new era of spaces.

Paramilitarism

In the Anglo-American policing context of which the Scandinavian countries are a part, there has been a strong historical tendency to demarcate visibly between the responsibilities and functions of the military and those of the police, together with clear distinctions in acceptable military strategies and tactics and those of the public order police. What has been the rule on the European continent has been the exception in Scandinavia. Nevertheless, we have been witness in Denmark and Sweden to a clouding of these long-accepted differences, although these developments are relatively recent. Denmark has taken the initiative in Scandinavia in developing explicitly paramilitary capacities for large-scale public order policing. This is a trend that we expect Sweden to follow (Björk and Peterson 2002, 2006).

The notion of police paramilitarism is highly contested. P.A.J. Waddington clarifies the fundamental difference between the use of force by the military and by the civil police:

> The military aim is to eliminate the enemy. This can be seen in military tactics, weapons and munitions that are designed to create a 'field of fire' in which the likelihood of survival is minimized. ... Civil police, however heavily armed they may be, do not aim to eliminate their adversaries who are still citizens, even if they are also armed criminals. Typically, if engaged by an armed adversary, fire is returned. Once resistance is overcome, further use of force is not only redundant but also illegal. (1999a, 154)

The aim of the Scandinavian police is not to eliminate their adversaries, but to contain, control and/or apprehend them. Despite this fundamental difference, I will employ the notion of paramilitarism in a specifically defined sense. 'Para' as a prefix can be defined as 'closely resembling'.[3] In my definition, 'paramilitarism' implies organization and tactics that closely resemble those of the military, while retaining significant differences. While I specify dimensions of 'closely resembling', it is important to keep in mind that this is always a question of more or less resembling. In employing the definition in reality, specific police organizations and functions will find themselves placed along a continuum, with the military at one end of the spectrum and an unarmed civil police force at the other. The definition offered here is limited to large-scale police operations in conjunction with public order policing, as well as police operations during exceptional events, for example, terrorist threats, hostage taking, confronting heavily armed adversaries, and so on. During these latter

---

3   *Webster's Seventh New Collegiate Dictionary*, Springfield, MA: G&C Merriam Company, 1969.

events, police forces today usually engage special police units, so-called SWAT teams, which more explicitly resemble the military in that they are armed with lethal assault weapons. The focus in this chapter is, however, upon the former, and the definition of paramilitarism will be specified in relation to policing major protest events. The dimensions of paramilitarism that closely resemble military organization and tactics are the following:

- the operation is strategically coordinated at the highest levels of the command structure;
- the command and order structure, where officers in the field are required to obey their superiors along a prescribed chain of command;
- while senior field officers can exercise tactical discretion, within the parameters of the overall strategic plan, in order to maintain operational flexibility in meeting unexpected situations, individual discretion on the part of rank-and-file officers is not allowed;
- both the strategic planning and the operational tactics implemented are inspired and influenced by military strategy and tactics;
- officers are routinely protected by the use of riot gear – helmets, body armament, gas masks and so on – as well as the deployment of heavy- and light-armoured vehicles.

The significant differences are:

- police do not aim to eliminate their adversaries: their aim is to contain, control and apprehend individuals breaking the law;
- the weaponry employed will be primarily of a non-lethal defensive character, for example batons, tear gas, water cannons, distraction grenades, etc. (with the exception of SWAT team weaponry);
- while police officers are required to obey orders from their superiors in the field, they are individually liable for their actions in using force.

For the analysis that follows, in addition to the advances in new tactical hardware and the development of tactical flexibility, the most important dimension or set of dimensions in the definition of paramilitarism concerns the hierarchical command and order structure, which precludes individual discretion among the rank and file. This dimension is in direct contrast to the bulk of routine public order policing that demands individual discretion on the part of officers policing singly, in pairs, or in small groups.

Case I: The police riots in Gothenburg

Researchers remind us that the overwhelming majority of contentious actions in Western democracies, even in a tumultuous period of contention, take the form of peaceful, orderly, routinized actions that break no laws and violate no spaces (cf. Meyer and Tarrow 1998). Most political acts of protest do not result in violence.

Indeed, most of the actions of activists on the streets and squares of Gothenburg were orderly and peaceful as described above. Three major mass demonstrations were conducted in a peaceful and orderly fashion, as were countless seminars and public debates. The public manifestations of protest were many and the overwhelming majority of these actions were peaceful, despite media reports that have left the impression that the Summit was dominated by acts of violence (cf. Parsmo 2002).

When violence does break out, authorities and the general public alike are eager to place the blame on some party in the events. But it is often difficult to determine who was 'responsible' for the violence when it did occur, or who lay behind its escalation. Responsibility is most readily assigned to protesters. However, activists are not the sole actors in riots, however instrumental they may be to its outbreak. Violence arises from interaction between protesters and responding authorities. Research since the 1960s suggests that police authorities often bear a major part of the responsibility (for example Skolnick 2002; Reiner 2000; della Porta 1998; Critcher and Waddington 1996; P.A.J. Waddington 1994; Skolnick and Fyfe 1993).

Direct physical confrontations between activists and police bring to the surface highly emotionally charged moments, inevitably leading to processes that in most cases will result in an escalation of violence. Peterson (2001, 1997b) analysed these 'moments of collective effervescence' as to their role in the construction of militant collective identities, as well as to how, enhanced by the explosive sociality of direct confrontations, they lead to a rationale of violence on the part of activists. P.A.J. Waddington turns the logic of these arguments towards the police, arguing that the baton charge, the favoured tactic employed by the police in Gothenburg during the Summit, easily leads to an escalation of violence.

> The reason why baton charges are difficult to control is known colloquially in the Metropolitan Police as 'the red mist'. This refers to a potential cocktail of psychological conditions which diminishes any person's self-control, and from which the police are not exempt. Baton charges require officers to act aggressively in conditions of relative anonymity ... they may be wearing protective clothing with visors to obscure their facial features; and they will almost certainly be acting, not as individuals, but an equally anonymous collective – 'the crowd', 'Them' – who will have insulted and physically attacked 'Us' – the police. Officers' anger and frustration will thus have been aroused, and a baton charge will allow retaliation in conditions which minimise individual responsibility. (1991, 177–8)

The events in Gothenburg revealed two groups 'high' on the potent 'red mist' cocktail – the masked, anonymous activists, and the masked, anonymous police. Embroiled in their violent bodily confrontations, a 'spiral of violence' became inevitable, both during the actual events and in their aftermath (cf. Peterson 1997). Retaliations from both sides of the struggle were surely evident in their head-to-head situations of combat. In our monitoring of the police in the field during this three-day campaign, we observed multiple acts of excessive violence, both physical and verbal, against activists assembled. Furthermore, these acts appeared to be highly arbitrary: many activists and onlookers found themselves beaten by batons or shoved to the ground simply because they were 'in the wrong place at the wrong time' (Peterson and Oskarsson 2002). These observations were corroborated after the event by testimonies and film documents.

Clive Emsley and Richard Bessel (2000) refer to French sociologist François Dieu and his typology of the violent force employed by police. The typology includes *la violence instrumentale*, which is the exercise of force justified by their legitimate authority; *la violence dérivée*, a by-product of the former when individual police officers are carried away by panic or accident and strike out indiscriminately at those who happen to get in the way; and *la violence déviante*, which are uncalled-for and indefensible exercises of force by individual police officers carried away by anger, frustration and revenge (Emsley and Bessel 2000, 4). These latter two categories include the actions of individual officers, however many, which may have triggered further disorder and hostility to the police in the situations that we observed. Nevertheless, they are both, in a sense, derivatives of the authorized employment of coercive force. We argue that they are both examples of the unprofessional exercises of coercive force, only the motives behind their exercise vary. *Violence dérivée* are violent acts in the heat of the moment, by-products of the legitimate exercise of police power, which has got out of control. *Violence déviante* are the premeditated acts of revenge and anger, by-products of the situations where authorized force has been instrumentally employed. Examples of the latter are the acts of violent harassment of the young people detained face down on the asphalt in front of Schillerska School, or when police officers childishly dumped ashtrays and fast-food scrap in the soup prepared by the activist kitchens.

While it is often unclear and controversial exactly how police should respond to public disorder in a democratic society, we do expect professional behaviour, even in the heat of the moment. Control and professionalism are intrinsically connected. The existence of highly disciplined public order police, in control of themselves and under the control of their superiors, is a precondition for the professional exercise of police force, even in the heat of the moment. The professional exercise of their mandate does not ring well with brutality, whether physical or verbal, or with arbitrariness. Our conclusion is that during many of the situations that arose during this three-day period, the police (or at least, many police officers) in the field were more or less out of control (Peterson and Oskarsson 2002). Violent collective protest involves interaction between the behaviour of 'rioters' and the agents of social control, that is, police authorities. Each side may under closer inspection turn out to be 'riotous'. What we witnessed on the streets of Gothenburg were not only riots perpetrated by a relatively small number of activists, but also police riots.

According to Emsley and Bessel (2000), riots are invariably attributed to 'agitators', or the blame is put upon 'outside agitators' as was often the case in the media accounts from the EU Summit in Gothenburg. And, of course, domestic as well as foreign agitators – that is, activists seeking confrontation with police authorities as a primary strategic means for protest – were present on the streets of Gothenburg.

However, their numbers were few, given the vast majority of activists who did not share this commitment to violent confrontation, but rather denounced this tactic. On the basis of our observations, we estimate the numbers of militant agitators to have been restricted to approximately 45 to 70 individuals (Peterson and Oskarsson 2002). While relatively small, this group bears a major part of the responsibility for the violence that broke out in Gothenburg 2001.

While riots are most often attributed to political agitators, authorities seldom attribute them to the wrongdoings of police. As Emsley and Bessel (2000) point out, on the odd occasion when authorities have acknowledged the role of police in the escalation of violence, it has been ascribed to the clumsy acts of individual 'rotten apples'. However, on the basis of their research, they argue that the root of many instances of disorder triggered or escalated by the police is found more in the cultures and structures of police institutions than in the faults of single, undesirable individuals within the ranks. Just as I argue that acts of excessive violence on the part of some activists is better attributed to the culture(s) of protest than to individual 'rotten apples', so is the case for acts of excessive violence on the part of police. It may be that the accumulated individual acts of activists lead to political riots, just as the accumulated individual acts of policemen lead to police riots, and only the number of acts and individuals vary, lending the riots their scale and proportions; but there are wider processes and structures that allow these acts to accumulate to the point where a riot breaks out. After looking more closely at the police riots in Gothenburg, I will evaluate whether they were the result of the acts of individual police or whether they find their roots in the prevailing police culture, wider processes and operational decisions.

Rodney Stark (1972) analysed police riots in the US and argued that they were unusual only in their relative infrequency. Stark argues that whatever ideas and practices officers bring to their more everyday police work, the 'culture of policing' is simply exacerbated during riots. Excessive acts of violence against persons who 'anger, offend, or frighten' police officers are commonplace. 'What is abnormal about police riots', according to Stark, 'is the number of policemen and civilians involved in a single incident during a relatively condensed time-span' (1972, 55).

Stark finds the preconditions for police riots in the cultural predispositions of individual police officers. I find this explanation woefully inadequate. A siege mentality did exist, that is, an 'us–them' mindset reigned, which tended to demonize adversaries. So while activists have a propensity to demonize police indiscriminately, the police in turn demonized activists, most often arbitrarily. The acts of some of the activists, which angered, offended and frightened many of the police officers mobilized in Gothenburg, enhanced a tendency to lump all of the activists assembled in the same category, that is, as dangerous criminal hooligans. A siege mentality does open the door to arbitrary and excessive acts of violence among individual officers, but it does not explain their collective occurrence. The existence of a police culture predisposed to perceive political activists as more or less criminal hooligans can underlie police riots, but other factors must come into play.[4] During the police riots in Gothenburg, other factors were decisive.

First, the vast majority of police officers mobilized for the campaign in Gothenburg was poorly trained in public order policing, and many were inadequately protected. Officers were drawn from the whole of Sweden, some with only inadequate training in crowd and riot control and others with none at all; the force assembled had no joint training. On the whole, aside from some specialized mobile riot units (some of which were immobilized behind the barriers surrounding the summit venue), the majority were unprepared for the situation with which they were confronted. Traditional police training in Scandinavia seeks to develop officers who can work independently and with little direct supervision. However, in dealing with demonstrations and mass protest manifestations – policing public order in large-scale operations – police are required to exhibit teamwork, impersonality and discipline that are seldom demanded in their routine work. These types of public order operations require highly disciplined personnel under a unified command control and coordination system. It is unreasonable to expect professional behaviour from poorly trained officers.

Second, dysfunctional operational tactics made control over the disturbances that blew up extremely difficult if not impossible. The use of impact techniques such as the baton charge and block charges of mounted police disperses activists to the four winds, bringing only a temporary control or a pause in a chain of events. The indiscriminate deployment of impact techniques impedes the arrest of activists in breach of the law and subsequently the ability to control and contain a violent situation.

Third, the overall operational strategy was more or less defensive and, above all, static. Rather than attempting to control situations, the police departed from a territorialization strategy designed to control places where situations could develop. This overarching strategy on the part of the police command undermined the police's tactical manoeuvrability, resulting in their inability to control quickly situations that developed outside the perimeters of their territorial occupations. Often locked behind their own walls of shipping containers, they lacked highly mobile and flexible tactics to address the militant action strategy of de-territorialization. This was perhaps most evident during the riots in the Avenue on Friday, but also during the two days of riots in Vasa Park, which culminated in the shooting of three activists. An account of the events that led up to the shootings bears out these arguments.

In the evening, a mass demonstration with over 15,000 demonstrators started its march through the streets of Gothenburg up the city's main avenue towards Götaplats,

---

4   By 'police culture', we mean how police officers see the social world and their role in it. This is an often-used concept in police research. Several researchers have pointed out that an important distinction should be made between 'cop culture' – the orientations implied and expressed by officers in the course of their duty – and 'canteen culture' – the values and beliefs exhibited in off-duty socializing. First, the attitudes and orientations expressed in these two situational cultures do not necessarily correspond. Second, there is not a one-to-one correspondence between attitudes and behaviour (e.g. Reiner 2000; P.A.J. Waddington 1999a; Hoyle 1998).

the main square. The police had taken extraordinary measures and blocked all the side streets leading to the avenue with steel shipping containers, as well as cordoning off the avenue with containers at the midway point. The single point of entry to the avenue and the square – with all of its shop and restaurant windows dramatically boarded up after the riots earlier in the day – was the street passing Vasa Park, which would lead the demonstrators to the square. The police employed a forceful strategy of territorialization with their effective containment of the Avenue and the terminus for the demonstration. Their objective was to cut off militant activists from entering and infiltrating the demonstration from the side streets as had happened during the previous evening's demonstration, thereby preventing violence from breaking out among the crowds of demonstrators. However, the demonstration remained peaceful, with only a small number of black bloc activists in its ranks.

Instead, the more militant protesters had once again converged in small 'packs' on Vasa Park, and the park became again the focal site for violent enactments. In order to avoid the vast crowds of demonstrators mingling with the militant activists converging, one of the containers was lifted from a side street and demonstrators were redirected through it, allowing them to leave without running into the militant activists. In response to the police's cordon of the Avenue, several hundred 'Reclaim the Streets' activists moved their planned street party from the Avenue to Vasa Park. When the police surrounded the 'Reclaim the Streets' manifestation and charged their ranks, the activists who were not detained (we could observe only a few solitary activists who were seized by the police) fled the scene in disarray.

At this point the black bloc 'packs', using the hilly terrain of the park together with a tactic to jam police communications, proceeded to disorganize the ranks of the riot police. There were over 700 police in the near vicinity, but with their communications temporarily disrupted, they could not coordinate their efforts (*RPS* 2001, 62–3). When police were called from one street to reinforce their besieged colleagues in the park, raids from other 'packs' quickly demolished their patrol cars and police vans. With their quick and violent confrontations and equally quick retreats, they managed to split the police into small groups that then became more vulnerable. At one point, when a group of 12–15 police officers was attacked with cobblestones, the police responded with gunshots. Film records have shown that the shots were fired after the situation had been relieved and the stone-throwing activists were at a distance. Three activists were hit and one critically wounded.

Police reinforcements eventually arrived, and the entire area surrounding the park and its perimeters was cordoned. This time, police entered the area in force; behind mounted police, they managed to press back the activists and slowly subdue the violence. Order was once again restored around midnight, but the costs were again high. Most of the shop and restaurant windows along Vasa Street and adjacent streets were smashed, and hospital spokespersons reported that they had treated 41 casualties – including both police and activists, among others the three wounded from gunshots.

These violent events vividly illustrate that while the police were in control of certain geographical places, they were not in control over the situations that erupted.

Furthermore, the police command had not delegated sufficient action authority to senior police officers in the field, which could come to terms with the flexible action tactics embraced by militant activist 'packs'. The police in the field were often physically immobilized and tactically paralysed in face of the rapid developments in the situations that arose. When situations are out of control, the likelihood of individual officers running out of control is greater.

This brings us to our last point. The command and coordination structure broke down during the campaign. Activists had jammed radio communication during some critical points in the events, posing problems in the field for coordination among the police. However, the most severe problems for action coordination were posed by the breakdown of the command and order structure. The operative command structure was heavily centralized to the person of police commander Håkan Jaldung, who was either located in the command room with visual contact via simultaneous video recordings of the events or hovering overhead in a police helicopter. The lack of operational command delegated to senior officers in the field inhibited their effectiveness, and perhaps most importantly, their authority over rank-and-file officers. In tense situations where police are unsure as to what to do, a state of confusion and demoralization arises, resulting in fear among officers, further undermining restrained and professional behaviour. Furthermore, a breakdown in the structure of authority of senior officers allows for situations where rank-and-file officers 'run out of control'. Skolnick and Fyfe maintain that acts of excessive violence in the field are invariably a result of the absence of strong first-line supervision (1993, 123). The acts of excessive violence we observed, both physical and verbal, as well as the acts of excessive violence reported in later testimonies, were all conducted by individual officers under the supervision of their superiors or by these superior officers themselves. Weak first-line supervision is most dramatically exposed in crises.

P.A.J. Waddington (1991) argues that if police officers are poorly trained, ill equipped and unsupervised, lacking clearly defined tactics or strategy, they may provoke as much disorder as they prevent. He claims that disorganized forays by police officers undermine police legitimacy and incite crowds. Placing emphasis upon the need for command and control to prevent police officers from getting carried away in the heat of the moment (what I call a police riot), he writes:

> Policing civil disorder engenders fear, anger and frustration amongst officers who are often too close to the action to understand what is occurring. The feeling that one has lost control and is at the mercy of unpredictable events only heightens anxiety. The opportunity to take forceful action allows not only for the expression of these emotions, but is exhilarating in its own right. For all of these reasons, it is essential that officers engaged in public-order situations are carefully supervised and controlled, for internal controls on behaviour are unlikely to prove reliable. (P.A.J. Waddington 1991, 137)

Together, these factors – deficiency in preparedness due to inadequate or nonexistent crowd control and riot control training, the lack of an operational strategy and a set of tactics which could control and contain unexpected situations arising in the field, the breakdown in the operative command and coordination structure which undermined the authority of senior officers in the field, as well as a police culture that readily demonized in an arbitrary manner the activists assembled in the city – exacerbated by the state of exhaustion in which many of the officers found themselves after over 12 hours of disturbances on Thursday in connection with the action against demonstrators at Hvidfeltska gymnasium, contributed to the police riots on the streets of Gothenburg. What we witnessed in Gothenburg was a tragic episode of the 'Keystone Cops'.

Aside from the violation of civil liberties that occurred as a result of the police riots, these liberties were further infringed upon in connection with the police tactic of mass detentions. Rather than lawfully detaining activists in direct breach of the law, a wide-net tactic of detainment was employed. Few arrests were made on the spot. Most were made at a later date on the basis of police video recordings. Nevertheless, vast numbers of activists were detained, many for up to six hours or more without charges being brought, a direct violation of their civil and political liberties. Perhaps the most blatant employment of this wide-net tactic was the action against Hvidfeltska School.

Day one of the protest campaign, 14 June 2001, the day of President Bush's arrival in Gothenburg for meetings with EC leaders, was tragically to set the tone for the days to come. On the evening of 13 June, the public prosecutor decided upon a raid of the Hvitfeldtska School on the charges that 'all', or alternatively 'almost all', of the activists billeted there were suspected of 'preparations for gross assault and battery and/or preparations for assault against civil servants, alternative, preparations for damages inflicted upon property'. This school, centrally located, was one that the county had put at the disposal of the coalition Gothenburg Action for housing visiting protesters and for their planned alternative conference.

The police's move on Hvitfeldtska School was an expressly pre-emptive measure. In contrast with the events to come on Friday, during which police reacted defensively, the sealing-off of the school and the subsequent detainment of its occupants was an offensive action taken to pre-empt anticipated actions by the activists housed there. As we shall see in the Danish case study, this action appears to have been planned primarily to counteract new forms of political contention, of nonviolent civil disobedience. In part, the police took the initiative with their surprise action in the hope of moving the scene of conflict to a geographical place far removed from the venue for President Bush's visit. They were successful in this respect. Furthermore, the action also paralysed Ya Basta's civil disobedience action planned for Friday, about which the police were particularly concerned. Most of the confiscated 'weapons' shown at the official police press conference proved to come from Ya Basta's supplies for making protective gear (foam padding and football helmets). During this press conference the police indicated that it was this organization that they were most anxious to neutralize before the planned events on Friday. However, the claim of Håkan Jaldung, commander of the uniformed police assembled in Gothenburg, that 'all', or 'almost all of the activists' housed in the school, 'were suspected of preparations for inflicting violence against government officials', was far from convincing. A great many of the young people housed at the school were from documented peaceful organizations and groups such as Attac, Friends of the Earth and the Field Biologists.

With a massive show of force, the police began cordoning off the area surrounding the school on Thursday morning. Steel shipping containers were quickly transported to the cordon and the area was effectively sealed off, with approximately 600 activists reported to have been sealed in. Around 100 to 150 were released during the day, after agreeing to a body search. Unrest broke out in the afternoon when a group of activists attempted unsuccessfully to break through the police cordon from the inside, while activists on the outside attempted to storm the perimeters. Confrontations ensued throughout the day and well into the night. The number of arrests and detainments remains unclear, but at the police press conference the following day it was reported that 453 activists had been detained, and of the 89 taken into custody on this first day of protest, 43 had been released. Only one of the arrested activists was later found guilty in the courts, of incitement to riot. In short, 453 activists were sealed in by the police, detained and charged indiscriminately with preparing violence against officers.

Selective police measures must be refined in order to avoid violations of civil and political liberties better; this would appear to be the key element for policing protest, which would not only maintain order using the minimum force required, but would safeguard the civil and political liberties inscribed in the European Convention's Article 5.1. The employment of non-selective procedures is at loggerheads with the general legal principles of policing. A wide-net tactic is not commensurable with the policing principles of law enforcement, as the law cannot, and should not, be brought to bear upon individuals who happened to be in the wrong place at the wrong time.

The Swedish police were wedded to the policing of territories. Faced with political protest tentatively anchored in the frontier-lands, their strategies and operational tactics were sorely inadequate. We will turn our attention now to the police campaign in conjunction with the EU Summit meeting in Copenhagen December 2002.

Case II: The paramilitarism of the Danish public order police

Since Kai Vittrup assumed command of the Copenhagen uniformed police in 1997, the Danish police have explicitly developed their public order policing along military lines. In contrast with the formation of specifically trained mobile riot police in most countries, including Sweden, all uniformed police in Denmark are trained in public order policing and riot control along paramilitary lines. At the same time, the government became increasingly concerned with rendering the police more accountable for their use of powers and the effective use of resources.

Concern with public order policing mounted after the Nørrebro riots in 1993 in connection with the referendum on the Maastricht Treaty, during which the police shot 11 protesters. After the event, which can be unequivocally designated as a major trauma for the Danish police, three major judicial investigations found them, to different degrees, unprepared and untrained to deal with major public disorder without the excessive use of force. The riots resulted in a growing gulf between the police and some influential and articulate middle-class opinion-makers, which contributed to undermining the legitimacy of the police force. The event was significant in converting policing into an overt political issue in Denmark. An influential civil and political liberties coalition gained strength, while the classical law and order coalition in turn lost some of its vigour (Ifflander 2002). It was against this background that Vittrup was appointed expressly to come to terms with what was deemed inadequacy in Danish public order policing. His appointment was in effect a mandate to completely restructure and develop public order policing capabilities for large public gatherings, demonstrations and disorders in order to come to terms better with *both* public order *and* civil and political liberties.

Vittrup's authorization can be described as a mandate to develop what Reiner (2000) calls a 'magic bullet'. According to Reiner, the 'magic bullet myth' is perpetuated by the notion that it is possible to develop tactics that deliver precisely the right degree of force necessary for effective yet legitimate order maintenance. It suggests that intelligently deployed policing measures can, with laser-like precision, excise disorder with minimal negative side effects for civil liberties. What this myth ignores, according to Reiner, is, first, that policing more or less reflects the conflicts and contradictions of the wider social structure, culture and political economy (2000, 108–9). In other words, policing alone cannot mitigate political conflicts that threaten the social order. Second, Reiner maintains that police work is more complex, contradictory, and even confused, than the 'magic bullet myth' allows (2000, 108–9). In the following pages I will assess Vittrup's 'magic bullet' as to its effectiveness in protecting a public space for political protest.

Vittrup was responsible for translating the wider strategic goals for the EU summit police campaign to an operational level that could, in turn, be executed through the police's tactical efforts. Vittrup (2002a and 2002b) has written and successively revised two volumes, *Strategi* and *Operation*: over 800 pages dealing with larger police campaigns. One can say that the Danish strategy and operational plan had been set years before Denmark assumed its chairmanship of the European Union. The Danish police's efforts can be accurately described as a textbook example of the implementation of Vittrup's ideas, in effect a paramilitary operation and command structure. The lodestar for his planned campaign was offensive: The police were to maintain the initiative during the summit, determining the time and place for the anticipated events and controlling their development.

The magic bullet for protest policing: A critical evaluation

According to Robert Reiner, when conflicts arise between police and activists over the appropriate policing of protest events, as was the case during the protest campaign we observed in Denmark, they most often stem from conflicting conceptions of public order and the quality of democratic processes (2000, 7). Contentious politics are intrinsically challenging to the quality of democratic processes, processes the police are compelled to support and maintain as the nation-state's coercive arm. A conflict on this point would seem inevitable. Conflicts over conceptions of public order are more negotiable, involving evaluations as to how well the balance between maintaining public order *and* protecting civil and political liberties are met. Order is politically defined. It is in regards to these evaluations that the Danish police and the activists gathered for the protest campaign during the December 2002 EU Summit meeting in Copenhagen differed and were more at less at loggerheads. The police were unequivocally satisfied with their policing efforts. Activists have, in turn, directed their critique at the police campaign, which can be summarized as concentrating upon two police operations: the deployment of what Vittrup calls the 'tactic of exhaustion' prior to Global Roots' so-called 'action day', and the police operation in conjunction with Saturday's mass demonstration 'for another Europe' (cf. Wahlström 2003b).

The newly formed Global Roots (Globale Rødder) is a Danish nonviolence/ civil disobedience network constructed along the lines of the action networks Ya Basta (Italian), Avanti (German) and Globalisering underifrån/Vita Overallerna (Swedish and Finnish). Global Roots planned and staged an 'action day' during the summit and was apparently regarded by police as potentially their greatest source of 'trouble'. The police appeared more concerned with containing acts of nonviolent civil disobedience than with their capacity to deal with an outbreak of riots, and from Wednesday evening onwards their efforts were concentrated upon the action day scheduled for Friday. The action day, to include a series of surprise nonviolent civil disobedience actions throughout the city centre, was only partially successful. The police implemented what they call an exhaustion technique (Vittrup 2002b, chapter 10.4), consisting of a series of forceful 'pinpricks' designed to put their opponents off balance and exert control over the planned event. Prior to the day, activists were repeatedly detained, individually and in small groups, by police patrols throughout Copenhagen's city centre. Questioned, forced to identify themselves, and in many cases body-searched, the activists felt themselves victims of police harassment, criminalized and put under suspicion. The legal help-group that was in place in Copenhagen reported that approximately 200 activists made contact with them in conjunction with complaints of police harassment (*Jyllands-Posten* 14 December 2002, section 2:7).

In addition, the police set in motion a surprise tactic on Thursday afternoon, cordoning off two bridges leading to central Copenhagen and directing traffic and pedestrians through a sluice. In particular, cars and buses with foreign plates were searched and their occupants questioned. Pedestrians and cyclists were questioned and backpacks and shoulder bags searched. Were the police tactics employed effective in thwarting Global Roots' planned series of symbolic civil disobedience actions? It would appear that the police were successful in pulling the rug out from under them. From the perspective of public order, the police were successful: the planned protest actions by means of civil disobedience were largely absent from Friday's events. An action against the multinational concern Danisco was carried out peacefully, together with a smaller action against the department store Illum, which was also undramatic. Two occupation actions, against the naval station Holmen and the Integration Ministry were called off after police detained some of the activists and confiscated the materials which were to be used (Global Roots press conference 13 December 2002).

The major event planned by Global Roots on Friday was the march against the venue for the European Union Summit meeting, Bella Centre, located several kilometres south of the city centre. Even in connection with this action, the police's employment of stop-and-search tactics was strongly felt. A number of the Italian civil disobedience activists, some of them long-time activists (including Luca Casarini, international spokesman for the Italian civil disobedience network), had been earlier arrested on the streets, and the remaining Italian contingent was now reluctant to demonstrate. It was this group who was to have taken the lead on the front line of the march against Bella Centre. Far less experienced activists were forced to take their place at the last moment, donning their homemade protective gear.

When the march, which included approximately 800 activists, approached Bella Centre after almost three hours in the bitterly cold winter weather, they were confronted by a solid wall of police cars and 11 armoured vans blocking the boulevard. Behind the vans, over a thousand police in riot gear were amassed. Here the police relied upon the technique of 'show of force' to disarm the potential for eventual violent acts and to discourage the demonstrators from attempting to force their lines. In short, their overwhelming display of strength was calculated to intimidate the activists. After admonishments to turn back and refrain from crossing police lines, the front ranks of activists put down their homemade shields, signalling the police of their nonviolent intentions. The march proceeded with the activists raising their hands in the air in a symbolic gesture, breaking through a symbolic line of police tape before stopping approximately 10–15 metres from the police cordon. At this point the activists came to a stop with their hands held high. Kai Vittrup, commander of the uniformed police in greater Copenhagen, ordered the cordon to open a corridor leading to the newly opened metro station. He invited the tired and cold activists to take the train back to the centre. Just as the civil disobedience activists relied upon symbolic gestures, the police countered with an equally symbolic gesture of hospitality that had been negotiated between the police and Global Roots during the march (Wahlström 2003b).

The well-organized and disciplined demonstrators, as well as the police, upheld the principle of nonviolence. The march broke through a symbolic police line, fulfilling their intent to carry out an action of civil disobedience and putting the police under no threat that their cordon would be forced. Translating the coercive relationship – the confrontation between the overwhelming force of the police, authorized by society to exercise coercion (although they were regarded by the vast majority of demonstrators as unauthorized) and the ranks of demonstrators armed solely with the vulnerability of their own bodies and their moral outrage – to, at least on the surface, a symbolic reciprocal relationship, allowed both sides in the struggle to retain face. Reciprocity is another distinct kind of power relationship. According to Muir, in a reciprocal relationship:

one individual overcomes the resistance of another by making an attractive exchange. He gives up something he values less and gets in return something he thinks has a greater worth to him. His exchange partner, meanwhile, because his scale of values is different, receives something that he desires more than what he has to surrender. Thus, both sides are reciprocally enriched. (1979, 47–8)

The two sides in this confrontation situation, through a bargaining process based on their knowledge of each other, struck a deal. The police exchanged the opportunity for the activists to defy their initial order, in order to avoid exercising coercion with their superior force. From the point of view of the police, this was an attractive exchange. The activists for their part satisfied their desire to execute a symbolic action of civil disobedience, while avoiding a physical confrontation with a hopelessly superior force. For the activists, too, this was an attractive exchange.

The potential for violence was effectively de-escalated by both parties in the confrontation with their show of restraint. However, for two action-oriented cultures – a police culture and an activist culture – to refrain from action is difficult. I observed a number of activists approaching the metro station who appeared to feel frustrated and cheated, ambivalent towards the display of hospitality on the part of the Danish police in allowing them to take the train. Some police officers also displayed a sense of frustration. A journalist reported that one officer said rather ironically to another: 'what's with them? Don't they dare come down to meet us? Isn't there someone who can go and tell them that they are more than welcome?' (*Jyllands-Posten* 14 December 2002, section 2:7).

Both of these cultures were trained and suited-up for action – demonstrators with foam rubber padding, homemade shields and football helmets, and police with full riot gear and armoured vehicles. In these situations, both cultures must rely on the discipline displayed by their members if violence is to be avoided. The demonstration organizers and march stewards exerted discipline, that is, control, over their rank and file, while discipline was similarly brought to bear by the senior police officers in the field. In this particular situation, two action-oriented cultures met with restraint, abstaining from action.

The tactic of exhaustion, Vittrup's translation of the guerrilla tactics of warfare to public order policing, is a central element in his 'magic bullet' recipe for policing contemporary protest. It is intended to disrupt high-risk protest actions before they are carried out. The success of its use to undermine the series of nonviolent civil disobedience actions planned by Global Roots rested upon harassment of activists and, most importantly, the detainment of key activists and protest materials prior to the event. First, I will look more closely at this latter condition for success, the high quality of information available to the police that enabled them to detain key activists.

A distinction exists, although hazy, between police knowledge and police intelligence. I argue that police knowledge of protest cultures and particular activist organizations and networks is fundamental for good public order policing. This knowledge, best won through direct contact with protest organizers and individual activists, is accumulated over time, and enables the police to dimension and plan their operations appropriately. Police knowledge of protest cultures also counteracts the formation of a 'siege mentality', which poses a direct threat to the protection of civil and political liberties and alienates police from their communities. This holds true for both senior and rank-and-file officers.

Police intelligence is of a different character. While knowledge implies a familiarity with various activist organizations' and networks' motives for protest, their organizational forms and their action repertoires, intelligence implies access to more detailed information as to specific planned actions. Much of police intelligence is now gathered on the Internet, yielding information that is of a general character and can be regarded as bridging the gap between police knowledge and police intelligence. However, detailed information and plans for specific actions, particularly high-risk actions for which activists risk arrest, whether these are planned violent actions or nonviolent civil disobedience actions, are not readily accessed. Detailed information can only be accessed through deep intelligence gathering, that is, through monitoring closed Internet sites, surveillance, wire-tapping and the use of informers and undercover police officers. This is the standard repertoire for intelligence services the world over. Some of the actions of the Danish police, with their deployment of the tactic of exhaustion prior to Global Roots' 'action day', were of a nature requiring access to detailed information that could only have been gathered through deep intelligence gathering.

Reiner (2000, 123) argues that governments' search for 'magic bullets' has led to the proliferation of intrusive forms of surveillance and the abuse of informers and other undercover tactics, both ultimately unethical practices and encroachments on civil liberties. Duncan Campbell (1980) has argued that the pre-emptive notion of crime prevention that prevails in all Western police forces today has virtually put all of society under surveillance. Any citizen, especially any socially uncharacteristic citizen, is a target for suspicion and observation (Campbell 1980, 65; see also Lyon 2003; Innes 2000; Sheptycki 2000; den Boer 1997). On the basis of my empirical materials, I cannot evaluate if this was the case in Denmark, even if I do raise the question.[5]

Secondly, in regards to the use of police harassment during the police operation prior to Global Roots' action day, while it appeared successful in putting activists off balance, it is nevertheless questionable along a number of lines. From a police perspective concerned with maintaining public order, the tactic proved successful in that it contributed to a defusing of the planned action day. However, from an activist perspective concerned with civil and political rights, it was far more problematic. First, the police were operating within a grey legal zone. According to the Danish justice code Section 750, police have the right to request that all demonstrators identify themselves. However, according to Section 792, they cannot search a demonstrator

---

5   Our interview with an official from PET, the Danish Police Intelligence Division, gave us literally no information as to PET's surveillance and intelligence gathering techniques, aside from their monitoring of activist organizations' and networks' Internet sites.

without first charging him or her with breaking a law, for example the law against bearing a weapon. The legal paragraph states that there has to be reasonable cause to carry out a visitation; but it is up to the individual officer to arrive at a judgement that reasonable cause exists. If the search has not led to a charge, the police officer is required to inform the demonstrator that the charge is dropped.

During the intensive stop-and-search tactics of the Danish police, approximately 41 demonstrators were placed under custody on minor charges. Activists reported being detained and searched repeatedly, in some cases by the same officers (see Wahlström 2003b). The number of arrests would appear to be far short of the number of detainments and searches carried out. Activists lodged over 200 complaints with the legal watch-group. The number of detainments and searches carried out is difficult to assess accurately, as activists have reported that they did not observe reports being written and filed, although filing a report on a stop and search is otherwise required of police officers. This is a fundamental safeguard built into the legal extension of stop-and-search powers, providing basic assurance for police accountability. These facts suggest that the stop-and-search tactic was employed as a pre-emptive police action (in this case a series of countless small actions) with the designed operational purpose of putting their opponents, in this case nonviolent civil disobedience activists, off balance. In other words, the use of a form of police harassment, which indeed operates within a legal 'grey zone', makes the tactic highly problematic from the perspective of civil and political constitutional rights.

Second, the use of the operational technique of exhaustion, in this case police harassment, is *per se* designed to strike against their *opponents*. Thus the exhaustion technique requires an easily identified antagonist if it is to be successful from both a public order perspective *and* a civil and political rights perspective. The stop-and-search tactic employed by the Danish uniformed police during the initial stages of the EU Summit seems to have been employed indiscriminately against any young person having what the police deemed a 'left-wing appearance'.[6] Reiner argues that a category, in this case young persons with a left-wing appearance, becomes 'police property when the dominant powers in society leave the problems of social control of that category to the police' (2000, 93). 'Police property' includes radical political organizations that the dominant majority see as problematic (Reiner 2000, 93).[7] A police force that cruises the streets fitting everyone with the appearance of a political

---

6   Reiner claims that police suspicion and stereotyping are inescapable as they are valuable tools in police work: 'the particular categories informing them tend to be ones that reflect the structure of power in society. This serves to reproduce that structure through a pattern of implicit discrimination' (2000, 91). Skolnick and Fyfe maintain that as a necessity and a consequence of maintaining a high state of readiness in order to avert violence breaking out, police develop a 'perceptual shorthand to identify certain kinds of people as symbolic assailants' (1993, 97). That is, their gestures or attire signal a potential threat. However, this perceptual shorthand and its typifying of citizens is open to breaches of civil liberties.

7   Reiner (2000) points out that a major pitfall for the police is to mistake a member of a higher-status group for police property. A demonstrator may turn out to be a university professor, a lawyer or even a EU parliamentarian, as was the case in 2001 when Swedish

activist/demonstrator into a lump category of symbolic opponents to be potentially detained and body-searched is treading upon a fine line between a police state and an open democratic society (cf. Skolnick and Fyfe 1993, 97). Furthermore, the struggle over the moral high ground between police and activists is clouded.

So public order was upheld, but at what cost to 'law' in the common phrase 'law and order'? Emphasis is more often than not given to the 'order' part of the cliché. However, under a regime of law, a legal system imposes restraints on the quest for order. The Danish legal system poses such restraints upon the police's order maintenance efforts. Did the pre-emptive public order policing employed with the Danish police's use of the exhaustion tactic, including arbitrary stop and searches, impinge upon civil and political liberties? It would appear to be the case.

Activists have also directed critiques towards the police in connection with the mass demonstration on Saturday. They were critical of the deployment of the plainclothes unit of public order officers, the so-called 'riot patrol', as well as the police's use of show of force during the demonstration. First, we will look at the activists' critique of the plainclothes officers, a specialized unit in the Danish uniformed police force. Skolnick and Fyfe (1993) warn that specialized units should be created only when particular tasks are so sophisticated that they cannot be adequately performed by what they call 'generalists'. These police researchers maintain that specialization has a number of pitfalls. First, specialized units tend to justify their existence and enhance their status by generating statistics, for example, the number of arrests made, without regard as to how they have been made. According to Skolnick and Fyfe, the quest for favourable statistics then often leads these units to break the rules. The cardinal sin is not breaking the rules, 'but to be caught breaking the rules' (Skolnick and Fyfe 1993, 190). Second, every time a new specialized unit is created, new agendas are built, and the route to the achievement of the police 'organisation's overall goal becomes hazier and less direct' (Skolnick and Fyfe 1993, 190). Third, when police departments build specialized units, 'whose names and roles are better suited to military commando squads' than to routine public order policing, the results are likely to be a 'swashbuckling style' that can escalate violence in the field (Skolnick and Fyfe 1993, 190).

The Danish specialized unit of plainclothes public order officers is not a new creation. It is a unit with a relatively long history, one that has been fraught with controversy. Perhaps the most serious controversy was in conjunction with the Nørrebro riots in 1993, where they were found to have played a provocative role that led to the escalation of violence. Their reputation as being the 'baddest' among public order police has followed them ever since. Within the activist culture in Denmark, the 'riot patrol' has become a symbol for repressive policing, extending to more moderate elements within the activist culture as well. Even within the police culture in Denmark, the 'riot control unit' is regarded as being made up of the fastest

---

police detained Per Garton in connection with a mass arrest in Malmö during a demonstration protesting EU finance politics.

and toughest officers; they are awarded a somewhat 'swashbuckling' image by their fellow officers (observations collected during training exercises in May 2002).

The question here is whether this specialized unit fills a function in Danish public order policing, given their symbolic image and reputation. First, their mere presence at demonstrations – among demonstrators they are readily recognizable in their left-wing disguises and occasional mask – frequently raises the emotional temperature in a protest situation, increasing its volatility and potential for violence. To what degree does their presence contribute to an escalation of violence? Secondly, to what degree does this unit have its own agenda at odds with the overall goal of the command level in Danish public order policing, which is committed to de-escalating volatile situations during protest events? This question brings us to our third point: how responsive is this unit to orders from field commanders?

I will offer here some reflections on these questions. First, my empirical materials[8] point conclusively to the fact that the presence of these plainclothes public order officers does heighten the emotional intensity in protest situations, especially in the presence of the more radical wing within the Danish protest culture. Secondly, it would appear that the unit has its own agenda during protest events. On the basis of the findings of the 'Stop Violence' questionnaire, their contacts with citizens differed markedly from those of their fellow uniformed officers. They were reported to be unresponsive and rude in contacts with Stop Violence stewards. One overly zealous plainclothes officer was seen being restrained from breaking into the demonstration and making a further arrest. There is some, albeit inconclusive, evidence that the unit at least unconsciously perpetuates its own myth, that of being the 'toughest and baddest' – they are living up to their image. Their 'undercover disguises' are not so much disguises, since they are readily recognized among activists, as they are symbolic uniforms of their status as the 'toughest and baddest'. And last, organizer reports from Saturday's demonstration indicate that the unit was unresponsive to orders from the field commander, Benny Hansen, to remain in the background. As mentioned, the empirical evidence is sketchy at best, but it does lead me to pose the question as to whether this unit's functions – surveillance and arrest – could not be carried out equally well, or better, by the 'generalists', that is, the uniformed public order police. The gains made with the deployment of this specialized unit appear to be heavily outweighed by the losses. The one identifiable benefit in a win-loss calculation is the fact that they tend to become the scapegoats for activist discontent with Danish public order policing. Activists tend to direct their sharpest criticisms towards the 'riot patrol', who become a welcome 'villain in the drama' of policing protest in Denmark; some of the 'heat' is lifted from the uniformed police in general and the senior command officers in particular. After this event, two officers from

---

8   The empirical materials included field observations (that is, during a mass training exercise, and during the protest events), interviews with activists, activist Internet sites, and a video recording of the activities of the 'riot patrol' during Saturday's demonstration 'for another Europe'.

the riot patrol were found guilty in the courts for illegal masking, and fines were levied.

Lastly, activists have also directed their criticisms towards the use of an operational tactic of intimidation that Vittrup calls 'show of force'. Show of force, as developed by Vittrup (2002b), is a technique designed and implemented to send a clear signal to activists that the event will develop in line with the police's premises. As such, show of force has the character of an ultimatum. Further negotiations are out of the question. It is a classic technique of intimidation with the primary purpose of preventing violent disturbances. Coercion is a means of controlling the conduct of others through *threats* to harm and/or through the *actual* exercise of force (cf. Muir 1979, 37). Intimidation is simply the psychological exercise of coercion on the part of the police; it is the threat of harm.

Show of force is executed with a large, visible and well-equipped riot force. Visibility is a key factor in enhancing the intended psychological effect of intimidation. Police vehicles – both the armoured and light-armoured vehicles of the Danish police – are put on parade, blue lights flashing, together with a large force of police officers in full riot gear. It is, in short, a massive display of police strength, used to frighten what the police perceive as potential 'troublemakers' in order to reduce the chance of violence.

Activists claim that police reneged on their promise to maintain low visibility during the demonstration if there was no indication of potential violence. Here, activists and police evaluate differently the potentiality of violence breaking out. While organizers felt confident in the peacekeeping capabilities of their march stewards, the police interpreted the very presence of a block of nonviolent civil disobedience activists, and in particular, a block of anarchist activists, as an indication that riots could break out. After the fact, we can conclude that the demonstration proceeded in an orderly fashion and that even after the demonstration divided and these two blocks of activists carried out illegal marches along unauthorized routes, no seriously violent outbreaks occurred. It is difficult to assess whether this was the result of the efforts of activists to 'police' themselves, or due to police intimidation with their display of massive force. What is evident from our observations is that activists were for the most part highly disciplined and march stewards were able to calm the ranks of protesters even in the face of what they perceived as police provocations, including the deployment of plainclothes officers and the subsequent arrests made within the ranks of demonstrators.

Show of force is not a directly coercive police tactic; rather, it is the indirect exercise of coercion. As the visualization of the threat of coercive force, it can be interpreted as a subtle intrusion upon civil and political liberties: a show of force can make peaceful protesters reluctant to exercise their right to demonstrate. The overt display of the 'mailed fist' of protest policing, which the Danish police force is not constrained to veil as was the case for British public order police in the early 1990s (P.A.J. Waddington 1998, 1994), is a political triumph of Danish police. Whereas the political climate that prevailed in England at that time compelled British public order police to keep their special mobile riot control units well out of sight in order to counteract potential charges of provocation, the same climate did not exist in Denmark in 2002. Here the political 'ceiling' was much higher, allowing the public order police far more latitude in their choice of tactics. A massive display of police force is part and parcel of the legitimate exercise of police power and the routine policing of protest in Denmark. This political leeway was won by the efforts of key senior officers after years of hard work to restructure the mode of protest policing in Denmark along paramilitary lines, together with their stated commitments to civil and political liberties.[9] In other words, their public image at this time allowed them to display a mailed fist, *if* it was at the same time clothed in the rhetoric of the velvet glove. Vittrup's 'magic bullet' for protest policing – a mailed fist wielded with a velvet glove – appears to have won the confidence of government officials, the media and the general public, even while scepticism remains within activist cultures. They had public sympathy on their side. At least for the time being, this variety of magic bullet is widely recognized in Denmark as legitimate routine public order policing. Darth Vader is in. However, even Darth Vaders must be subject to public accountability in their exercise of power, at least in liberal democratic societies. The degree to which this accountability is made transparent will in the long run shape

---

9   The successful restructuring of public order policing was won on the basis of two achievements. First, the restructuring and the new style of public order policing was accepted as a legitimate means to maintain order by the general public and government authorities in that it was perceived as a highly professional and disciplined exercise of police power in which order is achieved through a minimum use of force. To accomplish this, a number of changes were made in the Danish legal code, allowing the police greater leeway in instigating pre-emptive measures. *De facto,* the Danish police became political actors in that they would not only merely enforce the law, but they were instrumental in advocating policies that were enacted in law (cf. Bayley 1994, 126). The restructuring also demanded that considerable economic resources were allocated to the uniformed police. Bayley points out that there is much historical evidence that the police are much more readily given the resources they need to deal with collective threats to public order than they are to fight the kinds of crimes that victimize individuals (1994, 137). The restructuring efforts have even won considerable support within at least the more moderate activist cultures in Denmark as being a vast improvement on previous styles of public order policing. This was the external achievement. Second, the restructuring required that these changes be accepted internally, within the general institution of the police, and perhaps most importantly, within the prevailing police culture. As several of our informants have remarked, the biggest change was not in the acquisition of a more sophisticated 'hardware' for public order policing (i.e. armoured vehicles, new forms of teargas, protective gear, etc.), but the changes brought about in the 'software' of public order policing. That is, the mentality of the officers was transformed, with changes in how they perceived protesters and the legal sanctity of protest. In short, the officers on a management level were able to convince rank-and-file officers that this new style of policing was good public order policing. This latter achievement was not, and is generally not, easily won. On the basis of our field observations during an extended period of time, we argue that the professionalism and above all, the charisma, of key senior police officials, particularly police commander Kai Vittrup, facilitated the acceptance of this new mode of policing, and in particular, the gradual transformation of the software of public order policing in Denmark.

what is recognized as acceptable and non-acceptable forms of coercive police force in political policing.

Conclusion: The institutionalization of contentious politics

Spaces for contentious politics in the frontier-lands of contemporary societies are not given. The construction, protection and maintenance of spaces for challenges to the social and political order are vital for ongoing democratic processes, not only for the dissemination of the messages of protesters and the construction of public opinion, but also for the health of the democratic nation-state and transnational state. The legitimacy of these political institutions lies in their ability to enjoy the support of the populations they govern. Jürgen Habermas (2001, 1998) has pointed out that political legitimacy rests upon support for the formal processes and procedures of representative democracy, but it also rests upon the quality of the informal political communicative processes that take place in civil society. Subsequently, the temporary spaces that activists open for democratic discussions are underlying conditions for the legitimacy of the state's and transnational state's exercise of power. Paradoxically, a healthy liberal democratic state requires the voices of its challengers. Reconnaissance battles fought out in the frontier-lands both challenge and circuitously support the exercise of state/trans-state power.

Contentious politics opened by transnational summit meetings in the frontier-lands have, since Seattle 1999, increasingly become the stage for violent protest events. In Europe the meeting of the IMF and World Bank in Prague 2000 and the EU Summit in Nice the same year, the EU Summit in Gothenburg 2001 and the G8 meeting in Genoa shortly after, became witness to an escalation of violence on the parts of militant protesters and police alike. These dramatic protest events have become the subjects for critical analyses of policing protest (e.g. Björk and Peterson 2002; Gillham and Marx 2000). In these analyses the focus has been upon the police policing disorder. And as P.A.J. Waddington (1994) points out, commentaries on public order policing have tended to more frequently address violent protest events, resulting in an over-appreciation of the coercive and aggressive force of the police. But these types of protest events are just the tip of the iceberg in public order policing. Most public order policing is highly routine: few acts of violence occur, arrests are seldom made, and 'most operations are characterized by boredom among police officers rather than the exhilaration of battle' (P.A.J. Waddington 1994, 197). For example, the 2002 protest campaigns in Seville and Copenhagen were for the most part peaceful and orderly and the political policing was subsequently largely routine.

In what ways are spaces for democratic protest protected, alternatively threatened, by political policing? We will counterpose the two cases. Unquestionably, direct threats are posed to the public spaces for political protest in the event of serious public disorder and even more seriously in the event of police riots, as we witnessed during the EU Summit in Gothenburg. A deployment of 'Keystone Cops' in the action spaces of contentious politics poses serious threats to the civil and political liberties of activists. Excessive use of coercive force, together with non-selective forms of arrest, openly jeopardizes civil liberties. These were the outcomes of a policing public order control strategy wedded to the occupation of territorial spaces – a strategy that would appear to be out of tune with maintaining order in the frontier-lands of contentious politics. The second case, that of the police campaign in conjunction with the EU Summit in Copenhagen the following year, is far less dramatic. However, are these 'democratic spaces' even endangered by routine public order policing? Is Darth Vader a hazard for civil liberties? The tentative answer posed in this text is yes. The threats are, of course, subtler, but nevertheless, threats to civil and political liberties were incurred during the protest campaign in Copenhagen. The question then arises as to whether threats to civil liberties can indeed be wholly eliminated in the quest for public order in the frontier-lands of contemporary risk societies. Furthermore, can political challenges be posed within the prevailing notions of public order enforced by the police? How is contentious politics made 'safe and predictable'? What are the consequences for contentious politics that 'play by the rules'?

The liberal democratic state attempts to meet the challenges posed by activists through strategies of institutionalization. Meyer and Tarrow (1998) argue that authorities reduce the uncertainty and instability that can result when unknown actors engage in uncontrollable forms of action through processes of institutionalization. They delineate three distinct but complementary aspects of institutionalization.

1. *routinization* of collective action, such that challengers and authorities can both adhere to a common script, recognizing familiar patterns as well as potentially dangerous deviations;
2. *inclusion* and *marginalization*, whereby challengers willing to adhere to established routines will be granted access to political exchanges in mainstream institutions, while those who refuse can be shut out of conversations through either repression or neglect;
3. *cooptation*, which means that challengers alter their claims and tactics to ones that can be pursued without disrupting the normal practice of politics. (Meyer and Tarrow 1998, 21)

According to Meyer and Tarrow, these processes allow dissidents to lodge their claims and challenges *and* permit states to manage these challenges without smothering them.

As Meyer and Tarrow point out, police practice illustrates the processes of institutionalization in a microcosm. Demonstrators negotiate with the police the date and physical boundaries of their challenges. The police, in turn, representing the state, agree not only to tolerate them but to facilitate their march and protect them against eventual counter-movements. Even civil disobedience can be negotiated in this way, through agreements on the part of activists to eschew violence and agreements on the part of police to make their arrests without harming the activists. In short, both parts reach agreements as to the manuscript for action. Such agreements were forged in both Gothenburg and Copenhagen through negotiations between demonstration organizers and the police (cf. Wahlström 2003b). The routinization of activist practices through their cooperation with the police contributes to make protest relatively safe and predictable, which was more or less the case in Copenhagen, and less the case in Gothenburg.

A temporary public space for democratic deliberation is maintained and protected, but at what cost to the system-challenges posed by activists? Meyer and Tarrow are confident that routinization does not necessarily lead to inclusion and cooptation. That is, that the challenges posed are not necessarily lacking in force. They argue that, since movements can even pursue system-challenging claims *within* the institutions of the state, these routinized forms of contention are not *per definition* less challenging than those posed by non-routinized and even unruly forms of contention. 'Putting half a million people in the streets for an orderly demonstration may push policies in activists' preferred direction more than the dramatic and disruptive efforts of a few militants who firebomb opponents' offices or turn over cars' (Meyer and Tarrow 1998, 24).

This is an optimistic evaluation of the potential for contentious politics to maintain a voice in contemporary societies where protest has become relatively safe and predictable. And there is one primary argument that supports this optimism. Safe and predictable temporary public spaces for protest do invite a broader cross-section of citizens to voice their challenges. Potential participants who would otherwise be reluctant to become involved if the threat of violence was unpredictable would, at least hypothetically, be more inclined to join in the protest knowing that the threat of violence was more or less in check. At least in theory, the public spaces for democratic discussion and challenge are thus enlarged, in that they are made more readily accessible for a greater number of potential participants. Democratic processes are thus vitalized.

However, these very same spaces may at the same time be made less hospitable for protesters through the implementation of the 'show of force' technique. This was the case in Copenhagen. The massive police presence may have made some potential protesters reluctant to exercise their right to demonstrate. Many of those who did exercise that right felt themselves criminalized in the process. Wahlström cites one activist who claimed that: 'it seemed as if they [the police] were protecting Copenhagen against *us!*' (2003b, 31). In any case, contentious politics framed by a massed riot police leaves us with the impression that political protest is an unsolicited contribution to democratic discussions and at least potentially highly dangerous for the community in general.

This is the hopeful position in regards to the routinization of contentious politics. There are more negative positions. First, we find a forceful argument that contends that contentious politics rely upon the staging of political dramas. These dramas reveal the otherwise hidden power relations in society and make the challenges of protest visible to the polity at large. Political dramas are more effect-full if the manuscript is under-determined. The unpredictable, the element of surprise, amplifies the political challenges that come to life in the political dramas that are staged through protest. These challenges, which through their unpredictability make visible alternative political narratives, allow even relatively small groups of activists to enter public spaces of protest. Contentious politics is then not limited to the ability of protest organizations and networks to mobilize vast numbers of people.

Second, and perhaps most important, processes of institutionalization divide protest cultures. On the one hand, organizations, groups and activist networks that adhere to the 'rules of the game' set by the police are awarded a degree of recognition and access to some established political channels. The police will handle these activists with a 'velvet glove'. On the other hand, those who deny these rules and refuse more developed forms of cooperation are in turn marginalized by the established political channels and run the risk of meeting the 'mailed fist' – repressive forms of protest policing. In Copenhagen the autonomous network, and to a lesser degree the nonviolent civil-disobedient network Global Roots, were subject to the mailed fist of the Danish public order police, while the remaining groups and protest networks were met with the 'velvet glove'. These external dividing factors generate, more or less, internal divisions – processes of inclusion and exclusion – within protest cultures (see Wahlström 2003b; Wahlström and Oskarsson in this volume). They lead to divisions between the 'good guys' and 'bad guys' in protest cultures, where the categories find their basis in the prevailing power structures' definitions of 'proper and acceptable' forms of contention. The parameters of protest are inexorably set, not by the challengers, but by the state itself.

Chapter 4

The Policing of Transnational Protest in Canada

Mike King and David Waddington

Introduction

There are indications amidst a growing body of research that contemporary 'Western' public order policing is increasingly moving away from an overridingly reactive, incident-led orientation to one combining such a 'paramilitary' approach with a more proactive emphasis on intelligence-led contingency planning, negotiation and low-profile or 'soft hat' policing based on accommodation (P.A.J. Waddington 2003; della Porta and Reiter 1998a; McPhail, Schweingruber and McCarthy 1998; Brearley and King 1996; King and Brearley 1996). This chapter questions the consolidation of this trend in respect of the policing of transnational (and specifically anti-globalization) protest by examining key recent events in Canada, culminating in the 2002 G8 Summit meeting held in the remote Rocky Mountains location of Kananaskis, Alberta, and related protests in Calgary and Ottawa.

The chapter draws from archive research and interviews with public police agencies across Canada, conducted by the first-named author in the summer of 2003,[1] and is set out in three main sections. The first section outlines recent trends in 'Western' methods for the policing of public disorder, and then provides a brief overview of the nature of public order policing in Canada. A second section then evaluates the impact on police tactical and strategic thinking of key police–protester confrontations in the lead-up to the Kananaskis protests. The concluding section suggests that whilst elements of a trend from policing confrontation to accommodation can be identified, there are a number of qualifications (which we outline) against suggesting that this is a general trend in respect of the policing of transnational protest.

1   Mike King would like to express his thanks to the Canadian Department of Foreign Affairs and International Trade for funding part of the research on which this chapter is based through its Canadian Studies Faculty Research Program.

Changing trends in public order policing

Research relevant to policing developments in the United Kingdom (Wright 2002; King and Brearley 1996; P.A.J. Waddington 1994) and Europe generally as well as the US (della Porta and Reiter 1998a) suggests that the policing of public disorder generally is taking a 'two-pronged' approach. While it is clear that there has been a widespread retention of a paramilitary option to controlling actual or potential disorder, there has been a corresponding emphasis on proactive negotiation and accommodation, predicated on the heightened use of intelligence.

This approach to offsetting or, at worst, limiting the occurrence of disorder is exemplified in P.A.J Waddington's (1994) observational study within the Metropolitan Police Service in which he listened in on negotiations between senior police and protest organizers. Waddington noted how experienced specialist officers guilefully exploited various structural aspects of the negotiation (e.g. 'home ground advantage' and local knowledge concerning the most 'suitable' route for a proposed march) and made effective use of clever 'interactional practices and ploys' (such as exhibiting 'spurious friendliness' or helpful favours) to gain the compliance of the organizers. Then, during the protest itself, the police would display similar cunning to 'orchestrate' traffic – ostensibly as a courtesy to demonstrators – in such a way as to ensure that the march progressed along the route most preferred by senior officers. These tactics, allied to the presence of numerous accompanying officers, constant human and electronic surveillance and paramilitary units held in reserve usually ensured that demonstrations in central London were 'not only peaceful but *minimally disruptive*' (P.A.J. Waddington 2003, 409, emphasis added).

For these strategies to have the potential to work, though, it is necessary for demonstrator groups to have some degree of organizational structure, including representatives with the requisite authority to enter into negotiation with the police. Mawby (2002, 159) points out that, in the absence of such structural requirements, the police will depend more heavily on intelligence gathering as a means of 'second guessing' the opposition's intentions.

As P.A.J. Waddington readily acknowledges, the outwardly benign conduct of senior officers during negotiations conceals an otherwise unyielding resolution to exert firm situational control:

> On the face of it, public order policing in contemporary Britain remains a triumph of policing by consent. However, political protest is still largely conducted on terms determined by the police. In other words, their interests are served and in doing so other interests of the protesters are, at least, compromised. Protest is emasculated and induced to conform to the avoidance of trouble. In police argot, protest organisers are 'had over'. (P.A.J. Waddington 1994, 197–8)

Such sentiments are endorsed in interviews conducted by King and Brearley (1996) with public order specialists. According to one respondent, the contemporary approach to policing public order was now one 'of a more caring cop on the street in view of the public, with reserves all tooled up and ready to go in the backstreets'

(King and Brearley 1996, 78). This latter comment is indicative of the public order police's growing preoccupation with the cultivation of a favourable public image since the 1990s and beyond (Mawby 2002). Indeed, Mawby nicely illustrates this in the following concerning the policing of a 'Reclaim the Streets' demonstration in Sheffield, England, in 1997:

> despite the official line that the police operation had gone to plan, it appears that the police tactics on the day had not only angered city centre traders and shoppers, but also the rank and file police officers who were on duty. These different attitudes towards the policing of the demonstration highlight the tensions contesting the different meanings of policing. Whilst the rank and file officers wanted to engage in 'real policing' by confronting the protesters, the command team was anxious to avoid confrontation which would possibly amplify this local event to the national mass mediated theatre and damage the image of the force …. Although the official line of a successful operation was maintained in the media, behind the scenes, debriefings were occurring to review the general strategy adopted. (2002, 163)

The above also highlights the tension between policy and practice. This is an issue that we discuss later and touch on in the various events discussed in this chapter in respect of the translation of policy, comprising an increasing public order policing model shift towards accommodation, into practice on the ground.

There is widespread academic agreement that the degree of forcefulness and intolerance with which police tactics and strategies are mounted in any given public order situation may depend on the nature of the overarching 'public sphere' (Wisler and Tackenberg 2000), namely the political and media context that frames police attitudes and conduct towards dissenting groups. Generally speaking, police operations will be influenced by some combination of political pressure (with those parties exerting most political muscle typically holding sway) and a media-generated climate of opinion that either endorses or else delegitimizes the protesters and their motives. Dissident groups widely defined as problematic or marginal to the political mainstream are treated most harshly by the police (D. Waddington 1992; D. Waddington, Jones and Critcher 1989).

Further, P.A.J. Waddington (2003, 411) argues that there are certain 'occasions, locations and personalities' for which and on whose behalf the police would automatically and unquestioningly be prepared to 'die in a ditch' (i.e. risk injury, criticism and damage to their reputation). A state occasion involving royal persons and/or symbolic locations would be an example *par excellence*. According to Waddington, 'Proverbial "ditches" are not "dug" by the police … They are "dug" by others with the power to do so: the state that the police serve. Usually, the "ditches" are well marked on the political terrain and long established, but occasionally they are hastily created by powerful interests' (P.A.J. Waddington 2003, 411).

Indeed, this forms part of the body of 'police knowledge' (della Porta 1998, 1995), as does the stock of 'lessons learned' on the basis of key 'watersheds' in the history of police–protester engagements that may have induced moments of reflection on and reassessment of current policies and their practical application (King and Brearley

1996). It has equally been observed that the memories of such encounters and the 'lessons learned' from them may be just as influential in determining the orientation and conduct of protesters (D. Waddington and Critcher 2000; D. Waddington 1992; Jefferson 1990).

It is becoming increasingly evident that certain characteristics of the proliferating anti-globalization/anti-capitalist protests of recent years, as indeed even more so with respect to anti-nuclear or environmental protests (King and Brearley 1996, 102), have helped to confound police attempts to control public order via negotiated management. P.A.J. Waddington (2003, 414) has noted, for example, how the relative 'independence from class politics and socialist ideology' of some sections of the constituent 'new social movements' has made them less subject to the restraining influence of the labour movement than in the past. Indeed, this, allied to the fact that many of the new social movements are decentralized and lack formal leadership, has made it difficult for police negotiators to engage in meaningful pre-event liaison (Yeates 2001). Moreover, as we have previously explained, the sheer breadth and complexity of the political issues involved are making it increasingly difficult for the police 'to identify with any conviction a single, undifferentiated public in whose interests [they] can be seen to be acting and to whose common sentiments they can appeal for legitimacy' (D. Waddington 1996, 32).

In due course, we intend to illustrate both how these trends in contemporary public order policing and the complexities affecting the police management of anti-globalization protest were evident in police tactics and strategies used at the transnational protest events. To provide some contextualization for our discussion with regard to Canada *per se*, we now briefly outline public order policing developments there and the nature of the Canadian public order policing ethos in contrast to that of the US. This latter would, however, seem to play a somewhat subservient role to the more global moves towards transnational public order policing convergence discussed elsewhere in this volume.

Public order policing in Canada

Policing in Canada operates on three levels: federal, provincial and municipal. The Royal Canadian Mounted Police (RCMP) are not only the sole federal public police agency, but the territories contract out their policing tasks to them, as do the majority of the provinces, and indeed many of the municipalities too. The histories and traditions of the various police forces vary, but that of the RCMP is rooted in 'colonization and westward expansion'; this has had a major influence on the way that public order issues are policed (King 1997, 54, 57). Also, historically there has been greater recourse to military aid to the civil power provisions in the 'policing' of public order than has been the case in postwar England and Wales. In the past decade or so, though, there has been a noticeable reduction in this (which was to the fore during First Nations land claim protests of the early to mid-1990s) in respect of national protests, with the military taking more of a logistic (supply and provisions) role (King 1997, 57–8, 63). Further, since the 1970s there have been moves towards public order policing standardization and common training across the various police forces, although differences still remain, especially with regard to the deployment of guns and 'less lethal' weaponry (King 1997, 59–62, 72–3).

We have argued elsewhere (King 1997, 47) that public order policing in the mid 1990s regarding 'national' protest issues was, on the one hand, moving 'towards the institution and practice of more multi-agency, conciliatory, and consultative processes, but on the other hand an increasingly [para]military and *potentially* overtly offensive and escalatory public order formula'. It may well be that in the case of transnational protest though, rather than the military taking a 'back seat' in the policing operations, limited to support, logistics and participation on strategic pre-planning joint intelligence and command committees, one could find a return to the earlier national protest position of a more overt military engagement. Certainly this was the case in respect of the 2002 G8 summit in Kananaskis, albeit with the military operations presence being formally located with a supportive role to the police, as we detail later.

Despite these developments, and the colonial westward-expansionist root to much Canadian policing historically, there would seem to pervade a domestic notion, both publicly and in policing itself, of Canada largely being a 'peaceable kingdom' (King 1997, 54–6; Torrance 1986). Perhaps more accurately, this could be termed as 'a relatively peaceable kingdom' when compared to its nearest neighbour, the US. There is a marked contrast between the two North American states in respect of public order protest and the policing of that protest: Canada has had no urban disorder on anything like the scale experienced in the US; also, the majority of our Canadian police officer and intelligence officer interview respondents were at pains to distance Canadian policing from that of the US, regarding the latter as generally more public-alienated, overtly offensive, provocative and employing excessive force.

We now move on to examine developments in Canadian policing structures and practices occurring in the last decade with respect to transnational protest, through what our interviewees regarded as the seven key public order events leading up to, and including, Kananaskis.

Key public order events

As mentioned above, there follows an examination of seven major public order events that occurred in Canada between 1997 and 2002. The first instance involves national rather than transnational protest, but is seen as important given the subsequent Commission of Inquiry report and the timing of its publication. Further, some of the instances involve the presence of international dignitaries, but not all. Of the latter, the 2002 Kananaskis G8 'symbolic target' protests in Calgary and Ottawa are included as in marked contrast from the policing of Kananaskis itself. We have categorized the respective policing operations in their subheadings, and elaborate these in our conclusion. For ease of understanding, we provide a summary of the main issues we want to extract from the first four events, before moving on to examine the last three in greater detail.

Reactive, 'closed dialogue', 'hard-hat' policing: Saint-Sauveur and Saint-Simon, May 1997

Following the controversial policing by the Royal Canadian Mounted Police of school-closure protests in Saint-Sauveur and Saint-Simon, New Brunswick, in May 1997, a report by the Commission of Public Complaints Against the RCMP (CPC 2000) made a number of critical observations and recommendations for future practice.

Generally speaking, the report criticized the police for overreacting to the protests. The unnecessarily uncompromising nature of the police interventions reflected the need for a greater priority on 'open dialogue' with protest organizers and an enhanced commitment to warning demonstrators to disperse prior to the deployment of tactical troops. The report noted how, at Saint-Sauveur in particular, 'the situation was far from resembling a riot ... [it] justified deployment of the soft hats [only] ... There was no reason to deploy the Tactical Troop, the Emergency Response Team or the Police Service Dog Team' (CPC 2000, 169). Of equal relevance to our analysis of more recent events was the recommendation that officers engage in pre-event dialogue with relevant sections of the community (CPC 2000, 168). Such recommendations were subsequently accepted by the RCMP Commissioner (CPC 2001a; RCMP 2001) and duly incorporated into policies and guidelines.

From 'negotiated management' to overtly coercive, unaccommodating, externally-influenced policing: Asia Pacific Economic Cooperation (APEC), Vancouver, 16–25 November 1997

A subsequent CPC inquiry, this time regarding the RCMP's policing of an APEC conference in Vancouver during November 1997 (CPC 2001b), raised similar concerns to those expressed in relation to Saint-Sauveur and Saint-Simon. Whilst the onus for the policing of the conference was jointly devolved to the RCMP and the Vancouver Police Department (VPD), it was the former who held overall responsibility for security, including the safeguarding of the 18 Internationally Protected Persons (IPPs) in attendance. Further, the RCMP had sole command of policing arrangements for the final day of the conference on the University of British Columbia (UBC) campus. It is to those deficiencies, highlighted in the report, in policing arrangements and conduct on this final day that we turn our attention to here.

One major criticism by the report focuses on the poor quality of police pre-planning for the event. It states that despite the fact that there had been a two-year lead-in time in which to formulate police strategy, contingency plans for a possible breakdown of order at the UBC campus were only determined a mere two weeks prior to the conference (CPC 2001b, 437). Similarly, a 170-plus Quick Response Team (QRT), comprising RCMP and VPD uniformed officers and VPD bike squads, was formed only one week prior to the event. Indeed, QRT members were said to have received only 'a few hours' instruction on such matters as crowd control' and were 'never trained together' (CPC 2001b, 375–6).

Although protest against the conference had been peacefully conducted at various sites in Vancouver in the period up to the final day, a 'Threat Assessment Group' had warned RCMP senior officers that one particular group of protesters, known as 'APEC Alert', was likely to engage in 'civil disobedience, vigorous non-violent, protest action' (CPC 2001b, 112). In its report, the CPC Inquiry considered that police pre-planning did not pay sufficient heed to such intelligence. The report observed, for example, that a perimeter fence protectively constructed around the final meeting venue for 75 IPPs (including, contentiously, President Suharto of Indonesia) was not strong enough to be effective; nor was it guarded by sufficient numbers of police. Finally, there was no pre-formulated strategy for dealing with protesters liable to block one or more of the three exit roads leading from the site (CPC 2001b, 118–20, 126). Somewhat inevitably, the perimeter fence was breached due to a lack of police presence. With equal predictability, demonstrators blocked one of the exit roads, necessitating their removal by officers. In the latter case, protesters were given no time between the warning and the firing of an OC (pepper spray) canister. The Inquiry found that, in respect of this incident, 'pepper spray was not required to move the protesters. It should not have been used' (CPC 2001b, 352). As in the Saint-Sauveur and Saint-Simon report, the APEC Inquiry recommended that, following a clear warning by police, protesters 'should be given a reasonable opportunity to comply before the police take further steps' (CPC 2001b, 446).

In a further recommendation, which also resonated with the earlier Saint-Sauveur/ Saint-Simon report, the APEC Inquiry advocated that:

> The RCMP should continue to follow, and enhance where appropriate, its existing open door policy of meeting with the leadership of protest groups well in advance of a planned public order event, with a view to both police and protesters achieving their objectives in an environment that avoids unnecessary confrontation. (CPC 2001b, 445)

In accepting the main findings and recommendations of the report, the RCMP Commissioner indicated that, in the wake of the APEC conference, the force had conducted a major review of its public order planning and operational arrangements. Recently, it had committed itself to 'initiating ongoing consultations with other police agencies, nationally and internationally, to share information and to identify best practises in the provision of security at major public order events' (CPC 2002, Appendix B). The RCMP Commissioner further pointed out that his force was making increased efforts to engage protest organizers in pre-event liaison, reflected in the involvement of trained negotiators in dialogue with protest leaders at two recent events where conflict was avoided (CPC 2002, Appendix B).

However, Ericson and Doyle (1999) argue that the policing of the APEC event at UBC shifted from being initially based on 'negotiated management' consultative principles to that of governmentally and extra-nationally influenced exclusionary, coercive and preventative policing. In particular, they assert that not only was the Prime Minister's Office involved in influencing the policing operation to assure that protesters could not 'publicly embarrass' those political leaders of undemocratic regimes attending the summit, it had even given assurances to Indonesia to this effect. Further, they suggest that the presence of extra-national security services at the event placed additional pressure on the national police to ensure they were seen to 'control' the operation. Also, as part of their enhanced security remit, in addition to a number of protesters being subject to intensive pre-event surveillance, the police made pre-emptive arrests of 45 potential 'troublemakers', some even as long as one week before the event, the majority of whom were later released without prosecution.

Fortress-oriented 'show of force': Organization of American States Summit, Windsor, Ontario, 4–6 June 2000

In the wake of large-scale protests against the World Trade Organization (WTO) meeting in Seattle in December 1999 and the International Monetary Fund/World Bank congress in Washington in April 2000, an Organization of American States (OAS) Summit was held in Windsor, Ontario, in June 2000. This event was looked upon by police as an important precursor to the policing of the Quebec City Summit, scheduled for one year later.

Having noted how the Seattle policing operation was disorganized and easily disrupted by protesters, while the policing of the Washington event was more effective due to the construction of a perimeter barricade; those policing the Windsor summit also opted for the construction of an exclusionary fence (Killam 2001). This decision was also informed by police intelligence suggesting that 20–30,000 protesters were likely to attend Windsor. Accordingly, the six-block area of the summit site was cordoned off by a concrete-set eight-foot high continuous metal sheet (as opposed to APEC's separate chain-linked fencing). The policing operation involved 2,900 officers from the RCMP, the Ontario Provincial Police (OPP) and the Windsor Police, all of who had engaged in two days of preparatory training together. The number of protesters attending was far smaller than expected, with estimates varying between 2,000 and 6,000 (Killam 2001; NUPGE 2000), many of them drawn from trade union organizations. The policing operation was generally regarded as a success. There were only three minor confrontations between police and protesters, with the latter deploying tactical troops and pepper spray in each case (Killam 2001). Moreover, the total of 78 arrests was held to compare favourably with the 525 arrests occurring at Seattle and Washington, respectively (NUPGE 2000).

Killam (2001) argues that three 'key strategies' building on Seattle and Washington were fundamental to this outcome, namely: close partnership between the forces involved, intelligence-led policing, and a venue lending itself to the construction of an exclusionary perimeter. During interviews with police officers involved in the Windsor event, Killam was also told of their preference for a longer period of joint training, the standardization of communications equipment, and the presence of evidence-gathering teams as backup for tactical units. However, it is important to note that demonstrator turnout for the event was small. Also, a different interpretation was placed on events by some of those protesting against the OAS. For example, the journalist and political activist, Judy Rebick, complained that younger protesters in particular had been 'followed, stopped and searched' in a process of police intimidation (Rebick 2000). She and other protesters had been greeted on their arrival at the perimeter fence by a 'massive police presence':

> About 10 minutes into the speeches a group of the young people started snaking towards the fence arms linked. The group hoisted a banner up on the fence. That's all they did. No one climbed the fence. No one tried to push down the fence. And at that moment no one had even thrown anything at the cops. All they did was put up a banner and for that they were pepper sprayed. What was the crime? Decorating in the first degree? It was after the pepper spray that people started throwing things and let me tell you I felt like throwing something myself. (Rebick 2000)

Rebick reports two further incidents in which pepper spray was deployed against the crowd: first, when 20 people, mostly women, sat down in the road in an attempted obstruction of a police bus; and later, when angry protesters began yelling at police through the fence. According to her, the purpose of the huge police presence was 'intimidation, pure and simple': 'In Canada we have charter rights to free assembly. These rights were violated in Windsor to protect bureaucrats from countries where no such rights exist. We are told that free trade will bring democracy to autocratic countries. So far it seems to be bringing autocracy to us' (Rebick 2000).

A more accommodatory 'show of potential force': World Petroleum Congress, Calgary, 11–15 June 2000

One week after Windsor, the World Petroleum Congress in Calgary was attended by 3,000 delegates from 87 countries (CBC News 2000a). As in Windsor, an area of six square blocks was encased by six-foot high metal fencing. The event was policed without incident by the RCMP, Calgary Police Service (CPS) and Edmonton Police, with the CPS occupying the primary decision-making role. Pre-event preparation had been achieved with the help of a Protest Liaison Team, a Joint Intelligence Group and an Incident Management Team.

Reflecting on the WPC event, two years after its occurrence, the then chief of the Calgary Police Service, Christine Silverberg, commented that 'The intelligence component was absolutely key. Our purpose in WPC very much was one of prevention and de-escalation' (quoted by Scotton 2002). The police were evidently intent on taking no chances. Some 1,500 police officers were brought in from other areas. During the four-day conference, police 'spotters' were positioned on top of downtown office towers while helicopters busily circled overhead (Scotton 2002). Police intelligence estimates that no more than 2,000 protesters would be present proved not far wrong (*Risingtide* 2000), with numbers dipping to around 200 for a proposed 'day of action'. Generally speaking, the protest was conducted amidst a 'carnivalesque' atmosphere of 'colourful banners, puppets, masks and costumes' (Mahoney 2000), following exhortations by organizers for this to be a peaceful protest in order to 'get across the message of exploitation by oil companies' (CBC News 2000b).

Summary

It is apparent from the above reviews that Commissions of Inquiry into the police handling of demonstrations at Saint-Sauveur/Saint-Simon and the APEC meeting (both of 1997) highlighted basic shortcomings in a variety of police tactics designed to induce the cooperation of protesters. Regarding the former demonstration, police field commanders were criticized for needlessly escalating violence by their overzealous deployment of specialist units and police dogs. Senior officers were further counselled to engage in pre-event dialogue with protest organizers and to give demonstrators more adequate warning to disperse before sending in tactical troops. Crowd control officers at the APEC meeting were also roundly criticized. In this case, major deficiencies were observed regarding the poor quality of pre-planning and preparation for the event, particularly in light of intelligence to suggest that major 'civil disobedience' was on the cards. Police officers were further rebuked for not allowing demonstrators much time between the warning and firing of CS gas canisters. Finally, the CPC report noted how a specially constructed perimeter fence surrounding the meeting venue was not only weakly constructed, but also inadequately patrolled by police officers.

The problems of effective pre-planning, training and preparation had clearly been eradicated in advance of the Windsor demonstration of 2000. In the latter case, police sensitized to recent events at Seattle erected a much stronger and more effective exclusionary fence than the one breached by demonstrators in Vancouver. Participating police forces were better trained and more effectively coordinated, and intelligence was of a sufficiently high grade to be able to predict the size and tone of the demonstration. At the WPC in Calgary too, the police erected a six-foot high exclusionary fence. Intense pre-event planning, protester liaison and communication, and intelligence gathering, supplemented by real-time surveillance of protesters by bike teams and a decided saturation policing in initial 'soft hat' mode (Calgary Police Service interviews) helped to give police an even firmer control of the event. However, whilst Windsor constituted a fortress-oriented 'show of force' testing ground for Quebec City, to which we now turn, the WPC event in Calgary was a more accommodatory 'show of *potential* force', to be carried through to the Calgary policing of G8 which we consider later.

Exclusionary fortress-oriented policing: Summit of the Americas, Quebec City, 20–22 April 2001

The lead-up to the 2001 Summit of the Americas, held in Quebec City on 20–22 April 2001 (and indeed the policing of the event itself) was framed within the following extract of a report published by the Canadian Security Intelligence Service:

> as demonstrated by extremist animal-rights and environmental activists, security measures could prompt a rise in the scale of violence from smashing windows to arson attacks, the use of explosive devices, and even physical threats against individuals, including posting

warning letters purported to contain contaminated razor blades … it has been established that antiglobalists are organizing against a number of international meetings in Canada, including the April 2001 Summit of the Americas in Quebec City. Given the virulent anti-globalization rhetoric directed against the Organization of American States (OAS), the threat of Summit-associated violence in Quebec City cannot be ruled out. (CSIS 2000)

This report was supplemented by a pictorial account 'for security personnel only' released pre-G8 which outlines 'militant anti-globalization tactics' (CSIS 2002).

Interviews with police respondents confirm that four police forces were involved in the policing operation for the event. A majority of 3,768 of the 6,000 officers deployed were drawn from the RCMP, which accepted the main responsibility for operational planning, general coordination, public relations, dignitary protection and tactical liaison with the 680 army personnel also present. Also deployed were 2,750 officers of the Sûreté du Québec (SQ), charged with the task of civil emergency coordination, and coordination with provincial and local governments. Significantly smaller numbers of officers were deployed from the Ville de Québec (VQ), represented by 390 personnel, and the Ville de Sainte Foy police, by 75. The former's responsibilities included escorting and ensuring the safety of summit participants, while the latter's main remit was that of securing the airport.

Generally speaking, the main police priorities were the protection of visiting dignitaries and non-disruption of the summit. To this end, and in significant escalation of precedents set on previous occasions, a 6.1 kilometre security perimeter was constructed to cordon off the conference site from demonstrators. In addition to incorporating Quebec's natural fortress features, the construction also comprised a three-metre high chain link and concrete fence, tested to withstand 20,000 pounds of pressure (Chang et al. 2001, 20; Killam 2001, 30).

This strategy caused offence both to observers of and participants in the protest: 'Had the government deliberately set out to create a symbol of anti-democratic exclusion, they could not have done better. Letters to newspapers and calls to talk shows in both Quebec and English-speaking Canada regularly decried the construction of the wall as a naked attempt to silence popular opposition' (McNally 2001, 76–7).

In the week leading up to the summit, some 2,000 representatives of trade unions, environmental activists, women's groups, religious bodies and human rights associations came together for an alternative 'Second People's Summit of the Americas'. Delegates here engaged in a number of preliminary protest activities including a several-hundred-strong march by women (McNally 2001, 77).

With the commencement of the summit proper, the widely condemned 'wall of shame' became the preferred destination of participants on a six-mile march setting off from Laval University on Friday, 20 April, the first day of the protest. Comprised of, for the most part, students and youth activists, jointly organized by the Summit of Americas Welcoming Committee (CASA) and the Anti-Capitalist Convergence (CLAC), the march initially provided a colourful spectacle, conducted amidst a carnival atmosphere (Rebick 2001a). One female protester, dressed up as the Statue of Liberty, walked the entire route on stilts, while a group of women, calling themselves The Dandelions, wore T-shirts proclaiming 'The participant radical blossom that always blooms' (Rebick 2001b). Once in sight of the wall, a group known as the Medieval Bloc rolled forward a twenty-foot wooden catapult from which three teddy bears were projected at the police (Rebick 2001b).

Soon after their arrival, a small group of protesters set about forcing a minor breach in the perimeter:

> First a few then more climbed up the chain-link … and in a rocking motion pushed it down. By my watch it took less than five minutes for the hated fence to come down. The amazing thing was that only about 100 people rushed through the fence. The rest held back. It was the protesters not the police who held back the crowd. I was astounded at the discipline. (Rebick 2001b)

According to Rebick, fewer than 20 of the 3,000 now present were guilty of throwing stones or bottles at the police. Nevertheless, once the wall was breached, the police responded by firing a barrage of tear gas canisters into the crowd.

In the ensuing mayhem, demonstrators found themselves occasionally overwhelmed and, in some cases, the direct targets of tear gas canisters (McNally 2001, 77–8). Elsewhere, known activists, such as Jaggi Singh of the Anti-Capitalism Convergence, were picked off by police snatch squads (Klein 2001). Nevertheless, an attitude of defiance prevailed. The initial protesters were joined in solidarity by colleagues from the People's Summit (McNally 2001). Among the sights greeting new arrivals was a sit-down protest in which luminous peace signs pierced through the thick 'fog' of tear gas (Rebick 2001b). Marshals repeatedly explained to newcomers that anyone preferring the safer haven of a 'green zone' should veer left away from the wall. However, 'No one did. Thousands approached the perimeter. They ran when the tear gas exploded but they came back, time after time for two hours' (Rebick 2001b).

On Saturday, 21 April, the main day of the protest, 2,000 buses and a specially chartered train ensured a total turnout variously estimated at 25,000 to 60,000 (Anderson 2001; Killam 2001; McNally 2001). Unlike the previous day, there were two distinct (but overlapping) threads to the protest. In keeping with pre-event negotiations between labour leaders and representatives of the RCMP and VQ, a trade union-sponsored march followed a route that completely bypassed the perimeter fence. As McNally (2001, 78) points out, 'In addition to being inspiringly large, the union gathering was also tremendously colourful and festive in spirit. Banners, puppets and flags were everywhere; jugglers, clowns, artists and drummers filled the crowd with energy.' This component of the day's protest was policed according to a 'low-profile, soft hat' strategy (interview, VQ officer).

Such strategy was in sharp contrast to the policing of the relatively younger cohort of protesters converging, like the day before, though this time in greater number (7,000), on the perimeter wall. Indeed, here it was more like a 'siege-mentality', reinforced by bombardment with Molotov cocktails (Killam 2001), some of which ignited buildings inside the protective perimeter. In the course of protracted confrontation, police discharged a total of 5,148 teargas canisters and fired 903 plastic bullet rounds, and water cannon, tasers (stun guns) and pepper spray were also deployed (interviews with RCMP, SQ and VQ officers).

Daily press reports by a team of 40 observers assembled by the Ligue des droits et libertés (a Canadian civil liberties union) commented on the contrast between the police behaviour of the previous Friday, when tear gas was used in more restrained fashion to repel protesters threatening to breach the perimeter, and their conduct during Saturday, which was markedly more aggressive. As one reporter commented, 'Ligue observers noted a significant change in police behaviour around the perimeter fence on Saturday: tear gas was fired even before demonstrators approached the fence in volumes many times that of the previous day' (Boskey 2001). Observers further remarked on the regular use of plastic bullets, not merely to deter threatening individuals, but as a routine form of crowd control; and of the greater use of incursive forays, designed to intimidate and disperse protesters (Boskey 2001).

Rebick (2001c) maintains that among the most frequent targets of police aggression were sit-down protesters passively blocking roads and medics rushing to the aid of tear gas victims. Some protesters gave almost as good as they got. One participant recalls running excitedly from one scene to the next:

> Arriving at one spot I saw a guy run up and grab the fence, only to have a gas canister fired into the chain links explode in his face to send him flying to the pavement. Medics dragged him up an embankment and I watched them treat his bleeding face and arms. A few minutes later they were gone and I lobbed rocks and a beer bottle down on the riot cops then ran off down an alley with tear gas canisters exploding at my heels. (Morton 2001)

According to Rebick (2001b), hardly more than 100 protesters were engaged in 'front-line' activities of this nature. Nevertheless, as on the previous day, thousands of others signalled their collective defiance, in this case by 'pounding guardrails and posts with stones and placards in a deafening show of solidarity' (Rebick 2001c).

Such, then, were the main features of the Quebec City summit. Later, we mount a corresponding analysis of the key arrangements and activities involved in the policing of the Kananaskis G8 Summit and anti-G8 protests in Calgary and Ottawa, but first we consider an intervening public order event occurring in Ottawa in late 2001.

From 'conflict resolution' to post-9/11 'securitization' policing: G20/IMF and World Bank, Ottawa, 16–18 November 2001

Only four weeks notice was given that two important 'global' conferences would be held simultaneously in Ottawa in the third week of November 2001. The IMF/World Bank meetings were originally to have been held in Washington on 28–29 September 2001 but were postponed following the 11 September terrorist attacks on the US. Likewise, a conference of G20 ministers, originally scheduled to take place in New Delhi, was transferred because of India's disconcertingly close proximity to war-torn Afghanistan (CBC News 2001a). Contingency planning for the event was therefore vigilant of the possibility of the 'potential threat of terrorist actions'

(Ottawa Police Service 2002a). The primary concern of the RCMP was that of IPP protection, with the Ottawa Police Service (OPS), supported by officers from the Ontario Provincial Police and Metropolitan Toronto Police, taking the lead in respect of public order.

In the build-up to the event, the RCMP staged a conflict resolution seminar, led by academics from Ottawa's Saint Paul's University. Among its 26 participants were government officials, police agencies, and spokespersons for NGOs and other protest groups (Makhoul 2002). Separate discussions were held between the OPS and protester representatives. Finally, the perimeter fence around the G20 site was limited to waist height (CBC News 2001b). Such pre-emptive measures, though, proved out of step with the policing operation subsequently unfolding on the ground. The total number of 2,000 demonstrators actually attending the protests in Ottawa fell short of the 5,000 initially anticipated (CBC News 2001b). There was only one incidence of property damage – this occurring during a 'snake march' when a window of a McDonald's restaurant was put through (CPPC 2002). Nevertheless, there was a general feeling among protesters that the policing had been unnecessarily heavy-handed and not in keeping with the otherwise peaceful nature of the event (CPPC 2002).

After the event, a Citizens' Panel on Policing and Community (CPPC) was formed (later to become the Ottawa Witness Group) which made a formal request to the Ottawa Police Services Board for an inquiry into the policing of the protest. When this was denied, the CPPC held its own review, highlighting such problematic issues as: the decision to deploy 'hard hat' officers; the use of police snatch squads to make pre-emptive arrests; the open display of police machine guns; and the unnecessary use of tear gas, rubber bullets and pepper spray (CPPC 2002, 9). Of particular concern, though, was the (televised) use of police dogs against the crowd (CPPC 2002, 9). In giving evidence to the review, one CBC Radio News reporter complained that he was not only hit by a police officer but also bitten by a police dog (CBC News 2001b). The general feeling of indignation was epitomized by the comments of an administrator at Ottawa's First United Church, who explained: 'I've never been so afraid in my life …. We hadn't gone 20 paces from the staging area when police in full riot gear moved in on the crowd with out-of-control dogs. People were bitten, beaten, snatched out of the crowd. I really feared for my life' (quoted by Bird 2002).

The police sent observers – as did the organizers of the forthcoming G8 Summit in Kananaskis – to the public meetings staged by the Citizens' Panel (Bird 2002). In his interim report to the Ottawa Police Services Board, published shortly after the G20 events, the OPS chief expressed the view that his officers had acted responsibly in Ottawa, 'by deploying lawful tactics whose purpose and context may have been misunderstood by persons present' (OPS 2002a). Nevertheless, he continued by acknowledging that, 'As there will be future meetings in Ottawa, there is a clear need to enter into discussions with demonstrators in an attempt to develop a protocol that would help to guide police action and inform protest groups' (OPS 2002a).

The most tangible and far-reaching outcome of the Citizens' Panel recommendations and the OPS internal operations review was the publication of an 'Agenda for Excellence for Policing Major Events' (OPS 2002b). This document stressed three key objectives for OPS officers to bear in mind in their policing of major events, namely:

• to uphold the *democratic rights* of all individuals to freedom of opinion, expression, association and assembly as guaranteed under the Canadian Charter of Rights and Freedoms;
• to strengthen *community partnerships* through communication, consultation collaboration and transparency in planning and operations;
• to ensure the *safety* and security of our community and our members. (OPS 2002b, 2, original emphasis)[2]

A fundamental part of the recommended strategy for policing major events was that of 'crowd management' involving 'direct dialogue with protest organizers' (leading in turn to the establishment of a Major Events Liaison Team (MELT)), plus recognition of 'the potential for escalation through the use ... and presence ... of specific strategies, tactical units and "technical aids"' (OPS 2002b, 3). This 'Agenda for Excellence' also provided for discretion as to whether or not to make an arrest during an event, emphasizing that 'the potential impact of an arrest on broader crowd dynamics should be kept in view' (OPS 2002b, 6).

As we shall see shortly, such an attitude of contrition and commitment to principles of 'crowd management' and de-escalation on the part of local police following criticisms of their role in the Ottawa meetings was reflected in the superficially 'soft hat' arrangements for policing protests that occurred in Ottawa to coincide with the G8 Summit in Kananaskis. This is not to suggest, however, that previous 'lessons learned' – regarding the need for pre-event liaison with protest organizers, intensive pre-planning and intelligence gathering, real-time surveillance and the presence of adequate backup – were sacrificed in the process. Rather, as will now become apparent, these more pragmatic mechanisms were used to complement the 'protester friendly' tactics endorsed by the Agenda for Excellence.

Exclusionary, overt force policing compared with intelligence-led 'zero-tolerance' potential force policing mode: G8 Summit, Kananaskis, 26–27 June 2002

As mentioned earlier, following the G8 Summit in Genoa in September 2001, the Canadian prime minister, Jean Chretien, announced that the June 2002 Summit would be held in the remote Rocky Mountains village of Kananaskis, Alberta, 90 kilometres west of Calgary (Bergman 2002a). Whilst this relocation effectively

---

2 These objectives bear a close resemblance to the core elements of the 'negotiated management' model identified by McPhail, Schweingruber and McCarthy (1998) typifying the US public order policing shift in the 1980s and 1990s compared with that of 'escalated violence' of the 1960s.

denied protesters a primary focal point, it nonetheless created other symbolic sites of protest across Canada. For the purpose of this chapter, we focus on the policing of protest in two of these, namely Calgary (the closest city to the summit site) and Ottawa (the capital) in addition to the policing arrangements for Kananaskis itself.

Kananaskis
As with the Quebec City protest, a major policing task was to ensure an undisrupted summit. However, given the post-9/11 context, and the perceived threat of terrorism, Kananaskis consisted of the largest security operation undertaken in peacetime Canada (Bergman 2002b). Central to this operation was the now-familiar ploy of establishing an exclusionary mechanism.

The equivalent of Quebec City's perimeter wall was, for Kananaskis, a series of exclusion zones, patrolled by more than 6,000 military personnel and 4,500 police officers (Adelaide 2002). The first of these, a 'red' zone, referred to a two-kilometre radius around the core site of the summit, including the summit hotel and a local mountain trail. This zone was largely secured by military personnel, although responsibility for the security of buildings and the safety of the prime minister and IPPs was that of the RCMP according to its mandate. Beyond this, a 'blue' zone incorporated territory within a 6.5-kilometre 'no-go' area around the village. This was exclusively patrolled by the armed services. The final, 'yellow' zone, of 20 kilometres in radius, was jointly secured by army and police officers. This incorporated Highway 40 and Highway 1, which were both monitored by police checkpoints. In addition, the Canadian defence authorities established three surface-to-air missile bases as a last line of defence against any aircraft somehow managing to evade the squadron of CF-18 fighters patrolling a 150-kilomtre radius 'no-fly' zone (Adelaide 2002). The Canadian military were deployed in an operational capacity to such an extent that it might seem to exceed their post-mid-1990s logistics-support role to the police. Whether this may be a sign towards a future trend, or simply a 'one-off' post-9/11 instance, is too early to say. However, as we suggested earlier, military operational involvement in the policing of transnational events does seem worth monitoring to see if it starts to reverse the national public order policing trend of distanciation from one to the other. Our interview respondents stressed the role that the military played in this instance as simply supportive, as did the RCMP officer in charge of security operations for the Kananaskis summit when interviewed for *Canadian Security:*

> DND [the Canadian Department of Defense] operates solely in an assistance role in the security side to the RCMP; and to the city [Calgary] if it's under agreement. Their authority comes from us. They assisted the summit management office in logistics, and they assisted the RCMP in supplementing our ground security in the bush, supplementing our air threat capabilities and bringing in some of their specialized equipment, which we don't have. (McCutcheon 2002, 16)

Left-wing commentators criticized the heightened preoccupation with terrorism as a disingenuous attempt to intimidate activists and scare off broader popular support. Orpheus (2002) quotes an article in the *Calgary Herald* in which a senior Canadian army officer, Brigadier General Stenson, allegedly suggested how 'terrorists could very easily use "peaceful" protesters as a cover to slip into Kananaskis .... Given that threat, Stenson said he is very concerned that his soldiers might mistake a protester for a terrorist if there is a confrontation in the dark, forested environment of Kananaskis.'

Attempts by activists to set up a 'Solidarity Village' in Kananaskis County, capable of accommodating 15,000 protesters, were denied by local officials, who claimed that this would be in violation of government regulations (Adelaide 2002). In the event, protest at the Kananaskis perimeter zone was low-key. On day one, approximately 200 protesters drove in convoy towards the conference site, only to be turned back at the first checkpoint on Highway 40. A bus containing 30 postal employees intent on delivering some 400 protest letters to the G8 leaders reached the third checkpoint, where one of their members was arrested for obstruction. On day two, around 50 demonstrators attempted to breach the security perimeter and one person was arrested (*Pony Express* 2002, 14).

Calgary

In keeping with the precedent set by the WPC event and a commitment to avoiding the type of violence associated with other anti-globalization protests, the policing operation for Calgary was strategically 'soft hat', with an emphasis on intelligence and police–protester liaison. Intelligence activity was coordinated by a Joint Intelligence Group (JIG), comprising CPS and RCMP commanders and threat assessment officers, defence, customs and the FBI and other international security agencies. Correspondingly, specialist CPS and RCMP consultative units (for example the Activist Liaison Team, the Aboriginal Liaison Unit, the Community Relations Group (CRG), and CPS Community and School Liaison officers) were active in the build-up to the event. For example, in the weeks prior to the summit, the CRG mounted a consultative 'roadshow', though this was generally met with public scepticism (Kerr 2002, 7). As in Quebec City, police–protester liaison proved most productive in relation to trades union representatives, who complied with pre-demonstration notice requirements. Following the rejection of the application to set up a Solidarity Village, discussions between the CRG and other groups of activists broke down.

Adelaide (2002) reported how the police had denied all applications for permits for demonstrations in the week prior to the protest. In his view, this betrayed a cynical underlying motive:

> While to date the police have not arrested those who have protested peacefully without official permission, by refusing to give permits the police and city fathers have effectively given themselves the power to seize on any isolated instance of vandalism or violence to declare all the protests illegal and institute mass arrests.

Adelaide was equally suspicious of the RCMP's decision initially to allow an Amnesty International observer to observe police actions during the protest, only to withdraw cooperation subsequently on the grounds that the observer lacked 'the background and knowledge of the law required to make balanced and objective observations' (Adelaide 2002).

Certainly, police contingency planning allowed for the possible deployment of two RG12 armoured military rescue vehicles, two water cannons, a mounted unit, an RCMP field dog team, CS gas and line munitions (Bergman 2002b). The first line of response, though, was a low-profile Mountain Bike Unit. In the event though, the number of protesters never exceeded 7,000 and the public order unit was deployed in only one instance – when, on the first day of the summit, 30 demonstrators barricaded-in lunchtime customers at a downtown McDonald's. Other protest activities were overridingly peaceful and celebratory.

Prior to activities coinciding with the summit, an 'Alternative Summit' – the GSB (Group of Six Billion) People's Summit – of workshops and lectures took place on the University of Calgary campus from 21–25 June. Organized by the Alberta-based International Society for Peace and Human Rights, the principal objective of the 'summit' was to 'offer an alternative view of the planet's future; one that's not rooted in increased militarism and poverty, and decreased human and civil rights' (CBC News 2002). Marches and related activities occurring on the days of the official summit passed off peacefully. These included: a deliberately disruptive 1,000-strong 'snake march' through the downtown area; a 'protest picnic'; an improvised soccer match designed to paralyse an intersection; a symbolic 'die-in' highlighting third-world suffering through starvation and AIDS; a 'mud protest' in which participants caked their faces with mud; and a 'Global Knit-in', during which members of the Revolutionary Knitting Circle emphasized their commitment to the preservation of local crafts and social traditions.

The whole event therefore stands in clear contrast to the police–protester dynamics witnessed at Quebec City. As one RCMP G8 commander stated, 'We had a number of goals going into this and one was to reduce the level of violence. During the event, we didn't have to use any chemical weapons and we didn't have one broken window in Calgary' (*Pony Express* 2002, 16). However, our police interviewees also noted that the dynamics on the ground may well have been different if larger numbers of protesters had been present. As we shall now see, the G8 protest in Ottawa was policed to similar effect.

Ottawa

Given the absence of IPPs in Ottawa, the RCMP defined its role as that of protecting Parliament and other major institutions and buildings. The primary role of the OPS, meanwhile, was to ensure a safe and orderly G8 protest event, to protect persons and property, and to maintain individual safety and rights. To this end, the OPS operational plan specified how: 'Public order units will not be deployed or visible to protest groups unless directed to do so by Incident command. The Ottawa Police Service will maintain a "soft hat" approach to crowd management. The deployment of public order will be directly related to the actions of the crowd' (OPS 2002c, 7). Further dimensions of the police operation prior to and during the protest are described by Allen (2003), a sergeant in the National Security Investigation Service of the RCMP, who points out that the police were equally committed to ensuring that all park areas would remain open and that no new barriers would be erected in preparation for the event.

Allen (2003) acknowledges that the Ottawa protest had a 'serious potential for violence'. Demonstrations against the meeting of G8 finance ministers in Halifax one week earlier had been marred by violence in which 38 people were arrested and CS gas was used to disperse the crowd. Moreover, since February 2002, a protest group calling itself Take the Capital had publicly signalled its intention to inflict damage on named private and government buildings in the course of the summit protest. In the event, only five persons were arrested; there were few acts of vandalism and only one injury, which occurred when a police officer was dragged from his bicycle during a scuffle with protesters. Allen (2003) attributes such a successful outcome to three components of the policing operation: pre-event liaison and consultation; effective intelligence gathering; and a combined 'soft hat' and 'iron fist' approach to supervising protesters.

Pre-event preparation was underpinned by the activities of a joint RCMP/OPS MELT, dedicated to holding consultation meetings with protest groups, business representatives and other concerned or interested citizens. As part of this process, MELT officers held fruitful discussions with labour organizations but could not sustain contact with other anti-globalization groups. Indeed, it was subsequently alleged by protest activists that some constituent groups were visited by police officers advising them that they risked being arrested for participating in a non-permitted demonstration (Martin 2002).

Reflecting on one of the key problems confronting senior police officers, one protest veteran of the G20 Summit commented: 'I'm sure they're particularly concerned that they can't figure out who's in charge. I'm sure that's their key problem all the time – they don't understand that people can organize things cooperatively, because they don't work that way' (quoted by Campbell and Shahin 2002). This much was acknowledged by the OPS chief of police, who conceded: 'We're not sure where the main event is expected to be. But there is a movement afoot and our challenge is that we are going to have to move with whatever becomes targets' (Campbell and Shahin 2002). He added that 'We hope that we can work with some of the protesters. But some say the trust has been broken, though in some cases I'm not sure there was any trust [to begin with]' (Campbell and Shahin 2002).

Correspondingly, a Joint Intelligence Group (JIG), comprising participating police forces and other security agencies, was set up four months prior to the summit meeting. One major function of the JIG was to establish a 'vigorous program of information use', in which police and commercial databases and international intelligence from the Foreign Broadcast Information Service were used to provide information on participating individuals and groups and their possible tactics. Such intelligence was sophisticated enough to allow the JIG to identify and track all buses travelling to Ottawa prior to them leaving their cities of origin. Cars and vans known to be carrying persons violating arrest or parole conditions were similarly tracked en route to the demonstration. Meanwhile, details (including photographs) of any protester known to have a criminal record or otherwise warranting 'special treatment' were fed to officers on the ground.

In keeping with the superficially soft hat policy, tactical police squads were kept in buses and vans, close to the action, but out of view of the protesters. Nevertheless, Allen remarks that tactical police were permanently on standby, as part of an 'iron fist' approach dedicated to the safety of police officers, protesters and other passers by. As part of this resolute approach, the police kept up real-time surveillance footage via cameras positioned on tall buildings. This and video downlinks from an RCMP helicopter and OPS fixed-wing aircraft were transmitted to a central command centre.

Details of a temporary holding facility for police prisoners were widely circulated in advance as an intimidatory tactic designed to deter people from engaging in direct action. On arriving in their buses, protesters were 'greeted' by officers wearing jackets clearly marked 'police liaison'. Although outwardly friendly, police officers pointedly photographed each new arrival as an unmistakable statement of their intention. Finally, as part of a 'saturation' tactic, plainclothes officers infiltrated the crowd, providing tactical information while the march was in progress. Uniformed colleagues lined the route of the march, some of them openly parading cameras and other surveillance equipment. Anyone seen melting away from the march was immediately followed in order to thwart any possible intention to commit an act of vandalism.

As stated, these tactics proved decisive. On the first day of the summit, 3,500 demonstrators snake-marched through Ottawa's main financial and commercial sector, temporarily halting traffic in the process. During the same day, local activists staged an impromptu squat in an abandoned building as part of an appeal for a more widespread public housing provision. OPS officers took the decision not to arrest the occupants on condition that they refrain from causing any further damage (Martin 2002).[3] The highlight of the following day's protest, in which a total of 5,000 people was estimated to have been involved, was a 'No One Is Illegal' march, opposed to 'the criminalization, subjugation and exploitation of indigenous peoples worldwide by the industrial forces of the Western world' (Martin 2002).

Following the success of the police strategy, the Civil Liberties Association of the National Capital Region, in a letter from its president to the OPS deputy chief (CLANCR 2002), also formally recognized the 'greater effort' on the part of the OPS to 'protect legitimate dissent' during its policing of the G8 protest event. The letter continues: 'the approach of your force was the right one, and that by keeping the methods of dealing with potential violence out of sight (dogs, riot troops), you avoided a menacing appearance that can sometimes provoke demonstrators'.

This view was largely echoed by the Ottawa Witness Group (OWG) of voluntary non-protester independent observers in their report on the policing of the event (Witness Group 2002). In this they state that 'generally police interaction with marchers was professional. Police adhered to policy and used regular uniformed

---

3   They were, however, forcibly evicted at a later date (Witness Group 2002).

officers rather than riot police …' It further praised the involvement of MELT officers, maintaining that they 'proved to be a positive presence during G-8 events of June 22, 26 and 27 and defused some potentially difficult situations'. However, the report also highlights the intrusive nature of surveillance at the event: 'constant police videotaping provoked and intimidated, particularly when videotape teams waded into large crowds, and moreso when they captured on the tape people arriving in school buses' (Witness Group 2002). To this extent, it should also be noted that from our interviews with police officers in Ottawa, two main reasons were put forward for protester numbers being small: first, the heavy rain, and secondly, the pre-publicized intensive overt surveillance.

Conclusion

Ericson and Doyle (1999) have argued that despite the general trend towards a more visibly accommodatory public order policing in Western societies, including Canada, the policing of protest at transnational events where IPPs are present (instanced by the 1997 APEC Summit), and economic and trade interests are at stake, constitutes a special case and that policing will be more overtly coercive. Our study has found elements to support this (for example, Quebec City and Kananaskis); indeed we have also indicated that such policing operations were not simply overtly coercive, but even a 'show of force'. Further, the policing of the WPC event would suggest the need for a more local (as opposed to exclusively transnational or national) dimension. We could add that it would seem that the policing of transnational protest at events where IPPs were not present, although in some respects consultative and negotiated (with those more *institutionalized* protesters), was also covertly coercive.

We have accounted for this latter form by largely referring to a 'superficially soft hat' policing mode. On the one hand, this would support the depiction of a move towards a 'two-pronged' approach to public order policing mentioned earlier. However, it would appear from our studies of Canada that it is not merely a situation of policing with a 'soft hat', whilst the paramilitary units are held out of sight and in reserve, together with intelligence gathering pre-, during and post-event. Rather, it is more a situation whereby the policing operation is intelligence-led through risk analysis, consultation plus infiltration of 'non-negotiable' groups, intensive surveillance and pre-emptive removal of targeted leaders and potential 'troublemakers'. This also leads us to a notion of *potentially* and covertly coercive policing, which involves intrusive and disruptive policing practices. Further, as has been suggested in the case of the G8 protests in Ottawa, such disruptive policing, combined with widely publicized advance notice regarding the 'soft hat but zero-tolerance' and intensive surveillance on the day, presumably contributes to a smaller protester turnout.

We need briefly refer to the situation regarding protester numbers here too. At many of the events we have outlined, the number of protesters was small – and at times considerably less than police intelligence expected. In those cases where the police felt their 'superficially soft hat' operation had been successful, from our interviews they readily admit that things may have been otherwise if the numbers had been greater.

Finally, as we have indicated, it is also important to draw a distinction between policy and practice in respect of the contemporary public order policing form. Elsewhere (King and Waddington 2004), we have identified public order policing policy change in England and Wales that would support the arguments concerning an increasing 'liberalization' of the public order policing process. However, our research questioned the translation of such policy into practice on the ground as, in the particular instance we examined in some detail, policy was far removed from reality concerning pre-planning, liaison, negotiation and flexibility. Similarly, the more progressive policies we refer to in this chapter, incorporating Commissions of Inquiry and Citizens' Review recommendations, can be questioned not only by the reality of those instances of overtly coercive policing on the ground found, but also the covertly coercive and disruptive nature of contemporary 'superficially soft hat' policing.

Chapter 5

Aspects of the 'New Penology' in the Police Response to Major Political Protests in the United States, 1999–2000

John Noakes and Patrick F. Gillham

Introduction

Tens of thousands of protesters greeted delegates to the 1999 World Trade Organization (WTO) Ministerial Conference in Seattle. Protesters staged demonstrations throughout the four-day conference, but won what has come to be known as the 'Battle in Seattle' on the first day of the WTO meetings when they blockaded downtown streets for several hours, forcing the cancellation of the opening day's trade talks. Police and protesters clashed repeatedly during the four-day conference, particularly on the opening day when Seattle police made extensive use of less-lethal weapons to disperse the protesters – a process that took the better part of the day. Among the largest direct action protests in the US since the Vietnam War, the WTO demonstrations were the first of several mass demonstrations in US cities over the next several months, each featuring street clashes between police and protesters (Gillham 2003; Thomas 2000; Cockburn et al. 2001).

The WTO protesters' opening-day victory, the scale and intensity of the clashes between demonstrators and the Seattle police and the subsequent political activism inspired by the WTO protests have made *Seattle* a rich signifier for both activists and police. For political activists, it became an aspiration – a new standard for effective protests against which demonstrators measured their subsequent efforts (cf. Neale 2002; Kahn 2000). In the 'years of global justice protests' that followed the WTO protests, mass demonstrations were staged in numerous Canadian (Ottawa, Quebec City), European (Gothenburg, Prague, Davos and Genoa), and US cities (Washington, DC). In the US, political activists representing a wide range of national and international causes staged protests at the US national party conventions in Philadelphia and Los Angeles. Emboldened by *Seattle*, a subset of demonstrators in each city insisted on their right to disrupt these events, leading to repeated clashes between police and protesters.

Police interpret *Seattle* in terms as dramatic as those of protesters, including, as one high-ranking police official in Philadelphia put it, as 'parallel to Pearl Harbor to some degree' (Fisher 2001). More generally, police in the US characterized the WTO demonstrations as 'the start of a new genre of protests' with which they had little experience (Gainer 2001; see also Seattle Police Department 2000). For police, therefore, *Seattle* became a symbol of the worst-case scenario, the kind of situation for which they needed to retrain and retool so that it did not occur in their jurisdiction (Fisher 2001; Gainer 2001; Czech News Agency 2000). In the year following the WTO demonstrations, US police forces spent millions of dollars on new riot gear and sent representatives to seminars sponsored by the National Association of the Chiefs of Police and the US Department of Justice designed to 'provide public safety agencies with [the] skills, knowledge, strategies, and tactics necessary' to control a new breed of protester (Beasley, Graham, and Holmberg 2000; Burgess 2000; Montgomery and Santana 2000).

To better understand the strategic and tactical chess match between this new breed of protesters and police, we examine police strategies and tactics utilized during recent major contentious events in three US cities: the WTO in Seattle; the April 2000 IMF/World Bank meetings in Washington, DC; and the August 2000 Republican National Convention in Philadelphia. Our analyses are based on a careful reconstruction of the police response to protesters at these three events. Gillham (2003; 2000; 1999; Gillham and Marx 2000) observed the WTO and the IMF/WB protests and interviewed activists involved in both protests. Noakes (2001a, 2001b) interviewed high-ranking police officials in Washington and Philadelphia after the respective protest events in those cities. This primary source information was supplemented by extensive reviews of the newspaper coverage of each protest and a review of many of the official and activist documents produced in the aftermath of the clashes between the police and protesters.[1]

---

1   Newspaper accounts of social movements have been both a frequent source of data for social movement scholars (cf. McAdam 1982; Kreisi et al., 1995; Jenkins and Perrow 1977) and the subject of critical sociological inquiry (Ashley and Olsen 1998; Gitlin 1980; McLeod and Hertog 1998). Critiques of the use of newspaper accounts as a source of data have raised important questions about the validity of such a methodology (McCarthy, McPhail and Smith 1996; Oliver and Myers 1999). While we agree that newspapers are not 'passive channels of communication' (Oliver and Myers 1999: 39), for several reasons this is not a debilitating problem in this study.

First, we are using newspaper accounts to construct case studies, not to sample instances over a selected period of time. Because each of our protests received extensive press coverage, the question of media access is eliminated (Noakes and Wilkins 2002). Moreover, we have confirmed and supplemented the data obtained from newspaper accounts with information from other sources, including first-hand observations, official reports and interviews (Burgess et al. 2000; Seattle Police Department 2000; Gainer 2001; Sund 2001; Fisher 2001; Richman 2001). Second, many of the biases reflected in media coverage of social movements do not pose a serious problem for our analysis. Reporters' tendency to rely on official sources for information, for example, aids our research. Given the ease and frequency with which city and police officials are quoted in newspaper accounts of the police planning and response to the protests, a substantial record of official versions of events is available. Moreover, to the extent that police have an interest in sanitizing their actions, we obtain a conservative record of their

Policing philosophies and policing of protests

For most of the twentieth century, police in the US held an extremely negative view of protesters and exhibited little tolerance of the community disruption caused by political demonstrations. Police often over-enforced the law as a means of harassing protesters and rarely communicated with protesters prior to demonstrations. The primary, and often only, tactic employed to control protest was the use of force, escalating in severity until the demonstrations ceased (Schweingruber 2000; della Porta and Reiter 1998a). McPhail, Schweingruber and McCarthy (1998) have labelled such tactics the *escalated force* style of policing protests. By the end of the 1960s protest cycle, however, this approach was causing considerable problems for police, both *on* and *off* the job (P.A.J. Waddington 1998).

On the job, police began to question the effectiveness of escalated force tactics. Arrests and other uses of force by police during demonstrations often became the focal point of protester frustrations, escalating the risk for police and increasing the extent of community disruption caused by the protests (P.A.J. Waddington 1998; Barkan 1984). Off the job, after a decade of street clashes between police and civil rights, anti-war and other political dissenters, questions were raised about the integrity and legality of the escalated force style of policing protest from a variety of quarters. Several public commissions appointed to examine the causes and consequences of violence in American society, for example, criticized the repressive nature of the police response to political dissent. Moreover, in the US courts several legal decisions on public forum law extended the right to protest and placed limitations on state's ability to restrict these rights (Schweingruber 2000; O'Neill 1999; McPhail, Schweingruber and McCarthy 1998; Kerner 1968).

With the delegitimization of escalated force, new strategies for policing protest were needed. Decisions about how to police demonstrations are mediated by *police knowledge*, or how police 'construct external reality, collectively and individually' (della Porta 1998). This construction of reality by police shapes their role in the maintenance of social control. Most discussions of the role of police knowledge focus on the police perception and diagnosis of protesters, their tactics, and their motives. But Winter (1998a, 188) also documents how *policing philosophies*, or the 'conceptual principles and guidelines underlying police operations' shape the response of police to political protests. Winter illustrates this point in his analysis of the Federal Republic of Germany between 1960 and 1990 by contrasting regions with *Staatspolizei* philosophies, which understand the primary function of policing as serving the state and protecting it from opponents, with those with *Burgerpolizei* philosophies, which understand the primary function of the police as serving citizens. In areas of Germany in which the former predominated, political protests

---

actions from the newspaper accounts and our own interviews. Given that we are interested in documenting changes in police activities, the likelihood that our account underestimates the use of new, more forceful tactics by police gives us greater confidence that the changes we document are, in fact, real.

were perceived of primarily as threats to the state, and an escalated force style of policing protest was employed to discourage demonstrations. Protests fared much better in areas in which the latter philosophy dominated.

The crisis in policing protest in the US at the end of the 1960s protest cycle came at what sociologists of punishment and social control now recognize as the tail end of the penal modernist period of criminal justice (Garland 2001). Penal modernism, a *Burgerpolizei* philosophy that understands the police as 'an agent of reform as well as repression' (Garland 2001, 39), has its roots in the late nineteenth century but became the paradigmatic philosophy of criminal justice in the US after World War II. Its basic axiom is that criminal justice practices should encourage the understanding, rehabilitation and reintegration of offenders rather than seeking to merely punish them. Informed by psychological and sociological concepts that focused attention on the relationship between the individual and society such as relative deprivation, anomie, labelling, and subcultural norms, penal modernist criminal justice policies tended toward correctionalism (Garland 1985; Messinger 1968; President's Commission 1967).

The criminal justice system, of course, remained the legitimate purveyor of punishment. But, ideally, each offender was to be treated as an individual and each case decided on its own merits, with penal measures tailored to match the level of risk posed by offenders. Severe punishment remained an option, but those who were determined by penal institutions to pose little risk – because of their background, the extent to which they were embedded in society, or the extenuating circumstances of their offence – would be treated less harshly. The criminal justice system, thus, was a part of the welfare state. If delinquency was the result of inadequate socialization, substandard education or a lack of job opportunities, then flexibility in sentencing, the provision of social services and an extensive parole system were just and effective responses to crime (Garland 2001).

Penal modernism experienced its own crisis in the 1970s. Critics from a range of political positions questioned the criminal justice system's capacity to meet its correctionalist goals (cf. Wilson 1975; American Friends Services 1971). With belief in the possibilities of rehabilitating criminals declining and fear of crime increasing, the influence of penal modernism on criminal justice policy declined. In its place a new paradigm emerged stressing control, not understanding, of criminals and focusing on their incapacitation, not their rehabilitation. Reforms to the US criminal justice system over the last three decades have made punishment more punitive by eliminating indeterminate sentencing, establishing three-strikes-and-you're-out laws, and de-emphasizing correctional measures such as probation and parole (Simon 1993; von Hirsch 1993).

But the crisis in policing protests initiated by the delegitimization of escalated force tactics occurred before the end of the penal modernist period when the 'habitus … [the] working ideologies, [and the] trained responses and decisions' of police officials and criminal justice policy makers were still firmly rooted in the penal modernist worldview (Garland 2001, 38). Penal modernist ideology infused criminal justice institutions in an uneven and historically eclectic way. Given the timing of

Table 5.1   Comparison of three styles of policing protest

Characteristic	Escalated force (pre-1970s)	Negotiated management (1970–1990s)	Strategic incapacitation (current)
First Amendment rights	Denied to all	Stated top priority	Low priority (denied to transgressive protesters)
Toleration of community disruption	Low	High	Moderate (more likely to be tolerated for contained than transgressive protesters)
Communication	Low	High	High with contained; selective with transgressive
Use of arrests	Frequent	Last resort	Strategic; no longer last resort (used to incapacitate transgressive protesters)
Use of force	High	Last resort	Strategic; no longer last resort; expanded by use of less-lethal weaponry (used to incapacitate transgressive protesters)

Adapted from McPhail, Schweingruber and McCarthy 1998.

the crisis in escalated force, the policing of protest may have been the last facet of the criminal justice system to adopt penal modernist practices and principles. The escalated force style of policing of protest, which enjoyed pre-eminence into the late 1960s, violated nearly every key aspect of penal modernism. Police rarely considered the particular characteristics of protest groups or their causes. Moreover, they took a distinctly *Staatspolizei* approach to public order, tolerating little in the way of community disruption and ignoring protesters' political rights.

The key aspects of the *negotiated management* style of policing protest that emerged from the crisis of the escalated force style of policing protest, however, are clearly influenced by penal modernist philosophy (see Table 5.1). In direct contrast to escalated force, proponents of negotiated management counsel increased tolerance of minor community disruptions and the protection of the rights of protesters in an effort to minimize the disorder caused by both the demonstrations and the police effort to contain them (della Porta 1998; Waddington 1994). Moreover, they recommend that police officials negotiate the boundaries of acceptable protest with social movement group leaders prior to (and, if necessary, during) demonstrations, a process that, in the US, often began with the application for a permit to march or rally in public areas. It is during the permit process that the 'lofty principles' of negotiated management are reconciled with the 'practical bureaucratic guidelines for managing protests' (McPhail, Schweingruber and McCarthy 1998).

Several principles of penal modernism are reflected in negotiated management strategies and tactics. The emphasis on negotiating agreements with social movement organizers prior to demonstrations, for example, individualized social movement organizations and offered each an opportunity to demonstrate its commitment to cooperation and order. Moreover, police sought cooperation from protesters by offering to facilitate demonstrations and casting protesters as citizens seeking to exercise a constitutional right, not as opponents of the state. During the 1980s and 1990s in the US the deployment of negotiated management tactics and strategies resulted in a decline in clashes between police and protesters (McPhail, Schweingruber and McCarthy 1998). In fact, for many police agencies the need to use force to control a political protest had become a sign of police failure (Fisher 2001; Sund 2001; della Porta 1998).

Underneath this general trend toward softer, more cooperative police responses to protests, of course, there is a great deal of variation in how police respond to individual political demonstrations. The policing of protest, like all policing, remains selective, and there are numerous examples of protest policing in the last 30 or so years in which the police used extensive force to coerce demonstrators (McCarthy and McPhail 2005). In the US, for example, groups such as EarthFirst! and ACT-UP – both of which resisted cooperation with authorities – clashed repeatedly with police (Kaufman 2002). Given the range of police responses, sociologists often ask not whether the police response to political protests is harsh or tolerant, but under what circumstances police respond harshly (or softly) and why.

It is here that the second component of police knowledge – diagnoses of protesters, their goals and their tactics – becomes most clearly relevant. 'Shifts between tolerance and repression,' P.A.J. Waddington (1998, 131) argues, 'reflect the institutionalized standing of protesters.' In short, police distinguish between 'good' and 'bad' protesters. 'Good' protesters are those seen as ordinary, decent people protesting for a concrete goal that benefits themselves, particularly working men and women who have lost their jobs through no fault of their own (Waddington 1999b, 1998; della Porta 1998; Fillieule and Jobard 1998; Jaime-Jimenez and Reinares 1998). Police are more tolerant of minor lawbreaking and use softer tactics when confronting 'good' protesters, who, for their part, tend to engage in predictable demonstrations (Tilly 2000; P.A.J. Waddington 1999). Police are much less tolerant of demonstrations staged by 'bad' protesters, whether they are permitted protests or not. 'Bad' protesters include professional or political protesters, those seen as pursuing abstract goals or ones that will primarily benefit others, those who do not cooperate with police, and young protesters, who are characterized as ill-informed and easily manipulated by others (P.A.J. Waddington 1999; Fillieule and Jobard 1998; Jaime-Jimenez and Reinares 1998).

Police are also more likely to use force during protests that target international events or events involving political dignitaries. Demonstrations at such events carry extra risk for police, who face significant pressure to control such protests from state officials (della Porta and Reiter 1998a; P.A.J. Waddington 1998). The British police, therefore, forcibly resist protests near royal castles or 10 Downing Street (P.A.J. Waddington 1998). Ericson and Doyle (1999, 589) argue that the policing of international events 'may be affected by powerful extra-national influences', such as pressure from the governments of visiting dignitaries, thus leading to a harsher police response to protesters than normal in the host nation. Several social movement scholars also suggest that police are more likely to respond with force when facing the tactical innovations that often accompany new protest cycles (Tarrow 1998; Wisler and Kreisi 1998; McAdam 1983).

The introduction of new tactics, by definition, shifts the demonstrations from *contained* to *transgressive* contention and raises police concerns that they will lose control of the situation. Tilly (2000) categorizes protests that are staged by political actors well known to the police and who employ familiar tactics as *contained*; conversely political actors unfamiliar to the police and employing innovative tactics are categorized as *transgressive*. Good protesters are more likely to come from the community in which the demonstration is staged, thus increasing the likelihood that they are known to the police. They also are more likely to follow agreed upon cultural scripts (for example, picketing or marching along politically symbolic routes). Bad protesters are more likely to be from outside the community in which the demonstration is held and, therefore, more likely to be unknown to police (though 'professional' protesters often become well known to police, particularly with increases in electronic surveillance). They are also more likely to engage in innovative tactics (McAdam 1983).

The prevalence of transgressive protesters in recent mass demonstrations initiated a new crisis for those charged with the policing of protest in the US. While not as systemic as the delegitimization of escalated force, it raised essential questions about the limits of negotiated management. As long as most protesters cooperated with police and engaged in contained protests, negotiated management remained effective. But the extent to which recent protesters rejected the principles of contained protest compromised the effectiveness of negotiated management strategies. For police officials, the size, diversity and shapelessness of transgressive demonstrations made policing them more difficult. Moreover, police believed, transgressive protesters have begun to exploit certain aspects of the negotiated management style. As one of the primary street negotiators for the Washington police during the IMF protests complained:

> we would meet with [protest groups] at different times [during the protests], and frankly, while we were meeting trying to work out issues, other sub groups went about their anarchy .... So, on some days, it felt like [the contained groups] were tying me and my commanders up for three hours while [the transgressive groups] were out running amuck. (Gainer 2001)

Transgressive protesters not only refused to reveal many of their plans ahead of time, but their non-hierarchical, consensus-based decision-making process did not provide a 'good command and control over policy vis-a-vis what (the police) needed to have a negotiated settlement of each issue' (Gainer 2001).

The presence of a significant number of transgressive protesters at several recent major protest events in the US forced police to rethink their approach to policing protest. Because transgressive protesters would not negotiate their tactics and plans ahead of time, police had to manage greater uncertainty. Moreover, demonstrators also engaged in direct action protests aimed at disrupting the events police were assigned to protect. Unable to rely on pre-negotiated agreements with protesters and facing high-risk demonstrators, police expanded their strategic repertoire to include tactics not characteristic of negotiated management. But police did not simply return to the escalated force tactics of the past. In the same way that public order police in the early 1970s drew heavily on penal modernism when they needed new strategies and tactics to replace discredited escalated force tactics, when police were confronted by the limits of negotiated management they drew on the new penology, the paradigmatic criminological *episteme* of the late twentieth century.[2]

The new penology reconceived crime as a systematic phenomenon and elevated victims to a universal status (Feeley and Simon 1992; Garland 2001). Consequently, social control practitioners began to concern themselves less with why crime occurred and more with protecting citizens and corporations from criminal acts. To do so, they devoted considerable energy to developing new means of identifying and controlling groups that posed a risk to social order, managing the risk they posed, and improving the efficiency of penal systems. This new approach is summarized succinctly in Wilson's (1975, 153–4) claim that 'for crime reduction purposes, the most rational way to use the incapacitative powers of our prisons would be to do so selectively … longer sentences would be given to those who, when free, commit the most crimes.'

A distinct set of practices and policies have emerged to achieve these new penal ends. Resources, for example, have been aggressively diverted from low-risk to high-risk targets and deviant activities reclassified based on the new goals of the criminal justice system. Illegal drug use, therefore, is no longer viewed 'as an individual problem that can be remedied; rather it is interpreted as a factor used to classify the offender into a risk group' (Welch 1996). Similarly, three-strikes laws are 'based on a concern for managing aggregates of "dangerous" people' (Shichor 1997). In contrast to the penal modernist era, criminal justice officials seek to 'reduce the effects of crime not by altering either offender or social context, but rather by rearranging the distribution of offenders in society' (Feeley and Simon 1992, 458). Much greater emphasis is placed on preventing deviance from occurring, by minimizing the exposure of those defined as potential risks to criminal situations or, if this is impossible, by incapacitating them (Auerhahn 1999).

The rise of the new penology has influenced the policing of protest in several ways. During the 1990s, for example, police in the US had begun to incorporate the use of less-lethal weapons into their public order repertoire. This increases the capacity of police to incapacitate demonstrators during demonstrations without raising the risk of delegitimization associated with escalated force. As we will see below, the police adopted several strategies rooted in a new penological approach to social control during recent mass protest in the US. Before detailing these new strategies and tactics, however, it is necessary briefly to describe the protest events that constitute our three cases.

---

2   As is common in studies of social control, we refer to the entire criminal justice apparatus when we use 'penology', not simply the penal system (cf. Feeley and Simon 1992).

The return of mass protests in the US

In the remainder of this chapter we review the protest events in Seattle, Washington, DC, and Philadelphia and the police response to them. We will focus on the relative distribution of contained and transgressive protesters in each event. Contained protesters participate in protest events sponsored by well-known groups who have 'a stake in the orderliness of the political event' and, therefore, cooperate with police prior to and during demonstrations and employ familiar and officially approved tactics (McPhail, Schweingruber and McCarthy 1998). In contrast, transgressive protesters do not fully cooperate with police and often employ tactics that raise the level of uncertainty for police.

Before turning to the specific cases, we must distinguish between the two types of transgressive protester in our cases. Most transgressive protesters were organized under temporary umbrella coalitions set up to facilitate nonviolent direct action protests, such as the Direct Action Network (DAN) in Seattle and the Mobilization for Global Justice (MGJ) in Washington, DC. Though often anarchist in philosophy, these groups were committed to nonviolent direct action and disapproved of the purposeful destruction of property during demonstrations, which they saw as senseless and counterproductive in part because it garnered disproportionate media coverage – all of it negative (Fears 2000; Finnegan 2000; Jaffe 2000). A much smaller group of transgressive protesters did not renounce violence as a means of self-defence and destroyed property during demonstrations as a purposeful act of protest. The most prominent of these groups is commonly referred to as the black bloc.[3] Dressed in black clothing and wearing black bandannas or masks to cover their faces, black bloc members spurned negotiations with police as a matter of principle. Unless specifically noted, when we refer to transgressive protesters we are referring to the former, those committed to nonviolent direct action and opposed to the destruction of property during protests.

Seattle

In Seattle, protest organizers began educating and training activists weeks before the WTO Ministerial Conference, bringing together union, student, environmental and religious groups for numerous workshops, teach-ins and rallies. On the day before the official opening of the conference, several contained marches and rallies took place in Seattle, including a rally coordinated by the national and local offices of mainstream environmental groups promoting 'clean, green, and fair' trade, a 14,000-person march organized by a local affiliate of the religious-based Jubilee USA Campaign calling for the cancellation of international debt, and a late night rally and

---

3   Proponents of black bloc claim they are a 'tactic', not an organization (Info Shop 2004). For the purpose of this chapter, we, nevertheless, consider them a group in the sociological sense.

concert organized by People for Fair Trade, a campaign of Public Citizen (Gillham 2003; Smith 2001; Thomas 2000).

Early in the morning of 30 November 1999, the opening day of the WTO meetings, transgressive global justice activists affiliated with the Direct Action Network (DAN), organized in small affinity groups, chained themselves to one another and sat cross-legged in major downtown intersections and outside the hotels housing WTO delegates. Over the course of the morning they were joined by thousands of additional protesters and bystanders who occupied the public space surrounding the convention centre, small bands of black bloc protesters who vandalized corporate buildings in the downtown area, and the spillover from a legally permitted march sponsored by the AFL–CIO and the Sierra Club, which brought 30,000 more protesters into the downtown area. The direct action protests of DAN activists had brought rush-hour traffic to a standstill and, with additional protesters clogging the sidewalks, most WTO delegates were unable to reach the meeting site. Despite police orders to disperse, protesters held the blockades throughout the morning and continued to occupy the downtown streets even after police fired pepper spray, tear gas, concussion grenades and rubber bullets at the demonstrators, forcing the WTO to cancel its opening day schedule (Cockburn et al. 2001; Gillham and Marx 2000).

By the next morning, however, police had succeeded in retaking control of the streets, declared the downtown a 'no-protest zone', established a curfew, and along with the Governor of Washington, called in National Guard troops to assist overwhelmed police. These official actions did little to dissuade thousands of defiant and outraged protesters who returned to the streets over the next several days to protest at the police's tactics and attempt to disrupt the WTO meetings further. By the end of the week 500 protesters had been arrested, retailers had lost millions of dollars in sales and property damage, and the WTO meetings collapsed without any significant trade agreements being reached (Gillham 2003; Gillham and Marx 2000; Smith 2001).

Washington, DC

Inspired by the success of the 'Battle in Seattle', national activist organizations focused their attention on making the April 2000 joint meetings of the International Monetary Fund (IMF) and World Bank (WB) in Washington, DC the first major post-Seattle protest event (Gillham 2003; Burgess 2000). Annual demonstrations had been staged against the WB and IMF for several years, but they were generally small and primarily involved local church-based groups and DC-based national organizations like 50 Years is Enough. Known as the Mobilization for Global Justice (MGJ), the protests during the WB and IMF's annual spring meeting were structured similarly to the WTO protests in Seattle, with protest organizers negotiating permits for an MGJ rally at the Ellipse on the National Mall while some MGJ-affiliated affinity groups and the local Anti-Capitalist Convergence (ACC) trained for direct action protests aimed at stopping the WB and IMF delegates from attending the meetings (Gillham 2003).

On Sunday, 15 April, upwards of 20,000 protesters, many organized into affinity groups of transgressive protesters, unsuccessfully attempted to establish blockades around the World Bank building. On the advice of the Washington DC Metropolitan Police Department (MPDC), many delegates had arrived at the WB before dawn on chartered buses, foiling the demonstrators' efforts. Late in the afternoon, these transgressive protesters abandoned the intersection blockades and participated in several snake marches throughout the downtown area. These marches, which disrupted traffic and led to several clashes with police, eventually ended at the MGJ permitted rally on the Ellipse, where the transgressive protesters joined approximately 20,000 contained demonstrators (Dvorak and Ruane 2000; Fears 2000).

Demonstrations the following day were smaller, but still included a few thousand protesters. The day was characterized by sporadic clashes between police and transgressive protesters. It ended symbolically in the afternoon at a police barricade outside the World Bank building where a small group of activists successfully negotiated with police officials for the peaceful, choreographed arrest of approximately 400 protesters (Montgomery 2000a). In all, MPDC arrested 1,300 protesters and claimed a victory because the protests had been allowed to occur but had not unduly disrupted the IMF/World Bank meetings (Gainer 2001).

Philadelphia

Less than four months after the MGJ protests, a large contingent of global justice activists joined protesters advocating a variety of causes at the 2000 Republican National Convention (RNC) in Philadelphia. As in the two earlier protests, numerous national and local groups negotiated agreements with the Philadelphia Police Department (PPD) (Fisher 2001). In this case, a permitted rally in downtown Philadelphia drew several thousand participants on the eve of the RNC. But, as in Seattle and Washington, DC, transgressive protesters organized in affinity groups attempted to disrupt morning rush-hour traffic in downtown Philadelphia on Monday, 31 July, the opening day of the RNC. Several members of a group demonstrating in opposition to the United States Army School of the Americas, for example, blocked a major intersection in downtown Philadelphia. Around midday a local welfare rights group, led by 80 children and 20 people in wheelchairs, staged a four-mile march from City Hall to within a block of the sports arena in which the RNC was scheduled to begin that evening, despite having not obtained a permit to do so.

The most intense period of demonstrations, however, occurred on Tuesday afternoon when demonstrators, organized in clusters ranging in size from a couple of dozen protesters to upwards of 300, staged a series of surprise blockades. The scene was chaotic: as more than 100 protesters dressed as clowns and millionaires chained themselves together and sat down in the middle of an entrance ramp to the major crosstown expressway; other groups attempted to blockade the downtown hotels used by delegates or participated in one of several snake walks through downtown traffic, rocking cars, spray painting buildings, and setting fire to dumpsters. The demonstrations succeeded at bringing downtown traffic to a stop during the evening rush hour, but with the convention being held in a sports arena several miles from the downtown area they had little effect on the RNC. By the RNC's end, 400 demonstrators had been arrested (Couloumbis, Pangritis and Marshall 2000; Curet and Kennedy 2000; Marantz 2000; Newton 2000).

The police response to mass protests in the US

The police response to mass demonstrations in Seattle, Washington, DC, and Philadelphia was multifaceted. Whenever and wherever possible, police in these three cities negotiated agreements with both national and local contained protest groups, designating protest routes and setting demonstration guidelines (Fisher 2001; Gainer 2001; Seattle Police Department 2000). Impromptu street negotiations with large groups of trangressive protesters also resolved several tense situations in a mutually agreeable fashion (Montgomery 2000a; Postman, Rahner and Sorenson 1999). Moreover, police in each city often under-enforced the law in order to minimize the disruption to public order caused by permitted marches and, on a few occasions, facilitated unpermitted marches by familiar and usually trustworthy groups (Fisher 2001; Gillham and Marx 2000; Newton 2000).

When negotiated agreements between police and protesters could not be reached, however, police in each city used new tactics to break up the demonstrations and disrupt protesters' planning. These new tactics included: (a) restricting the access of both contained and transgressive protesters to large areas of public space adjacent to the primary event venues or in symbolic spaces where direct action protests could draw considerable attention or cause significant disruption; (b) aggressively enforcing laws and regulations in an effort to disrupt the preparations of transgressive protesters; (c) employing various means of force, including arrests and less-lethal weapons strategically to rearrange or incapacitate transgressive demonstrators; and (d) utilizing intensive prior and real-time surveillance in an effort to neutralize the uncertainty generated by transgressive protesters. We see evidence that these techniques became part of the strategy of the Seattle police after the WTO protesters succeeded in shutting down the opening day of meetings. In Washington, DC and Philadelphia such tactics and strategies are evident throughout the protest events. We turn now to a more detailed discussion of each tactic. Space limitations will not permit an exhaustive review of how police departments in each city responded to their respective protest event. Instead, we have chosen to illustrate each tactic with representative examples.

No-protest zones

It took Seattle police until nearly midnight to clear the streets of protesters after the first day of the WTO protests. Police then began enforcing an expanded no-protest zone around the WTO meeting venue, pushing demonstrations far enough away that they no longer could easily interfere with the delegates' movements. Having learned from the Seattle experience, police in Washington, DC and Philadelphia announced extensive restrictions to protester access to public space in their respective cities. Most notably, oversized no-protest zones were announced well in advance of events and without prior negotiations with contained groups. In addition to restricting access to a large area surrounding the site of the RNC, Philadelphia city officials also granted the Republican Party first rights to all public spaces in the city during the convention, effectively pre-empting legal protests in public parks and symbolic sites, such as the Liberty Bell or Independence Mall. Protest organizations went to court to reduce the size of the no-protest zone in Philadelphia, but they never gained access to the area near the site of the RNC (Levy 2000).

Over-enforcement of the law

Washington, DC and Philadelphia police vigorously enforced city regulations to disrupt the preparations of transgressive protesters. The MPDC, in conjunction with city fire inspectors, raided and closed a convergence centre established by the MGJ as a temporary housing and meeting places for nonviolent, transgressive global justice demonstrators (Drake and Mizejewski 2000). Similarly, the Philadelphia Police Department (PPD) also teamed with city fire code inspectors to raid and close a building used by transgressive global justice protesters as a puppet factory and convergence centre (Slobodzian 2001). All 75 occupants of the building were arrested during the raid, which was timed to prevent a non-permitted demonstration planned for that afternoon from occurring. Police also seized several large puppets and other props built for use in the demonstration. Police had learned about the planned demonstration and the props being made from undercover state troopers, who had infiltrated the site by masquerading as union carpenters opposed to globalization (Fisher 2001; Betz 2000).

Strategic use of force

The most significant deviations from the negotiated management tactics, however, involved the frequent and *strategic* use of force. Under the negotiated management style of policing protest, force is to be used only as a last resort to control protesters who will not cooperate with police. There is considerable evidence from these cases, however, that the use of force, both in terms of arrests and the employment of weapons, was used not as a last resort, but rather strategically to temporarily incapacitate and rearrange protesters. In Washington, DC, for example, the MPDC arrested everyone on a single block (over 600 people) for marching without a permit on the night before the IMF meetings began, despite having allowed unpermitted marches on several previous days (Drake and Mizejewski 2000). Many who intended to protest the next day were not released for 23 hours – one hour short of the statutory deadline for charges to be filed and well after most of the first day's demonstrations had concluded (Drake and Mizejewski 2000).

In addition to the arrest of the occupants of the convergence center noted above, the Philadelphia Police Department used arrests strategically in another way. When confronted by demonstrations by groups without permits they selectively arrested protesters from groups unfamiliar to the police (such as those opposing the School of the Americas) while letting protesters with whom they had long-standing relationships (such as the Kensington Welfare Rights Union) demonstrate.

The use of less-lethal weapons by police in Seattle and Washington, DC is also noteworthy (see Dvorak and Ruane 2000; Fears 2000; Keary and Williams 2000; Beveridge 1999; *News Tribune* 1999; Postman, Broom and King 1999). Less-lethal weapons 'use some controlled force to interact with some aspect of the human body to temporarily affect it' (Kenny 2000). A wide variety of these weapons have been developed for military use, from acoustic bullets to robotic land probes (Duncan 1998; Lewer 1995; Starr 1993). Similar weapons have been used to quell civil disturbances in parts of Europe and elsewhere for a number of years (Mettress and Mettress 1987).[4]

Seattle police employed a wide range of less-lethal weapons including pepper spray, rubber bullets, tear gas and concussion grenades as soon as they realized they had lost control of the downtown area to WTO protesters. Though global justice demonstrators in Seattle held their ground for most of the first day, the SPD's assault eventually succeeded in dispersing the protesters and chasing them outside the downtown area. Police officials then established a much broader no-protest zone and enforced a curfew. While protesters challenged both the geographic and temporal restrictions on demonstrations, the SPD succeeded in moving the conflicts outside the downtown area, thus allowing the WTO to proceed with its scheduled meetings. Having established a broad 'red zone' prior to the IMF/WB protests, police in Washington, DC used pepper spray to keep demonstrators from breaching barricades and to disperse protesters when police found themselves outnumbered (Drake and Miszejewski 2000; Montgomery 2000a).

Use of surveillance

The best example of the use of surveillance information to incapacitate demonstrators strategically was in Philadelphia, where police targeted three alleged 'ringleaders' for pre-emptive arrest based on intelligence information it had obtained on local and national activists (Fisher 2001). Each of the three was charged with conspiracy to commit crimes, though police testified in court that they had ignored those who

---

4   By the early 1990s, all police forces in major US cities equipped their police officers with at least one authorized less-lethal weapon (Crime Control Digest 1992a). While it took some time for less-lethal weapons to become a regular part of the arsenal used by US police during protests, today's well-armed police officers face demonstrators with rubber bullets, pepper spray, beanbag launchers, paint-ball guns and concussion grenades (Alexander and Klare 1995-6). The most frequently used less-lethal weapons are pepper spray and rubber bullets.

actually committed the crimes that resulted in those charges (Harris and McCoy 2001, 2000; Commonwealth vs. Kathleen Sorenson 2000). Prosecutors requested and received extremely high bail ($1 million in two of the cases, $500,000 in the other) by citing information in defendants' intelligence files as evidence that they 'facilitate[d] the more radical elements to accomplish their objective of violence and mayhem' (quoted in Kinney and Couloumbis 2000; see also Commonwealth vs. Sorenson 2000; Harris 2000a; Harris and McCoy 2000; Kinney 2000). Unable to raise these extremely high bails, the alleged ringleaders remained in jail until after the RNC had concluded, at which point judges reduced their respective bails to $100,000.

Discussion

The police use of force against transgressive protesters was, in many ways, predictable because police would, by definition, diagnose transgressive demonstrators as 'bad' protesters. In each city, professional organizers from groups such as the Ruckus Society, Public Citizen, and the Rainforest Action Network helped train activists – many young and, in the eyes of the police, easily manipulated – and coordinated demonstrations. Moreover, abstract goals such as 'global justice' would primarily benefit those in less-developed countries, making the police suspicious of the motives of those in the streets of US cities. In addition, the targets chosen by the protesters in these three cases included events of international and national importance, featuring diplomats, trade representatives and political leaders. Finally, transgressive protesters did not fully cooperate with police, employing innovative tactics and refusing to negotiate away their right to disrupt the events they targeted.

If the use of force by police was predictable, the same could not be said about either its form or function. The social scientists who documented the shift to negotiated management never claimed that the use of force by police had been eliminated altogether, but they did claim that it had been relegated to a tactic of last resort to be used primarily against uncooperative protesters (della Porta and Reiter 1998a; McPhail, Schweingruber and McCarthy 1998). Otherwise, within the policing protest literature, the police use of force was a largely un-theorized activity. As a result, the only logical conclusion was that the use of force by police could be situated on a continuum between its employment under the escalated force and negotiated management styles. As such, the contemporary use of force by police during protests was portrayed as a temporary and situational return to escalated force tactics. But the use of force during recent global justice protests does not sit comfortably on the continuum between escalated force and negotiated management. Important aspects of the strategies and tactics of police in these three cases are rooted in neither the escalated force nor the negotiated management style of policing protests.

Instead, we argue, they reflect a third response to political protests, which we refer to as the *strategic incapacitation* style of policing protests. Strategic incapacitation is a variation on the selective incapacitation philosophy of social control, which is distinguished by two of its facets: First, the utilitarian focus on preventing deviance rather than avenging the offence, rehabilitating the offender or deterring others from committing the same act; and second, its selective focus on those deemed most dangerous (Miethe and Lu 2005; Auerhahn 1999). From the selective incapacitation perspective, for example, incarceration is a means of preventing the offender from committing a criminal act again. It is not rehabilitative and need not be a means of revenging the offence. If the sentence is harsh, as it is in many states with three-strikes provisions, the length of sentence is intended not as a means of retribution but rather as a reflection of the perceived dangerousness of the offender (Shichor 1997).

The *strategic* incapacitation style of policing protest is also selective but recognizes the dynamic nature of relations between police and protesters and the contingent nature of who and what is dangerous. Dangerousness may attach itself to particular protesters, protesters using specific tactics, or protesters in a particular place at a particular time. Moreover, dangerousness is only relevant when political demonstrations are about to occur or are occurring. Therefore, the targeting of transgressive protesters and, in particular, their leaders, in an effort to prevent or severely restrain demonstrations without necessarily causing permanent harm or engaging in extensive punishment of the protesters is one of the central tenets of strategic incapacitation (Noakes, Klocke and Gillham 2005). But contained protesters, like those on the streets of Seattle after DAN had succeeded in closing down the downtown area, may find themselves the target of such tactics, as well.

In the remainder of this chapter, we elaborate on three central aspects of strategic incapacitation: risk assessment, temporary incapacitation and the rearrangement of offenders. One long-term police strategy to decrease uncertainty is surveillance. 'Information work' plays a key role in strategic incapacitation strategies. During the escalated force era, for example, it was used as a means of gathering information that could be used to delegitimize or expose groups' efforts to force social change (cf. O'Reilly 1989; Powers 1987). During the negotiated management era, the primary use of information work was to allow police to maintain public order while under-enforcing the law (della Porta 1998; della Porta and Reiter 1998a; McPhail, Schweingruber and McCarthy 1998). Della Porta (1998), for example, details how the Italian police use new technologies to let troublemakers know they are being watched, anticipate where trouble will occur, and record protest events so that police can arrest those who commit violence after the protest has ended, when doing so is less likely to spur continued additional unrest.

Although police continue to use new technologies to these ends, information work has taken on an additional function in this new era. Intelligence information circulating among the FBI and police departments in each city provided authorities with information on:

> who might be consistent rabble-rousers, the course of funding for the groups, and then, the discussion of their tactics ... how they communicated, how they moved about the city,

how they took over intersections, who was likely to be behind that. What they did with puppets, and all the techniques they used. (Gainer 2001)

The extent of this information work allowed police to assess risk and identify individuals and groups who were later subjected to various strategic incapacitation tactics, a practice referred to by one observer as 'political profiling' (quoted in Scher 2001).

Police also seek to rearrange and incapacitate protesters for as long as possible without incurring the costs associated with punishing the offenders. By rearranging we mean creating obstacles to participation in demonstrations. This can be done by arresting protesters or by use of physical barriers to control protesters' actions. So, for example, large no-protest zones demarcated by fences, mobile barriers and police in riot gear work to rearrange protesters. Incapacitation is also achieved when force is used to disable protesters temporarily or otherwise make it impossible for them to participate in demonstrations. The most obvious example of incapacitation occurs when police use less-lethal weapons against demonstrators.

Arrests intended to keep protesters out of demonstrations have aspects of both incapacitation and rearrangement. For example, the mass arrest in Washington, DC temporarily immobilized several hundred protesters on the eve of the WB/IMF demonstrations. Similarly, the arrest of 75 protesters at a Philadelphia convergence site was timed to disrupt direct action protests planned for the following day – the date and time of which police had learned from an undercover officer who had infiltrated a protester convergence site (McCoy and Harris 2000a, 2000b). We contend that these arrests were intended to incapacitate rather than punish demonstrators because only rarely did these arrests result in prosecutions or, when the accused did end up in court, in convictions. Those arrested on the eve of the IMF/WB meetings, for example, were all released within 24 hours, after payment of only a $50 collateral bond, which nearly all of them subsequently forfeited without penalty (Drake and Mizejewski 2000; Wagner 2000). After the IMF meetings had ended, another 150 protesters were released after prosecutors agreed to reduce each charge to jaywalking, which carries a $5 fine (Montgomery 2000b). Similarly, charges brought against numerous direct action protesters were dropped or dismissed when Philadelphia prosecutors were unable to connect specific people to specific crimes. In the end, the 400 arrests in Philadelphia yielded only 24 misdemeanour convictions (Harris 2000b; Harris and McCoy 2001).

Though police officials are quick to remind observers that the failure of the courts to convict defendants 'is never dispositive on whether we had a right to arrest them in the first place' (Whitman 2001), in many cases it appears as if the police made little effort to punish those arrested, ignoring such basic police procedures as establishing a clear chain of evidence (Drake and Mizejewski 2000; Montgomery 2000b; Wagner 2000). As one exasperated Philadelphia municipal court judge instructed the district attorney's office: 'You're going to have to have somebody come in here and testify that somebody did something wrong' (quoted in Harris 2000b).

Less-lethal weapons also function to temporarily incapacitate protesters without risking the dangers of traditional firearms. The most frequently used less-lethal weapons are pepper spray and rubber bullets. Pepper spray includes a highly concentrated resin derived from cayenne that temporarily disables a target by causing intense pain, irritation of the eyes, swelling of the throat, temporary paralysis of the larynx, and loss of vision and balance (Jett 1997; Cook et al. 1994/95). But the most serious effects of pepper spray last only about an hour, after which nearly all people make a full and speedy recovery (Zollman, Bragg and Harrison 2000; Jett 1997). Rubber bullets are 'cylindrical projectiles resembling chunks of sausage, fired from a .37 millimeter gas gun' (*Crime Control Digest* 1992b, 5). When fired at the ground, the rubber chunks ricochet into crowds, striking protesters in the shins and thighs and leaving a painful welt (*Crime Control Digest* 1992b; Metress and Metress 1987). Fatal injuries can occur when projectiles strike people in the head (Wedge 2004), but if used as designed they should not cause the death of a victim.

At first glance it may appear that the use of less-lethal weapons is consistent with the move toward softer means of policing. There were, for example, no reports of serious injuries as a result of the use of less-lethal weapons in Seattle or Washington, DC. If, however, less-lethal weapons are used more readily than more lethal means of force would be or if, when police decide on their response to a demonstration, they use less-lethal weapons where once they would have arrested protesters, negotiated mutually agreeable solutions or allowed the protesters to demonstrate unimpeded, then the use of less-lethal weaponry represents an increase in the use of force by police in response to protests. But this is not a return to escalated force tactics. The use of force is not an end in itself, nor is it indiscriminate. Instead, rearranging and incapacitating protesters allows the police to control and defuse protests without risking the delegitimization crisis faced at the end of the escalated force era.

The differences between the 'new penology' and penal modernism are reflected in the new strategies and tactics adopted by police to respond to the new breed of protesters. Paraphrasing Feeley and Simon's (1992, 458) analysis of changes in the dominant philosophy of crime and punishment over the past 30 or so years, we argue that the new approach to policing transgressive protesters encourages police 'to reduce the effects of [protests] not by altering either [the protesters] or the social context, but by rearranging the distribution of [protesters]'. There were, of course, differences in the police response in our three cases. During the April 2000 IMF/World Bank protests in Washington, for example, DC police arrested more protesters than their counterparts in the other two cities combined. Moreover, the Philadelphia police were the only force not to adorn its officers in riot gear and employ less-lethal weapons. Our argument is not that the police response in each city was identical, but rather that when the negotiated management style of policing protest faced a crisis posed by an increase in transgressive protesters in the late 1990s, various police departments drew from a common police philosophy to help construct innovative approaches to controlling demonstrations.

Conclusion

In the months following the WTO demonstrations in Seattle, mass demonstrations were staged in several US cities, coinciding with major national or international events. Protesters in Washington, DC and Philadelphia, inspired by the success of the WTO demonstrations, tried to replicate the tactical innovations introduced by protesters in Seattle by, among other things, deploying loosely coordinated affinity groups to disrupt the targeted event. At the same time the success of the WTO protests also led police to re-examine their approach to policing protests. The negotiated management strategies that police relied on to control protesters were rooted in penal modernism, the dominant police philosophy of post-World War II America. But the influence of penal modernism on the criminal justice system had faded in recent years and a new policing philosophy, referred to in the sociological literature simply as the 'new penology', emerged to take its place as the paradigmatic philosophy of social control.

Faced with a crisis in policing protests following Seattle, police had to devise new strategies for controlling political demonstrations. The tactics they developed are deeply rooted in the new penology. As a result, the policing of protests in the US now has a dual quality. To the extent that protesters are willing to negotiate the scale and scope of their demonstrations with police, and demonstrations are contained, police continue to adopt a *Burgerpolizei* approach, operating primarily as promoters of the political rights of citizens, facilitating the right to protest and protecting First Amendment rights. But the presence of uncooperative protesters or acts of transgressive contention leads police to adopt a *Staatspolizei* strategy of control in an effort to reduce uncertainty and maintain order. Transgressive protesters, for example, are more likely to be arrested in an effort by police to incapacitate them for as long as possible. That arrested protesters on our three cases were rarely prosecuted, and when prosecuted rarely faced a concerted effort by police to convict them, suggests that the primary purpose of the arrests was to rearrange or incapacitate transgressive protesters, not to punish them. In addition, transgressive protesters found their access to public space constricted, their preparations for demonstrations disrupted by overzealous and targeted enforcement of laws and regulations, their leaders targeted for their pre-emptive detention, and their demonstrations subject to less-lethal weapons fire. These new police tactics, developed to control transgressive protesters, are consistent with neither the escalated force nor the negotiated management approach to policing protests. Instead, they form the basis of a third approach, which focuses on the strategic incapacitation of protesters.

Chapter 6

Negotiating Political Protest in Gothenburg and Copenhagen[1]

Mattias Wahlström and Mikael Oskarsson[2]

Introduction

The police strategy of trying to negotiate with protesters before political protests, and to maintain continuous communication with them during these manifestations, is today widely used in many Western countries. However, with a few exceptions, such as P.A.J. Waddington's *Liberty and Order* (1994) and McPhail, Schweingruber and McCarthy (1998), among others, this specific aspect of protest policing has remained relatively under-studied. This chapter will explore the practices of negotiation that occurred between police and protesters in connection with two EU summits in Scandinavia – in Gothenburg in June 2001 and in Copenhagen in December 2002. Our aim is to improve understanding of the role of negotiations in relation to these kinds of large protest events, and to provide some tools for analysing some of the problems that are likely to emerge.

While this chapter contains comparative elements, it primarily uses the two case studies to complement each other with different aspects of negotiation. Our description of these aspects is structured along three general stages of negotiation between police and protesters: *entering communication*, *reaching agreements*, and the *practical outcome and subsequent evaluation* of the negotiation by the parties. In practice, there is certainly an overlap among these stages – the choice to re-enter communication with the police can always be reassessed, and attempts to reach new agreements will often persist during a protest event, after practical outcomes of earlier negotiations. Therefore, while we have tried to structure the major part of our analysis along these lines, we will still have to go back and forth between the stages in order to make certain processes intelligible.

To create a rough model of the workings of negotiations, we will use as a starting point Elinor Ostrom's (1990) analysis of criteria that must be met to create

1   This chapter is based on two separate studies, some results of which are also published in Oskarsson (2002) and Wahlström (2003a, 2004).

2   We would like to thank Abby Peterson, Donatella della Porta, Herbert Reiter and the other participants in the protest-policing workshop in Fiskebäckskil, Sweden, 2004, for their generous and very valuable comments on earlier versions of this text.

an enduring solution to 'social dilemmas'. According to Ostrom, when there is a conflict concerning the use of finite collective goods, a sustainable resolution has three prerequisites: (1) one must be able to supply new institutions, or *sets of rules*, that all the involved parties can accept; (2) the commitment of each party has to be *credible* (when accepting the rules, one must have reason to believe that the others do not simply break the rules when it suits them); and (3) the actions of the parties relating to the agreement must be *monitored* (1990, 42–5). The dilemma faced by the parties in Gothenburg and Copenhagen related to how they could work together to find an acceptable solution to the conflict of values that emerged between the demand for public order, on the one hand, and the constitutional rights to free speech and to demonstrations of political protest in preparation for the EU Summit on the other. Appropriate levels of both public order and civil rights may be regarded as two forms of collective goods, although they possess certain properties that distinguish them from the collective goods that Ostrom has in mind.

A collective good has the property of being accessible to all, once it has been produced. The good may, in other words, be consumed by all and on equal terms in time and space (Olson 1965). To begin with, the demand for public order is a collective good that is not exploitable in the same manner as fish in a pond: it can, in principle, be enjoyed by an unlimited amount of people without becoming exhausted, as long as everybody agrees to the meaning of 'public order' and to who are its legitimate defenders. Of course, these questions are subject to serious symbolic conflicts that tend to become manifest in the context of certain political protests. And it will not help for some groups to agree to the terms of the maintenance of public order if another group has a strong intention of challenging these terms.

In similar fashion, and unlike other social dilemmas, the right to demonstrate means that one cannot impose limitations on who may appropriate these goods. The right to demonstrate is a 'collective good' that is protected by the Swedish and Danish constitutions (although more weakly in Denmark; cf. Björk 2004) and thereby lacks 'clearly defined limits' of access, which are required in order to achieve a lasting institutional solution to the value conflict between public order and civil liberties (Ostrom 1990, 90–92). It should also be noted that these values are not always to be seen as standing in opposition to one another. The right to demonstrate and the freedom of political opinion require a situation where public order can be maintained in order to minimize the effects of encroachments and provocations by others, including those to which the police themselves contribute. The police easily find themselves trying to accomplish a slightly schizophrenic task – to protect the state and the constitution while at the same time protecting those challenging the state and certain other actors' constitutional rights (such as the EU delegates' right of assembly). Thus, agreements on universal rights such as the right to demonstrate mean that even arrangements that fulfil Ostrom's three conditions run the risk of breaking down, to the detriment of those who intended to consume the collective goods in question.

If we examine more closely Ostrom's three conditions for resolving a social dilemma, we furthermore discover an important obstacle to realizing the third condition, that of *monitoring,* in relation to political demonstrations. The possibility of police and citizens sharing responsibility for the supervision of an agreement essentially boils down to a practical question of how far the police are willing to go in a specific instance, as regards the acceptable level of public (dis)order. Any agreement is at constant risk of being jeopardized as soon as the police feel forced to invoke their legally specified preferential right of *on the spot* interpreting and *defining* the extent to which an activity is a breach of agreement or a threat to public order. The significance of this fundamental limitation is that the problems are interrelated, and hence neither of the other two conditions may be realized either: '[w]ithout monitoring, there can be no credible commitment; without credible commitment, there is no reason to propose new rules' (Ostrom 1990, 45).

The notion of 'credible commitment' of the negotiating parties can be interpreted as the level of *trust* they have for each other in this situation. Trust, or in this case perhaps more often *lack of trust*, based on experiences from past interactions, will strongly influence all stages of negotiation, but especially the parties' willingness to enter negotiations. The evaluation of the outcome also affects parties' future trust for each other. In this chapter, we will use Piotr Sztompka's (1999) analysis of trust (elaborated below) to interpret how crucial parts of each party's knowledge of the other are constructed.

Finally, at least in this kind of social dilemma, the *political performances* that protesters wish to stage play a crucial role in the negotiations and in the improvisatory drama performed for the wider polity. This knowledge can be expressed in Goffman's (1974) terms by the *frameworks* that both the police and the activists rely on to order their experiences and expectations of each other. These frameworks are shaped by their past experiences and are built upon the accumulated knowledge of each other in ongoing *learning processes*. Each party's 'knowledge' (cf. Berger and Luckman 1967) of itself and 'the Other' will be analysed as *police knowledge* (della Porta and Reiter 1998b) and *activist knowledge*, respectively.

This framing of the actions of the opposite party and of the self will not be regarded as an entirely passive process. First, the correct interpretations of others' actions are likely to be discussed within the groups. Second, through their political *performances*, both police and activists are also actively trying to shape the framings of themselves and their actions. These framings will often be contested for political reasons (cf. Benford and Snow 2000). When, for instance, a conflict between the police and protesters arises, it is very important for each party to appear morally superior to its antagonists (cf. P.A.J. Waddington 1998, 129). The political performances of protesters highlights the fact that both groups enter communication despite a lack of trust, as well as explaining why particular groups abstain from negotiations regardless of their actual trust that the police will keep their part of agreements.

There are, of course, no value-neutral criteria for determining whether or not a specific negotiation has been successful. One party may be quite satisfied, while the other afterwards feels that it has been cheated. A completely successful negotiation would, in our opinion, ideally satisfy all involved parties, and generally involve a minimum of violence in connection with the demonstration.

The empirical material for this study consists of participant observations of protests in Gothenburg and Copenhagen during the EU summits, and of meetings within the police and activist networks. We have also used text sources, such as reports from meetings and material from the Internet, and interviewed 20 people altogether. Among these were police from Gothenburg as well as activists from Gothenburg and Copenhagen, some of whom had been to meetings with police, while others belonged to organizations critical of any such contacts. Interviews and participant observations were carried out both before and after the EU summits in question. Several respondents have wished not to remain anonymous but, for the sake of simplicity, only their first names are presented in the text. Occasionally, we have chosen only to present the group affiliation of the cited individual; in most cases this is due to the sensitive nature of the information. Any reader curious for additional facts on events during the protests we describe will find more details in Abby Peterson's chapter in this volume.

Entering communication

To understand the conditions under which the different parties in Gothenburg and Copenhagen, respectively, entered (or did not enter) negotiations, we need to look at prior experiences that are likely to have shaped their understanding of their current situation. In the literature on protest policing, the notion of *police knowledge* has been raised (della Porta 1998; P.A.J. Waddington 1998). The knowledge accumulated by the police is a vital factor in relation to their capacity to carry out their work in a way that generates public confidence. Police knowledge may be understood as an institutional 'filter' that comprises both the police's perceptions of their own mandate and their understanding of the society around them. In connection with political demonstrations, police conceptions of the characteristics of 'ordinary/good demonstrators' and 'professional/bad demonstrators', respectively, are a key factor in relation to how they will interpret events and act in different situations (P.A.J. Waddington 1999b, 1998, 1994; della Porta 1998; della Porta and Reiter 1998b). In a complementary manner we apply the notion of *activist knowledge* to denote the corresponding views of the activists, that is, their views of themselves and, more specifically, of their relationship to the police.

It is essential to keep in mind that this 'knowledge' is not static, but subject to the *learning processes* of each group; it is shaped by the experiences of police and activists alike, at the same time as the experiences to some extent are shaped by existing knowledge. If there is to be any point in developing the use of dialogue and negotiation, it is vital that the police realize that through their own actions they may both calm tensions and provoke (even peaceful) demonstrators. Breaking down the mutual distrust and moving beyond earlier, negative experiences of the actions of one's antagonists requires a well-developed capacity for communication and an ability to adapt to the demands of a given situation.

In order to understand this process, we need to develop our notion of *trust*.[3] Piotr Sztompka (1999) describes trust as a *bet*, which makes it more than just a belief in the reliability of others, but also a willingness to act 'as if' one could actually be completely sure of others' future actions, even if one cannot. To *trust* someone generally implies, furthermore, that the actions of this person will somehow be beneficial to us, directly or indirectly. Conversely, when we believe that others' actions will do us harm, we talk rather of *distrust*. In this article, the word *mistrust* will be used to indicate the state of uncertainty in the actions of others, and hence the unwillingness to make any bets (cf. Sztompka 1999, 26–7). In the analysis we will focus on the dimension of trust that Sztompka (1999) describes as a *relationship* between actors, as opposed to the *psychological* disposition to feel trust in others in general, or the rules and practices in a *culture* regarding trust. In the discussion of relational trust between actors, Sztompka's three primary reasons for trust will be taken into consideration: (1) *reputation* – what is known of an actor's past actions; (2) *performance* – the present actions and results of the actor; and (3) *appearance* – the actor's presentation of her own trustworthiness. If we follow Sztompka's line of thought, activists' knowledge of the police has to be considered an important factor for their framing of police behaviour, especially with respect to the trustworthiness of the police's actions.

In Gothenburg, the police authority initiated the formation of a Contact Group relatively late – less than three months prior to the EU Summit meeting in June 2001 – and the group started working only about six weeks before the meeting. This so-called 'psycho-tactical unit' consisted of six persons, men and women in equal proportions. The group established contact with two large protest coalitions: Gothenburg Action and Network 2001. The Contact Group's objective was 'to have constant and immediate contact with those stewarding demonstrations both prior to and during the demonstrations in order to be able to prevent deviations from the demonstration permits applied for and/or to intervene in the case of criminal activity' (Operational Order 27a, Västra Götaland's Police Authority). The Swedish police's plan to initiate a dialogue with demonstrators prior to the EU Summit in Gothenburg, and to conduct negotiations with them during the course of that summit, was based on a traditional view of 'law and order' issues; this is partly revealed by the police's official designation of the Contact Group as a 'psycho-tactical unit', underlining their ambiguous mandate. As late as March 2001, the idea of using dialogue and

---

3   The use of the notion of trust in this context has been criticized on the grounds that it is actually not important for the choices of activists in relation to the police, since there is never any trust in this relationship anyway. This criticism is justified in the sense that activists *may* enter negotiations for tactical reasons without a huge amount of trust, as we too will argue below. However, in another sense the criticism misses the point since (1) some organizations actually *do* have a significant amount of trust in the police, even if they may reassess it later; and (2) in demonstrating at all, most people show in practice a 'tacit trust' that they at least will not be shot dead in the street by machine guns (which, as we know, has happened).

negotiation remained a non-question for those in charge of the police operation. Thus the idea came to the fore at a late stage of the police's preparatory work, and the way it was put into practice gives the impression that the use of this approach was more a question of 'necessity' than of any genuine conviction as to its merits. It would have been relatively easy for the leadership of the police operation to inform themselves at an early stage about the methods and techniques of negotiation developed by other European police forces for use in the context of particularly high-risk protest actions.

One task of the Contact Group in Gothenburg, which lay outside the operational order presented above, involved providing information to the personnel who would be drafted into the police operation. These informational meetings were intensive and important, both as a means of presenting the objectives of the Contact Group, and to provide general information on the various organizations and groups that intended to go to Gothenburg in order to participate in demonstrations. At one of these informational meetings the leader of the Contact Group, superintendent Göran Nordenstam, emphasized amongst other things the need to maintain a nuanced image of the demonstrators and avoid contributing to 'triggering' incidents of various kinds. The image he presented of the demonstrators was that the overwhelming majority ('95 per cent') had absolutely no intention of causing problems for the police, whilst the remainder did constitute a problem to varying degrees (field notes, 2001/05-23; see also Contact Group report (Kontaktgruppens erfarenhetsberättelse)). Police knowledge can be used to break down stereotypes or at least nuance the perceptions of protesters, not only among staff officers but, perhaps most important, among the rank and file.

Prior to the summit in Gothenburg, while there was a belief among many activists in the value of dialogue with the police, some groups expressed serious doubts, primarily based on the heavily criticized hard-line policing in connection with a protest in April the same year in Malmö, also connected with the Swedish presidency of the EU. The leadership of the Malmö demonstration, which had had some practical communication with the police prior to the event, afterwards expressed serious doubts about participating in further talks with the police: 'Of what value is a smiling chief of police, when at the same time we should count on his planning to batter protesters to pieces with batons?' (Evaluation cited in *Betänkande av Göteborgskommittén* 2002, 249). In other words, while the Swedish police seemed to have had a reasonably good *reputation*, at least within some activist groups, their *performance* in Malmö at the EU finance ministers' meeting just a few months before radically diminished reasons for trust, which was somewhat compensated by their reasonably favourable *appearance* during the brief negotiations.

In contrast to Gothenburg, the Danish protest groups and networks had direct contact with senior police officers in charge of the operation, including chief constable Kai Vittrup (head of the uniformed police in greater Copenhagen). Additionally, regular meetings between police and protesters began earlier in Denmark; NGO Forum Stop the Violence had their first meeting with the police as early as February 2002 (http://www.ms.dk/ngoforum2002/stopvold/politidialog01.htm, 26 May 2003), almost a year prior to the event, compared to the approximately six weeks that lay between the creation of the Contact Group and the EU Summit in Gothenburg. Both the Danish police and most protest groups had comparatively strong beliefs in the value of dialogue from the start.

The non-hierarchical character of the campaign coalitions, as well as the organizations and activist networks included in them, was a complicating factor (just as in Gothenburg – see the following section). Even though the autonomous group Global Roots was a member of both the Initiative for Another Europe and the NGO Forum Stop the Violence, it had not taken part in any of the coalitions' meetings with the police. In order to achieve a separate meeting with Global Roots, the police contacted one of its members. Global Roots' reply to the police was also sent to the press. It stated that they would not agree to a private meeting with the police; however, a public dialogue through the newspapers was suggested. According to Global Roots, the police did not show any interest in such a dialogue. The main reasons expressed by Global Roots for carrying out a public dialogue were that there would not be a 'picture of unanimity and fraternization where this is not the case' (email from Global Roots to the Copenhagen police on 8 August 2002), and so that their members could follow the entire discussion and approve of all of the organization's statements.

The Danish case can be used to explore further the mechanisms of trust in connection with negotiations. Our exploration starts with an assessment of the history of contacts between the police and factions within the protest culture in Copenhagen. Mikkelsen (2002) and Karpantschof and Mikkelsen (2002) maintain that the style of protest policing has become generally less 'tough' during the last decades, while at the same time a relatively hard line has been taken towards certain groups and protest forms. This comparative toughness appears to a large extent to have been directed towards groups that occupied land and abandoned houses in Copenhagen from the late 1960s until the 1980s. The occupations resulted in no small number of violent confrontations (Mikkelsen 2002, 71–5), although one should keep in mind that political violence in Denmark has still not been very extensive from a European perspective (cf. della Porta 1996). Experiences from the conflicts of the last decades between police and protesters seem to some extent, according to the interviews, to continue to pervade, for instance among members of Global Roots and the Anarchist Federation, especially in the form of *tactical* knowledge (Johannes, Global Roots). It is difficult to assess how much influence these experiences have on the current views of the protesters, but it does not seem farfetched to assume that the police will have to accept that they cannot easily rid themselves of the burden of historical experiences of coercive force in their attempts to approach these groups: 'We don't prefer a dialogue with the police, because the experiences we have of the police are enormously bad. There are many people that have had bad experiences of the police that reach many years back in time' (Jacob, the Anarchist Federation).

Incidents from the last decade's conflicts are, however, probably the heaviest burden for the police. Relations between police and protesters in Denmark suffered a serious, and still unhealed, wound on 18 May 1993. The police fired into a group of 200 people involved in a violent protest against the Maastricht Treaty, and are said to have wounded at least 11 people (see, for instance, http://www.amnesty.org/ailib/aipub/1994/EUR/180294.EUR.txt, 25 February 2003). According to all sources connected with protesters that have been found in the research for this chapter, the plainclothes riot squad – the 'riot patrol' – played a decisive role in escalating the situation. While several activists made a clear distinction between the character of the police chief constable at the time and the current chief constable, many were still extremely suspicious of the plainclothes police.

It is important to keep in mind that protesters' views of the police in their home country are also affected by impressions from protests during earlier transnational events abroad, obviously policed by foreign police forces. In addition, transnational events are visited by large groups of activists of different nationalities, who to some extent will project their domestic relations with the police onto the police force in charge. The EU Summit in Gothenburg and the G8 Meeting in Genoa are two events that appear to have been important reference points for the protesters as to how the police could be expected to behave in Copenhagen in December 2002. Both events resulted in highly negative narratives, again largely due to the police's use of firearms against demonstrators. What also seemed important for many protesters in relation to a dialogue with the police was the raid that was carried out by the police in Gothenburg at Hvitfeldtska School (see below and in Peterson's chapter). This clearly made a poor impression on many activists in Copenhagen:

> Our experience is [...] that the Swedish police didn't wish to have a real dialogue, but that the purpose of the 'dialogue' was only to present the police as generous and accommodating, while they in reality planned and carried out violent encroachments on the political rights of the activists. (email from Global Roots to the Copenhagen Police, 8 August 2002)

Before the EU Summit in Copenhagen, opinions of respondents in this study varied somewhat regarding the expected relationship between the actions of the police at the imminent meeting and those during the meetings just mentioned. Some stressed how the Danish police commanders differed from their Swedish colleagues, in that the latter did not have 'the same reasonable, pragmatic approach that Kai Vittrup has had' (Lars, Attac). Others, for instance members from Global Roots, could see no reason why the Danish police would act differently from the police forces in neighbouring countries.

Regarding the police's current *performance* (cf. Sztompka 1999), there was activist knowledge of more recent episodes that, for some, were promising. At smaller demonstrations during the year, the police seem to have 'performed' generally well, from the perspective of the protesters, and the communication in the field between police and protesters seems to have gone more or less smoothly.

But then again, among the more recent experiences there were also those that might have exacerbated some groups' distrust of the police. In the fall of 2002, police were criticized for excessive violence and failing to show a search warrant during raids at two premises connected with the radical activist environment (http://

www.ulydighed.dk/dk/prb%F8rnehus.htm, 26 February 2003). People also felt criminalized by police accusations of having found materials for making bombs on one of these occasions (http://www.ulydighed.dk/dk/prballegade.htm, 26 February 2003). These incidents play an important part in the contact between activists and the police. Members of Global Roots contrast this behaviour with the police's statements about the desire for a dialogue and protecting the right to demonstrate. 'One hand dishes up coffee and lemon biscuits, while the other strikes the battle drums' (email from Global Roots to the Copenhagen Police, 8 August 2002). In light of the raids, the benevolent attitude of the police might look like a facade, behind which repressive intentions lurk. As regards the *appearance* of the police – Sztompka's (1999) third precondition for relational trust – we could, for instance, see how the attempts of the police to present a friendly attitude do not seem to have alleviated the distrust of the protesters to any significant extent.[4]

The experiences described above can be said to be a part of the total 'activist knowledge' that contributes to the frameworks protesters use to interpret police behaviour and predict their future actions. Whether an invitation to a dialogue is regarded as an attempt to manipulate or as a genuine effort to create understanding is likely to have strong influence on the response to said invitation. The decisions that the different activist organizations and networks have taken on this issue can be understood in large part from this point of view. The corresponding *distrust* that the police may have had towards particular activist groups appears to have less influence over their choice to *enter* communications with the activists; the information-gathering function of dialogue and improved chances of making activists stick to their demonstration permits remain, despite their underlying distrust.

However, the level of trust and intentions of information gathering are not the only explanations for *if, when* and *how* parties enter negotiations. For instance, an unofficial motive for Global Roots' strategy of trying to initiate a public debate was, perhaps surprisingly, that the group *expected* the police to break their promises and assurances:

> We *knew* they were going to break the agreements. That was why we wanted to have the discussion in the press. Make the police write: 'We will be non-visible.' They didn't want to write that anywhere, did they. […] It was a precondition for our media strategy that they would [break their agreements]. If we thought the police would be so sound, as they said they would be, then we would make a laughing stock of ourselves. (Claus, Global Roots)

This brings us to the analytical focus of the next section: the *performances* that the parties wish to stage in connection with negotiations.

---

4   Even though it would be wrong to underestimate the effect of the *appearance* of the police on protesters' distrust or mistrust, it is worth noting the distrust with which most interviewees looked upon the attempts of the police to be accommodating.

Reaching agreements

It is not just the parties' level of trust and their ability to deal with Ostrom's dilemma that affect negotiation. An analysis of the material of this study suggests that the *performances* (Goffman 1959) that the protesters wish to stage are equally important in this context. The nature of these performances may differ between different activist organizations and networks, and they have crucial implications for both in-group coherence and out-group political influence. They will therefore greatly affect the way in which the group approaches police contacts and deals with negotiations. We can here distinguish between highly *institutionalized* groups (Meyer and Tarrow 1998), whose standard mode of protest today is normalized and relatively uncontroversial, and less institutionalized groups that challenge the norms of the political system, not just in terms of content but also through the *form* of their protests. The latter type of groups and networks should be regarded not simply as a threat to the democratic process, but rather as an element that vitalizes the protest climate and makes protests more inspiring and less routine. From this aspect, the 'negotiated management style' of protest policing (McPhail, Schweingruber and McCarthy 1998) need not be entirely beneficial to the protesters: 'It is in reducing costs for protestors that the police most effectively exercise power; for they subtly invite demonstrators to emasculate the force of their protest' (P.A.J. Waddington 1994, 199).

Among the more institutionalized groups involved in the protests, one can notice an interest in reducing the anxiety of members who risked being intimidated by threats of violence during the EU summits. A working and trusting dialogue with the police, as well as within the coalition, can be viewed as a performance that gives the members a sense of safety when they go out demonstrating.

Many of the participants (probably the majority) in NGO Forum Stop the Violence and its Swedish equivalents appear, furthermore, to regard violence as something that must be avoided in connection with demonstrations. Aside from being considered bad in itself, violence is viewed as a crucial obstacle to expressing one's political message: 'Naturally, the experience is that in the end all kinds of violent behaviour harm the police. [...] But it damages all kinds of positive political messages even more' (Mads, the Danish Red–Green Alliance). Since a working preparatory dialogue was assumed to increase the chances of a nonviolent summit, there were obvious reasons for seeing it through.

The acceptance of a dialogue was furthermore a performance that conveyed a picture of the participating organizations as legitimate democratic actors. Conversely, a refusal to take part in a dialogue would have implied a performance that showed the organizations in a bad light: 'If we had rejected any dialogue with the police, we would [...] look like someone who had something to hide, who had a hidden agenda' (Kenneth, the Danish Red–Green Alliance/Attac). Additionally, in cases of the police breaking the agreements reached during preparatory negotiations, these could be used as a starting point for a performance that disrupted the police's framing of their actions as democratic and legitimate (cf. P.A.J. Waddington 1998, 129). The latter strategy is particularly consistent with the interests of many non-institutionalized groups.

During the meetings between the police and NGO Forum Stop the Violence, perhaps the most important question for the protesters concerned police visibility during demonstrations. Both parties seem to have agreed throughout the meetings that the avoidance of 'massive visibility' would considerably decrease the risk of violence breaking out (NGO Forum Stop the Violence's notes from a meeting with police, 29 August 2002). Furthermore, NGO Forum Stop the Violence put forward a demand that the police wear numbered helmets, something the police opposed, with reference to demands from their workers' union. Criticism was also levelled at the border controls that the police planned to set up to prevent potentially violent protesters from entering the country.

While preparing their own activities, other groups and networks like Stop the Union, the Initiative for Another Europe and Attac had their own meetings with the police. As Stop the Union had held its protests earlier in the year, the results of certain discussions with the police could be passed on to later meetings with NGO Forum Stop the Violence.

The press did function as a channel for further communication between police and protesters; for example, protesters seem to have been quick to respond through press releases to a couple of public announcements made by the police. Even apparently appreciative statements about protesters in the press could provoke reactions. In the media, prior to the summit, Kai Vittrup commended Global Roots' nonviolent protests and expressed the hope that their attendance would be high. To this, the latter replied angrily: 'We wish to be spared from those kinds of comments; we don't think it is the task of the police to characterize political organizations at all' (http://www.ulydighed.dk/index.html, 24 November 2002). A reason for this reaction, as suggested by the quotation itself, is their unwillingness to participate in the distinction between 'good' and 'bad' protesters (cf. della Porta 1998, 241–5).

In an open letter of 8 August 2002, Global Roots put a couple of questions to the police concerning issues that it wanted to clarify. To make more explicit its own intentions when invited to further 'open' negotiations, the group presented a set of 'rules' to which it intended to adhere during its proposed civil disobedience actions. No violence, in the sense of 'physical harm', would be used – not even in defence. There would be no destruction of property and, if the action disrupted traffic, ambulances and fire engines would be allowed to pass (email from Global Roots to the Copenhagen Police, 8 August 2002). The open letter to the police presented Global Roots in a favourable light, while possible replies from the police would have given them the means for effectively criticizing the legitimacy of the police.

Media attention was subsequently used by members of Global Roots to try to make known how badly they felt they were treated by the police. By the first day of the Copenhagen protests, the group had already planned an official complaint and perhaps a lawsuit against the police (Claus, Global Roots). Such criticism can be seen as a part of Global Roots' general strategy of trying to represent conflicts in society through their protests, which has also been decisive for their attitude regarding closer contact with the police. Too intimate a relationship between the police and the group could damage the performance they are trying to stage in their confrontational protests:

> We have an idea of wanting to show the conflict, and as it is the police that represent those that we are in conflict with – all the 'evil ones' – it is them that we want to get at. And *that* is really hard, if we sit down drinking coffee with them and so on. (Johannes, Global Roots)

It is important to remember that the performance has two different goals. First, members wish to act out the conflict between those with power and those without. Secondly, distancing themselves from the 'Other(s)' – in this case the police – is of vital importance for the construction of their collective identity (cf. Peterson 2001, 55–6). A clear-cut conflict with authorities contributes to the experience of a 'we', and consequently the coherence of the group would be risked by too close a relationship with the police. As the specific attitude towards the police seems to vary among individual members of Global Roots, closer contact between the police and a less scrupulous faction of the group could furthermore lead to serious internal conflicts. In regard to the hypothetical question of what would happen if it were discovered a that faction had 'directed' a civil disobedience action together with the police, Claus in Global Roots answers:

> It would be devastating. [...] Because it would cause great internal problems in the environment. And it would probably also create divisions. That is, if an individual became known as someone that enters into agreements with the police, people wouldn't cooperate with that person again. It would give rise to problems, that's for sure.

According to the views presented here, a confrontation between a civil disobedience group and the police requires, like ordinary plays in Goffman's (1974, 123–55) analytical framework, that the parts in the play have *information states* that do not coincide. If the characters in a play share information states, any plot is made impossible; one knows that the actors know exactly what is happening and is going to happen. Political drama differs in that each actor is assumed to be at least partially ignorant of the other's plans and actions. Communication that removes the element of surprise from the police blunts the edge of the political performance, at least if it becomes known. If the police lack information and lose control, this can, according to some, be clearly advantageous: 'One way or another, it wouldn't have hurt if the police had lost some of their control, and a situation occurred that they couldn't control. [...] It's when they lose the overall picture and control, that there is a hotbed for funny things to happen' (Johannes, Global Roots). This highlights the importance of control over situations (see Peterson 2003b), rather than giving priority to control over territories.

However, herein lies a potential conflict. At the same time, Global Roots has a principle that implies the need to be as open and attentive as possible with respect to their activities, in order to prevent a rift between themselves and the public (http://

www.ulydighed.dk/dk/herfra_min_faerden.html, 26 April 2003). This attitude has obviously been an important reason for their decision to write open letters, as well as for the openly declared intentions therein – presented to generate public sympathy for their actions. However, as discussed above, the group must balance its actions so as not to appear to have a close relationship with the police. Presenting intentions is in line with the principle of openness; but the appearance of having entered into agreements with the police is bad for credibility, at least internally and within the radical environment from which they recruit.

Accordingly, the fierce way in which Global Roots reacted in relation to the sometimes accommodating attitude of the police does not give the impression of being simply a response to the categorizing of 'good' and 'bad' protesters; it also appears to be an attempt to establish a *team performance* (Goffman 1959) wherein the police are expected to play the part of an adversary. If the police as an institution have a positive attitude towards the group, or if it suddenly looks as though they have a relationship based on trust, they break with their role in the team performance, and the sought-after framing of their relationship 'collapses'.

Global Roots risked such a collapse during their action against the summit venue in Copenhagen. They chose not to assume a more confrontational attitude and gave the protest a peaceful ending, which meant taking the risk that the performance would be perceived as an expression of understanding between themselves and the police. Furthermore, an agreement was made with the police during the march that demonstrators would be allowed free passage to the nearest metro station at its conclusion. The police's choice to stand by their promise and open a passage to the station after the manifestation could also be viewed as a break with their possible part as the 'bad guys', irrespective of their actual reasons.

It should be noted that Global Roots' view differs from that of the 'Non-violence Network' in Gothenburg during the EU summit in 2001. The latter made extensive agreements with the police, at least in connection with one of their actions (Oskarsson 2002, 94–5). Together with the observations of P.A.J. Waddington (1994), this shows that the analysis of how this kind of civil disobedience ought to be carried out is not uncontroversial.

The Anarchist Federation in Denmark shares some of the content of its protest performances with Global Roots, namely the wish to reveal to the public the illegitimacy of the police. Like Global Roots, it also appears to have a need to reassure itself of its distance from the police, as the police play an important part in the anarchists' political struggle: 'It is they [the police] that represent the power structures we demonstrate against' (Jacob, the Anarchist Federation). This distancing also creates a kind of Catch-22 situation concerning the relationship between trust and the willingness to communicate: 'If it were the case that one could have a demonstration that the police didn't break into, there would be no reason to talk to them, would there?' (Jacob, the Anarchist Federation).

Regarding the shape of its performances, the Anarchist Federation subscribes to a plurality of methods; but one can notice a difference compared to Global Roots, in that the anarchists' performances are not so obviously built upon active conflict with the constabulary. To the question of whether it is preferable that the police do not act forcefully towards their demonstrations, Janne from the Anarchist Federation answers:

> I don't know how much media attention we would get, and I don't feel that is unimportant, but it doesn't matter as much to me as to be able to come out with one's point of view, and to be able to attend to that instead of all the time focusing on the police attacking anytime.

From the Gothenburg case, we learn that *trust* has an impact not only on the choice of entering negotiations, but also on the process of reaching agreements. We will also show that *access to information* is an important factor for successful negotiations. One chief goal, common to both the Gothenburg Contact Group and the demonstrators' networks, was the agreement that the networks' own stewards should be responsible for maintaining order during the demonstrations. According to the coalition Gothenburg Action, the more inclusive of the two primary coalitional networks, its own principal concerns related to disorderly elements among its own demonstrators: neo-Nazis who were expected to disrupt the demonstrations in various ways and, as events surrounding the EU Finance Ministers' Meeting in the Swedish city of Malmö earlier the same year had shown, provocative and heavy-handed action on the part of the police (interview, Gothenburg Action). The police promised not to make the same mistakes that had characterized the Malmö Summit. The Contact Group would be the only body of police present in direct connection with the demonstrations and had promised the representatives of the demonstrators' networks that any other police would be kept at a safe distance from the marchers' routes through the centre of Gothenburg.

The actions of the Swedish Communist Party (KPML(r)) during the EU Summit exemplify how a relationship of trust may be built that accommodates agreements in the negotiations. The Contact Group and the leadership of the police operation in Gothenburg had complete faith that the party's stewards, together with other groups of stewards within Network 2001, would maintain order in the ranks and keep their promise not to allow demonstrators to mask their faces, as well as not participating in any hazardous actions against objects whose security the police were keen to safeguard. The Communist Party, which on ideological grounds harbours few positive feelings toward either the bourgeois state or its 'apparatus of violence', nonetheless trusted the police to keep their word. This trust was probably based on the reputation and performance of the Swedish police as being restrained in relation to orderly demonstrations. Both parties, including the whole of Network 2001, have since stated that their agreement remained intact throughout the EU Summit (interview, Network 2001; evaluation, Network 2001; evaluation, Västra Götaland Police Authority).

How, then, did Network 2001 and the police come to a consensus regarding the conditions necessary to sustain such collective goods as public order and the right to demonstrate? The fundamental attitude of the network was of central importance, but this was also true of the police's faith in the commitments made by the network.

This faith was made possible in part by the fact that some of the network's leaders had local roots and had previously maintained direct contacts with the police in connection with earlier political demonstrations – and in part by the fact that the group of individuals mobilized by this network constituted a more traditional section of the activist population, including a large proportion of older members of political organizations. Both these factors served to create a substantial level of predictability in the actions of the network and contributed to a circulating flow of information between the Network's leadership, the police Contact Group and the leadership of the police operation. Police knowledge, as well as activist knowledge, of the *reputation* and *performance* of the other party led in this case to a relationship of trust.

The question is whether the work of the Contact Group and the broad mobilization of Gothenburg Action served to increase, or to reduce, the levels of insecurity with which the two parties had to contend while the dialogue continued. As long as the dialogue was focused on the maintenance of order in connection with the demonstrations, both Network 2001 (the other major coalition) and Gothenburg Action made it clear that, until and unless they sought assistance from the police, they themselves would handle order among their ranks. Against the backdrop of what had for several months been regarded as public knowledge, the Contact Group had good reason to question the leadership of Gothenburg Action about activities that were planned to take place outside the sanctioned demonstrations.

Here the police's need for information and Gothenburg Action's non-hierarchical structure stood in direct conflict with one another. The Contact Group felt that the leadership of Gothenburg Action was not putting all its cards on the table. In interviews with the Contact Group and the leadership of Gothenburg Action, a picture emerged indicating that the latter was not prepared to accept responsibility for anything that happened either prior to or after the demonstrations for which permits had been issued. In light of the groups that had joined the Gothenburg Action coalition, it was not particularly surprising that the leadership was reluctant to collaborate in providing the police with an 'intelligence advantage'. Just as the Contact Group had no decisive influence over the operational activities of those in charge of the police operation or of individual police officers, Gothenburg Action could not control events outside the organized marches. Nor could the Contact Group provide Gothenburg Action with information on the intelligence that *inter alia* was serving as the basis for the police leadership's perceptions of the threats that existed.

From the point of view of control, the perseverance shown by the Contact Group was rather pointless, since certain of the groups associated with the coalition were explicitly autonomous – that is, they were independent and planned their actions to take place outside the sanctioned demonstrations. Stated bluntly, the leadership of Gothenburg Action had no mandate to conduct discussions or to come to an 'agreement' with the police, either in relation to actions aimed at gaining illicit entry into the summit venue, or regarding any other types of action at locations where EU politicians would be present. In the course of the interviews, the leaders of Gothenburg Action described having known more than they had told the police; in addition, they reported that they had never regarded revealing details of planned political actions to the police as an option. 'We didn't want the police to exploit the information' was the underlying motive for not informing the police about the 'Reclaim the Streets' party on the night of 15 June, for example (interview, Gothenburg Action).

Gothenburg Action had adopted a platform of nonviolence, but the substance of this stance was limited, since the group was not particularly interested in any discussion with the Contact Group on actions that took place outside the demonstrations. It was here that the risk of direct confrontation was imminent. Gothenburg Action would not, or could not, accept any responsibility for exercising territorial control over autonomous groups; even if there had been a desire to do so, such an ambition would have been impossible to realize fully in the field.

To conclude the Swedish experiences of the negotiations, the principal problem affecting the relations between the Contact Group and Gothenburg Action was their unwillingness to share *vital* information:

> Negotiators who are not aware of what the other party would regard as an acceptable outcome cannot always be expected to come to and agree upon an efficient outcome if only a *minimum amount of time* and energy is to be devoted to the negotiation process. Each will devote time to misleading the other regarding their own preferences whilst at the same time attempting to work out what lies behind the other's misleading declarations of preference, and both will thereby be committed to a strategy that may involve setbacks in the form of missed chances to reach an acceptable agreement. (Miller 1996, 66, emphasis added)

The ambiguous mandate of the psycho-tactical group formed to negotiate with the protest networks in Gothenburg, which included the gathering of intelligence, clouded the working relationship that the group attempted to initiate and secure with protesters. In particular, a sense of trust was undermined by the group's intelligence-gathering function during their contacts. While the negotiating group operative in Copenhagen did not as clearly have this 'double function', even Danish activists were sensitive to this matter. The protesters complained of attempts by PET (the Danish security police) to contact members of Attac, the People's Movement against EU and Stop the Union at their home addresses. The aim of these visits was believed to be to gather information concerning potential threats from other organizations. In connection with this, NGO Forum emphasized that it had nothing to hide, and that all information of interest could be found on the organization's homepage.

Good information and communications are central requirements for the establishment of trust in interpersonal relations. Some are of the opinion that asymmetries in levels of access to information have a directly damaging impact on the effectiveness of negotiations. In order to achieve equilibrium, the parties attempt to induce their counterparts to give up information in various ways. If they are successful, conditions are created that are conducive to successful negotiations (Miller 1996, 65). From the police perspective, the flow of information constitutes the very 'life-blood' of the organization; police are generally unwilling, even among themselves, to share information (P.A.J. Waddington 1999b, 100). This general unwillingness to share information may be explained *inter alia* by the need for police personnel to maintain their autonomy in relation to their commanding officers within the organization (Lipsky 1980).

Intelligence work and obtaining information are fundamental to the existence of hierarchies, but at the same time constitute a crucial obstacle to the effective functioning of the hierarchy in question, that is, to its ability to reach settlements with parties both within and outside the organization itself (cf. Miller 1996, 175). By contrast with collaborations between equals, the informational imbalance is ultimately based on the asymmetrical power relations between state and citizen, and in this particular case between the police and demonstration organizers. Negotiations without sufficient information exchange run a serious risk of failure, since each party's desires depend to some extent on the other's.

In relation to the more traditional methods used in investigative and intelligence-gathering work, the more open activities of the Contact Group in Gothenburg may be regarded as means of information gathering with the potential to produce valuable resource savings. If this is combined with a general unwillingness to provide relevant information to one's counterpart in the negotiations (which may be regarded as something of a 'reflex' action on the part of the police), then it does not differ in any essential respect from approaches already found in the police's more traditional methodological arsenal. A genial tone of voice and 'ever so good' intentions on the part of the police will not be sufficient to alter this.

To sum up this part, the degree to which an agreement can be reached in negotiations between police and protesters, as well as the nature of this agreement, basically depends on the *performances* that each party wants to stage. A certain amount of *trust* is definitely beneficial, but since neither of the parties involved generally wishes to disclose sufficient *information*, any agreements will most likely be very limited and unstable. When the police are represented by a contact group instead of by the commander of the operation, and when activist groups are predominantly non-hierarchical, negotiations will suffer from unclear *representativity* and weak *responsibility* of the participants.

Practical outcome and evaluation

In regard to the Contact Group's role during the protest events in Gothenburg, the group suffered from its unclear mandate and role in the overall operative strategy of the Swedish police. It received the worst possible start in its negotiations with activists when the police cordoned off Hvitfeldska School (housing many visiting protesters during the EU summit) on the eve of the summit and President Bush's official visit. The group had not been informed as to this proactive move on the part of the police, intended to stop activist attempts to gain access to the summit area. Had the Contact Group been informed, it would have had time to activate the leadership of Gothenburg Action and also the local authority, which had been very obliging in making the schools available for the demonstrators' use.

Instead, the Contact Group, and particularly its leader, Göran Nordenstam, was drawn into the process with only a limited opportunity to affect developments. Rather than being given the chance to enter into discussions with the leadership of Gothenburg Action and others who might have been able to prevent events from taking a violent turn, the Contact Group had to face a barrage of accusations from the leaders of Gothenburg Action about the limited value of dialogue and the failure of police to communicate and honour their agreements. This was not a good beginning for the dialogue during the protests, which nonetheless proceeded once the chief of the police operation shifted his position on the use of the Contact Group following pressure from activist negotiators. Subsequently, the dialogue was again broken off by the police chief, and in the days that followed the Contact Group was used off and on. A general impression is that the Contact Group was used by the Swedish police commanders when it suited their pragmatic needs; when it did not, they bypassed it.

As is the case with so many aspects of the events during the EU Summit in Gothenburg, the way in which the negotiations at Hvitfeldtska have been described by the demonstrators' networks and the Contact Group respectively must be understood in the light of the parties' earlier collective experiences, their access to relevant information and their distinctive roles. The nature of the threats as perceived by the police, supplemented by 'fresh' intelligence relating to the nightly meetings held at Hvitfeldtska, inspired the police's concern (interview, Gothenburg Action). The police perceived a problem inside the school to which they judged that they had to react in the context of their ongoing assessment of the situation. But instead of turning to the only available resource that might have resolved the conflict or nuanced their assessment, the leadership of the police operation acted in accordance with an action-inspired logic that is well documented in the field of police research.[5] Despite being repeatedly ignored or bypassed, the activists' negotiators persisted in trying to maintain contact with the police, probably because there was nothing they could lose with this strategy (from the point of view of their specific interests – see the discussion about *performances* above).

Among the collection of conceptions, values and practices that make up police culture, an attitude of suspicion and the 'us and them' stereotype constitute distinctive characteristics (P.A.J. Waddington 1999b, 97–102). The Police Authority's evaluation of the EU Summit operation in Gothenburg provides us with a concrete example of the use of stereotypes. The evaluation concludes with a glossary of terms and abbreviations. Of particular interest here is how the Police Authority defines and employs the term 'activist' as 'a person who committed or made preparations to commit crimes between 11th and 16th June 2001 in Gothenburg'. Even if several unrelated criminals, like drunken drivers and wife-abusers, could be called 'activists' according to this definition, it would be passable if the evaluation had only employed this definition in a way that took account of the rulings made by prosecutors and the

---

5   For an introduction to the literature on the action-focus and a number of the other distinctive characteristics of the police culture, see Reiner 2000; P.A.J. Waddington 1999b.

courts. In the section on the events at Hvitfeldtska, however, the evaluation speaks of 'a hundred activists' (*EU 2001-kommenderingen* 2002, 79). The prosecution service has dismissed a great many of the cases relating to persons arrested in the school grounds. At the time of writing, only one person has been sentenced for a crime committed inside Hvitfeldtska School. In addition, it is worth noting that (at least in Sweden) the term in ordinary usage generally includes groups and individuals whose words and actions are expressive of a commitment to the fundamental principles of Swedish democracy.

It is quite natural to utilize stereotypes and simplifications as a means of making the complexities of the real world more readily comprehensible. The use of the term 'activist' in the above example, however, must be regarded as completely inappropriate. For one thing, it stigmatizes the thousands of peaceful demonstrators who regard themselves as 'activists'. Far more serious, however, is the fact that the Police Authority, in spite of judicial rulings, nonetheless persists in the context of an official document in contending that these 'activists' are to be regarded as criminals. To put it in rather cautious terms, the possibility of employing more developed forms of dialogue and negotiation in connection with political demonstrations will require a readiness on the part of the police to reflect on the stereotypes that contribute to their image of themselves as an organization and of the social reality that exists outside this organization.

However, given the conditions faced by the Contact Group and the demonstrators' networks, the dialogue between the two was relatively successful. The initial doubts harboured by representatives of the Contact Group turned quickly into a much more optimistic attitude and, over time, into an increasingly strong faith in the merits of dialogue. In spite of the limited time available, the Contact Group and Network 2001 succeeded in reaching an agreement that remained open and stable throughout the days of the summit. In this particular case, the joint experiences of earlier collaborations between the two parties were more important than the generally obstructive effects of the time pressures involved. When it came to the relationship between the Contact Group and the 'activists' in the leadership of Gothenburg Action, however, there existed a degree of suspicion beneath the surface that the two parties never managed to overcome. Following the cordoning off of Hvitfeldtska School, Gothenburg Action's trust in the police had sunk to near zero, although the dialogue with the Contact Group was maintained to the last. Despite the problematical relationship with Gothenburg Action, the Contact Group nonetheless came to the conclusion that the use of dialogue in relation to political demonstrations can make a difference by comparison with the more traditional methods otherwise employed by the Swedish police (interview, Contact Group).

In Copenhagen, the police had a generally reasonable approach towards the demonstrators – most unannounced demonstrations (for instance Global Roots' demonstration from Christiania to Enghave plads, 13 December) and changed routes (Global Roots' and the Anarchist Federation's to Vestre Fængsel, 14 December) appear to have been accepted. However, during some of the demonstrations the communication seems to have been less effective, particularly in relation to the anarchists' own demonstration on Saturday, 14 December and other occasions when plainclothes police officers were involved (cf. Wahlström 2003a). These incidents have been publicly highlighted by protesters as examples of communication breakdowns or of the police's failure to keep to agreements (see http://www.cph2002. org/side/82, 16 January 2003).

Three months after the EU Summit in Copenhagen, protesters' narratives of the actions of the police were still dominated by: (1) how the police had broken promises made to the protesters; (2) how the police acted in an unnecessarily provocative way especially during Saturday's demonstrations; as well as (3) how the police outside the demonstrations had harassed protesters by, for instance, raising checkpoints in the streets to carry out identity checks and searches. Some had the view that the Danish police after all had done better than their colleagues in Gothenburg and Genoa, but this idea seems to have fallen somewhat into the background in the conversations and consciousnesses of the protesters as a result of what they deemed condemnable behaviour on the part of the police.

The most elaborate examination of what many regard as breaches of promises by the police was made by the Initiative for Another Europe (http://www.cph2002. org/side/82, 16 January 2003). Although it concerns only their own demonstration on Saturday, it gives several instances of police behaviour that allegedly came into conflict with what was said in the preparatory communication (see above). The criticism is primarily directed at: (1) the police being palpably visible during the whole demonstration; (2) plainclothes officers moving close to, and perhaps also within, the demonstration before organizers were given the opportunity to counteract unacceptable behaviour by protesters; and (3) the police failing to carry out adequately their duty of keeping the demonstration route free from traffic.

It was perceived that the massive police presence, particularly the presence of plainclothes police, criminalized the peaceful demonstrators. Majbrit (the People's Movement against EU) emphasizes that the duty of the police at demonstrations is primarily to protect the right to demonstrate – 'But the picture was different. It seemed like they were protecting Copenhagen against *us*.'

The criticism against the plainclothes police is moreover claimed to be a question of security. People who want to express their political opinion publicly ought to feel assured that they are not monitored without their knowledge: 'In this country it is the case, when you want to demonstrate, and that's a constitutional right, that you should be sure that the person walking next to you is not an officer that takes notes of what you think and what you do' (Kenneth, the Danish Red–Green Alliance/Attac, quotes from a press interview with chief constable Kai Vittrup).

Furthermore, it can be observed that the Copenhagen police, in spite of preparatory communication with the activists, contributed in several ways to a somewhat restricted democratic space for many protesters. Perhaps the most obvious of these were the checkpoints set up in the city and along some roads, where people with a 'suspect appearance' were stopped, asked to identify themselves and were searched (cf. Peterson's chapter in this volume). Observations and respondents' testimonies support the picture of the police in practice making a selection based partially upon foreign appearance and speech, partially upon the dress code that is common in some activist circles. In Copenhagen during the EU Summit, the police were ubiquitous, and after the summit stories circulated about some individuals being stopped several times within a few hours. Again, it is a question of people feeling criminalized and feeling that the police 'marginalize people that don't follow the fashion from *Eurowoman* or *Femina*' (Majbrit, the People's Movement against EU). Mads from the Danish Red–Green Alliance makes the following assessment: 'Their conduct was quite as repressive as in Gothenburg. They were simply cleverer.'

The arrests by the police have also been looked upon by, for instance, Global Roots as a breach of promise and a breach of the law (http://www.ulydighed.dk/dk/Pressemeddelelser/2002/EU-topm%F8de/19-12%20civile.htm, 13 February 2003). Kai Vittrup seems actually to have announced: 'No arrests may be carried out without reasonable cause. [...] That kind of action is nothing that we have planned in the least' (http://www.tv2lorry.dk/nyheder/nyhed2002.asp?Id=4383, 30 April 2003). Hence it is understandable that some, in this light, regard the actions of the police as a breach of promise.

It might be interesting to connect the police behaviour with P.A.J. Waddington's (1994, 198) observation that the police's power over protesters consists of the latter being considerably more dependent on the police than vice versa. He uses this to explain why so many anti-establishment left-wing organizations seem to accept the negotiation tactics of the police. Let us specify, however, in what ways do the protesters need the police, and could these needs differ between different groups?

According to P.A.J. Waddington, the needs of protesters lie primarily in what the police do *not* do, for example, not making arrests for minor offences and not restricting the activists in ways that make protesting difficult. The protesters are, in other words, dependent on the police being helpful, having a pragmatic interpretation of the law and not escalating possible confrontations. As we have seen, this is important both for broad participation in demonstrations and for conveying their political message. Larger and more institutionalized groups, but also the anarchists, appear to have this need. The latter are, nonetheless, more prepared to pay the costs for not having their subversive power emasculated (cf. P.A.J. Waddington 1994, 197–9).

Global Roots, for their part, also seem to be interested in, for instance, not having their protest actions stopped before they have even commenced; but their need for the police lies perhaps more in the police's dramaturgical part as an adversary. This could go as far as regarding an absence of resistance from the police as a possible disadvantage for the performance. Johannes from Global Roots, for example, humorously comments on the alternative lines of action of the police at the Bella Centre: 'If they had kept away, it'd just have become an even greater fiasco, because then we'd just have stood there [laughs].' Of course, the group's need for a conflict with the police should not be exaggerated, but it is striking that they hereby encounter an alternative that raises the dividends of the protest action if the police act aggressively towards them, instead of being helpful.

Additionally, several protesters had learned from their experiences in, for example, Gothenburg, and were trying to find ways of solving Ostrom's (1990) problem of *monitoring*; hence the creation of the 'monitoring group' in Copenhagen.

> The photographs that came out of the clashes that occurred in Gothenburg were photos that the police had taken, and it was the police who chose what was published. That was why the photo of that officer sitting on a horse, on his way to being struck on the head by a cobblestone, was on the first page of all the papers the day after. That was the police's own photo. We wanted to have a counterpart to that. (Johannes, Global Roots)

This strategy was regarded as relatively successful. However, in the future, the groups involved would try not to link the criticism to just one demonstration (as was the case on this occasion), but would use the material to expose the general behaviour of the police during a protest campaign (Johannes, Global Roots). In Goffman's (1974) terms, one can say that the 'police-critical' performance that followed the summit could become even more effective in establishing the intended framework of the police's actions.

The question is whether the sanctions that protesters can impose on police can be severe enough to have a real effect on their actions. P.A.J. Waddington examines research about media influence on police behaviour, and notes (1999b, 202–3) that media attention might prove influential in this respect, even if seriously discredited police forces sometimes start acting in ways that confirm the negative picture of them. However, one must keep in mind that the sanctions that protest groups can muster are generally indirect and weak in comparison to the sanctions for deviant behaviour from the police and legal system.

While it appears that the learning processes of the activists may lead to better qualifications for solving the problem of *monitoring*, the low level of trust in the police makes the problem of *credibility* harder to manage. It is possible, however, that the protesters taking part in contacts with the police will try to improve their capacity to control the actions of the police, for instance by means of more accurate forms of documentation of the meetings:

> We tried to take notes at those meetings, but have had to state afterwards that they're not binding, those reports. So I would probably adopt a legal stance. [...] The police would of course never tie themselves down to a legal contract, I realize that, but I think that I would be tougher, and a bit more bossy, in the way I will negotiate with the police the next time. (Majbrit, the People's Movement against EU)

Concerning the question of trust, all of the activists interviewed in Copenhagen *after* the summit report having a low degree of trust in the police. How this trust has been affected by the incidents presented in the last section differs, however, from individual to individual. Only one person – Majbrit (the People's Movement against EU) – is positive that her trust in the police has generally diminished as a consequence of the behaviour of the police, since before the summit she thought that they were going to keep their promises. Even among non-demonstrators, for example the NGO Forum Stop the Violence's 'Stop-the-violence stewards', there were indications of an altered level of trust (Majbrit, the People's Movement against EU). An internal inquiry concerning the experiences of this group provides some, albeit weak, confirmation for this fact (http://www.ngoforum2002.dk/www_settings/index.asp?id=533, 7 February 2003). The loss of trust by those having participated in negotiations with the police appears to be not only on an intellectual level, but also on a personal and emotional one.

> When you sit with a human being on the other side of a table, and he sits there and promises you something that he doesn't keep the day after, you automatically become disappointed on a human level. [...] I also felt cheated. Because I had wasted my time. I think it's irritating that the NGO group used up so many resources in discussions with the police, and such hard efforts that we have put in on our nonviolence strategy, while the police just don't give a shit, to put it plainly. (Majbrit, the People's Movement against EU)

Other activists are inclined to say that their trust in the police has not changed much, as it was already at such a low level: 'Before, I knew that you couldn't trust the police, and now I know that you can't trust the police. So it's the same' (Johannes, Global Roots).

However, even those whose trust in the police had been diminished by the experience did not foresee any decisive changes in their organizations' approach to future negotiations and contacts with the police. The reasons for this are: (1) that preparatory contacts provide the organizations with material that can be used to criticize the police, in case of renewed breaches of promises; (2) that negotiations nevertheless can contribute to mutual trust (at least among parts of the police and the networks); and (3) that they need, nevertheless, to have contacts of a practical nature before demonstrations, which supports P.A.J. Waddington's (1994) remarks regarding activists' dependence upon the police.

This increases the risk of different factions moving further apart within the already fragile 'rainbow coalitions' (cf. Peterson 1997). The anarchists, for instance, felt that they had a rather weak position in the negotiations in the Initiative for Another Europe, and that they accepted agreements that more or less compromised their politics. For these reasons, several anarchists seem to be sceptical about again being part of a coalition like the Initiative for Another Europe. The Anarchist Federation officially declares:

> [d]uring the summit, the police broke all the promises they had given to those NGO's naive enough to start negotiations with them in the first place. [...] This is not in the least bit surprising to us. But we hope that some of these organizations now have [sic.] learned that it is never possible to make deals with, or trust, the police. Those who haven't can fuck off. (http://www.resist.dk/action.asp?execute=thetext&id=Summit_Epilogue.asp, 17 February 2003)

When it comes to the outcome of the negotiations, our empirical material confirms the point that we emphasized in the introduction regarding the police's preferential right of interpreting situations on the spot, which implies a pragmatic approach to any agreements reached. Limited control of the rank and file is also a 'problem' for negotiators from both parties. The evaluation of the parties can be used in the subsequent media struggles and will contribute to ongoing learning processes that affect future tactics and mutual levels of trust.

Conclusions

Negotiations that take place in connection with political protests must be understood in light of the political conflicts underlying present-day supranational political protests. These are problems that must be solved within the framework of the political system and cannot reasonably be handled by forces whose principal task is the maintenance of public order. The obstacles to the creation of mutual trust between police and protesters are an ever-present reality and are likely to remain so in the foreseeable future. A further problem is that the emphasis placed on risk, surveillance and security in today's society, in a world where national borders are no longer much more than lines on the map, tends to give priority to discursive practices that place matters of security before the individual's constitutional right to protection from unreasonable curtailments of civil liberties (cf. Ericson and Haggerty 1997, chapter 2).

The focus on security, in combination with asymmetric relations between police and protesters based on their respective legal powers and access to intelligence, entails definitive limits on the kinds of joint agreements that such parties are able to reach. Thus the social dilemma so cleverly solved by Ostrom (1990), in favour of a self-regulatory institutional arrangement to secure collective natural resources, is not so easily resolved when it comes to the fundamental dilemma faced in connection with political demonstrations.

Another factor highly limiting the possibilities of negotiations is the lack of authority that both police and protester negotiators may have in their own groups and organizations. It is not surprising if both parties are suspicious of agreements that are easily overridden by superior police officers or ignored by a peripheral group in a network. This problem is accentuated by the transnational character of the protests. If activist negotiators have little influence over several groups in their national network, they may have even less influence over visiting groups from other countries. This is not to say that the protest organizers have *no* influence whatsoever over their foreign comrades – on the contrary, observations from Copenhagen indicate that there was widespread respect for the plans and ideas of the local organizers.

We argue that the reasons for activists' *mistrust* and *distrust* in relation to the police were found in their knowledge of the police's use of coercive force and breaches of promises in past decades and in other places, as well as in the performance of the police during the period immediately prior to the summits. This was particularly problematic in Copenhagen, where the protesters' distrust could not easily be amended by the (spurious?) friendliness of the police.

In several instances, however, we can see that both police and protesters try to maintain communication despite lack of trust. This line of action is made understandable by pointing to the different forms of *political performance* that the parties wish to stage. More institutionalized groups and networks, perhaps most of all, want to establish a peaceful relationship with the police, this being regarded as constructive for recruitment and conveying their political messages. The police in Sweden and Denmark also wish to convey their good and democratic intentions through a peaceful relationship with political protesters. Meanwhile less institutionalized groups and networks often prefer to stage a conflict with, or at least a dissociation from, the police. These groups have different needs for the police, manifested in their differing attitudes towards 'playing the game by the rules' set by the police.

In both Denmark and Sweden, there was widespread opinion among protesters that the police had broken promises made prior to the summits. By many, they were also considered as having acted provocatively and repressively. The Swedish police, however, received a great deal of support in the mass media during, and immediately after, the summit, which probably affected the high level of support they received in opinion polls (Weibull and Nilsson 2002). In Denmark, protesters responded to the repression by attempting to impose sanctions on the police in the form of negative media attention, and by lodging complaints to the minister of justice and the director of public prosecutions. At the time of writing, the only 'successful' legal sanction against the police was a trial of two Danish plainclothes policemen who were masked during a demonstration where the mask ban was in force (*Politiken*, 23 April 2004). The constables were fined.

In this chapter we provide reasons to emphasize not only the need for sufficient time for negotiations prior to major protests, but also the limits to how much trust can be achieved through a preparatory dialogue between the parties, no matter how much time the participants have at their disposal. To begin with, protesters need to be motivated to spend a great deal of time on contacts with the police, which is not likely to be the case. Many of the respondents in this study were sceptical precisely because of the time-consuming nature of negotiations (as they might not lead to much anyway). The nature of the political performances that each protest group tries to accomplish may also in some cases provide little room for close contacts with the police.

The protesters' evaluations of the police after the EU summit in Copenhagen finally point to the importance of actually sticking to one's promises. If the police wish to build up some trust in activist circles, it does not matter what they say as long as, in practice, they act repressively towards protesters. This study indicates how counterproductive it is to begin to create a trustful relationship around the negotiation table, which then turns out to have little correspondence to reality. A protest event never occurs in a vacuum, but takes place against a background of experiences from previous protests, which determines what the actors expect. 'You do not trust a person to do something merely because he says he will do it. You trust him only because, knowing what you know of his disposition, his information, his ability, his available options and their consequences, you expect he will *choose* to do it' (Dasgupta 1988, 55–6; emphasis in original text).

Clearly, the negotiations in both Gothenburg and Copenhagen had several common and specific problems, and may even have had adverse effects on long-term relations between the police and some protest groups. However, to some extent they appear to have been favourable in terms of safeguarding civil rights and political opportunities for many protesters, particularly since they made it possible for some groups to feel secure in entering the public space. Nonetheless, some protest actions were barely affected by the preparatory communication between the police and the coalitions. The dialogue did not prevent the police from acting in ways that on several occasions restricted the protesters' opportunities to make themselves heard in the public sphere.

References

Interviews

Sweden
Göran Nordenstam, 9 August 2001, Police Contact Group.
Peter Jigström, 5 September 2001, Planning Staff.
Jan Strömqvist, 9 November 2001, Network 2001.
Lennart Ronnebro, 12 November 2001, Police Contact Group.
Hans Abrahamsson, 4 December 2001, Gothenburg Action 2001.
Anders Svensson, 13 December 2001, Gothenburg Action 2001.
Gunilla Gevreus, 13 December 2001, Police Contact Group.
Gerd Brantlid, 2 January 2002, Police Contact Group.
Håkan Jaldung, 18 January 2002, Chief of the police operation at the Gothenburg
    summit.
Annika Tigeryd, 22 January 2002, Gothenburg Action 2001.
Magnus Hörnqvist, 23 January 2002, Gothenburg Action 2001.

Denmark
Kenneth Haar, 1 December 2002 and 11 March 2003, the Danish Red–Green Alliance
    and Attac.
Lars Bohn, 1 December 2002, Attac.
Nikolaj Heltoft, 2 December 2002, Global Roots.
Johannes Brandt, 3 December 2003 and 8 March 2003, Global Roots.
Mads Hagen, 3 December 2002 and 10 March 2003, the Danish Red–Green
    Alliance.
Jacob Larsen, 15 December 2002 and 11 March 2003, the Anarchist Federation.
Janne Sørensen, 11 March 2003, the Anarchist Federation.
Claus Pedersen, 9 March 2003, Global Roots.
Majbrit Berlau, 10 March 2003, the People's Movement against EU.
Correspondence by email with Pil Christensen from Global Roots.

Personal reports and evaluations from the Contact Group and the demonstrators' networks

Contact Group report (Kontaktgruppens erfarenhetsberättelse), 1 November 2001.
Anders Svensson, 'Göteborgs-händelserna 2001'.
Network 2001, 'Aktiviteter vid EU:s toppmöte i Göteborg', November 2001.

Official documents

Rikspolisstyrelsens utvärdering av EU-kommenderingen i Göteborg år 2001 [The National Police Board evaluation of the police operation at the Gothenburg summit in 2001], Stockholm: RPS.
EU 2001-kommenderingen, 'Utvärdering. Polismyndigheten i Västra Götaland' ('The evaluation of the Gothenburg police operation conducted by the Police Authority of Västra Götaland').
'Kommenderingsordrar (KO) från Polismyndigheten i Västra Götaland i anledning av EU-mötet i Göteborg 2001' ['Operational orders from the Police Authority of Västra Götaland issued in connection with the Gothenburg EU summit in 2001'].
KO 200 – EU 2001, 'Central operational framework in outline' (applicable 5–17 June 2001).
KO 27a, 'Order for the Contact Group' (applicable 16 June–5 July 2001).

Newspapers and journals

Aftonbladet, 8 April 2001.
Dagens Nyheter, 8 April 2001, 23 April 2001.
Göteborgs-Posten, 12 June 2001, 3 January 2002.
'Dagarna som skakade Göteborg', *Två dagar*, 27/01, supplement to *Göteborgs-Posten*, 15 September 2001.
Josefsson, Dan and Fredrik Quistbergh, 'Göteborg 14–16 juni. Dagarna som skakade Sverige', *Ordfront Magasin*, 9/2001.
Politiken, 23 April 2004.

Chapter 7

Formalizing the Informal:
The EU Approach to Transnational
Protest Policing

Herbert Reiter and Olivier Fillieule

Introduction

The increasing number of global justice protests, their explosive growth, their reliance on direct action repertoires, and the frequent clashes between demonstrators and police have raised among sociologists the issue of mass demonstrations and the maintenance of law and order. Other chapters of this volume were dedicated to the question of whether we are witnessing a profound transformation in forms of political participation and/or methods of management of public order within democratic states – or, as partisans of the movement affirm, a 'criminalization of social movements' (e.g. George 2001; Palidda 2001; Petrella 2001). The present contribution is inspired by the observation that not only at the national but also at the transnational level, in particular within the European Union, the global justice movement is perceived as one of the 'new threats' alongside terrorism: the European Police College (CEPOL), established by the Council Decision of 22 December 2000, affirms in the welcoming section of its website its aim to reflect, along with the priorities specified within the Council Decision, those emerging in light of the summits at Gothenburg and Genoa and the events in New York on 11 September 2001.

The history of political protest has been characterized by a dual opposition: on the one hand, between condemning violent troublemakers in the name of the rule of law and denouncing repression in the name of the freedom of expression, freedom of assembly and the right to civil disobedience; and on the other hand, between the legitimacy of elected representatives and the legitimacy of the street. In this connection, it should be readily apparent that the indigenous categories contributing to the collective production of a discourse concerning the 'transformations in the forms of political participation' should be constructed by the researcher as a subject of study rather than taken at face value. In other words, as Pierre Bourdieu has suggested in relation to the legitimacy of strikes, the struggles over classification correspond to 'a strategy reflecting biases that cannot be adopted by science without danger. There is a political manipulation of the definition of the political. *The issue at stake is itself an issue at stake*' (1980, 258).

This symbolic battle over meaning seems all the more important for the transnational aspects of protest policing, characterized by a lack of transparency and a weakness of public (and even scientific) debate. This holds true also for those aspects attributable to the EU, one of the more structured and regulated IGOs, in fact often described as a postmodern attempt at statebuilding. The very police powers coming to play in EU protest policing are ill defined and there are few, if any, public fora of debate on these issues. A similar picture emerges if we look at the *transnational* protest rights of the citizens of the EU: protest rights are formalized in the European Convention on Human Rights and in the EU Charter of Fundamental Rights.[1] However, until recently the concrete forms and boundaries of protest rights were rarely tested beyond the national level. Consequently, the declarations contained in the Convention and the Charter are not supported by a consolidated *practice of transnational protest rights*. In an interview with the German weekly *Die Zeit* (5/2005), Ralf Dahrendorf observed that the institutions of freedom dear to him were not transferable to the larger spaces we are really living in. The construction of a democratic EU is certainly a conflictual process, as had been the construction of the nation-state: citizens' rights are the result of social struggles (Bendix 1964; Marshall 1950).

In the following, we shall concentrate on the specific scenario of transnational protest policing represented by the conflict between the EU and the GJM. A first part of our contribution will be dedicated to the characteristics of justice and home affairs within the EU, in particular police cooperation, and to the development of an EU approach to public order policing. In the second part, we will discuss the characteristics of the GJM and their specific impact at the transnational level; the EU protest policing measures taken in reaction to the incidents in Gothenburg and Genoa; and the impact of 9/11 on EU protest policing and on EU justice and home affairs in general. In the concluding section, we will attempt to sum up the emerging tendencies in EU transnational protest policing.

The development of EU transnational policing

Police cooperation and justice and home affairs

The origins of transnational policing have been located in the aftermath of the 1848 revolutions, in particular in the *Polizeiverein* of the German states directed against democratic aspirations (Deflem 2002, chapter 1). Cooperation, however, was not restricted to the boundaries of the German Confederation or to the informal exchange

---

1   The right to protest in Europe is protected by Article 11 of the European Convention on Human Rights, which accords such practice an 'eminent' 'fundamental place' (CEDH, 26 April 1991, Ezelin, Series A, No. 202, pp. 23, 51; Com. EDH, 10 October 1979, *Rassemblement jurassien contre Suisse*, DR, vol. 17, p. 105). Article 12 of the EU Charter of Fundamental Rights (proclaimed in December 2000 in Nice) protects the freedom of peaceful assembly and of association 'at all levels', i.e. also at the EU level, 'in particular in political, trade union and civic matters'.

of information between European governments: France and Prussia, for instance, collaborated in 'liberating' Switzerland from refugees by organizing transportation to Great Britain and the United States, routing French revolutionaries through German territory and Germans through French territory (Reiter 1992). While subsequent developments in international policing, most notably Interpol, have excluded the political element of 'high policing', the beginning of closer police collaboration among the EU Member States in the TREVI-groups since 1976 was caused by the threat of terrorism, not by the emergence of transnational 'common' crime. It was, in fact, the exclusion of 'political' crime from Interpol's operational brief (in 1992, 80 per cent of Interpol messages were generated within European countries and 40 per cent within EU countries) that led to the TREVI-groups (Sheptycki 1995, 620).

Police cooperation among EU Member States developed as a form of intergovernmental collaboration outside the EU institutions, in fora like TREVI or (since 1985) Schengen (the agreement between a group of Member States gradually to abolish internal border controls). The intergovernmental character of this collaboration brought about deficient public debate, opaque decision making, and a lack of democratic accountability. These shortcomings were pointed out in a December 1989 resolution of the EU parliament stating that:

> The secret discussions, without democratic control by parliamentary supervision, on matters of police action, internal and external security and immigration, namely those effecting refugees, by member states acting outside the competence of the European institutions, within fora such as Schengen, TREVI and the Ad Hoc Immigration Group, violate the aforementioned conventions [on legal rights] and democratic principles. (McLaughlin 1992, 483)

However, this and subsequent resolutions were ignored by the above-mentioned groups.

Moreover, there has been a tendency to delegate decisions to expert committees, providing the police with opportunities to expand its professional autonomy and playing the nation-state off against the EU (McLaughlin 1992). This tendency contributes to a downplaying of the political implications of transnational police collaboration within the EU: 'Harmonization', for instance, has been likened to Habermas' notion of 'the scientization of politics' whereby issues become a technical problem examined and managed by restricted groups of bureaucrats, experts and professional lobbyists (Sheptycki 1995, 630).

Three sets of forces (and discourses) have contributed to a more distinct EU dynamic in this area (Walker 2003a, 123ff.): First, a new internal security discourse has conceived of the EU as a self-standing 'security community'. Second, as the EU broadened its competencies, functional spillover into the police sector could be observed, an obvious example being the measures against counterfeiting that were connected with the introduction of the euro. More specifically, one of the first studies on EU police cooperation had already advanced the hypothesis that the increased legislative and social policy profile of the EU would encourage protest directed against European institutions and policies, which in turn would enhance the law enforcement capacity of the Union in the long term (Anderson et al. 1995, 110). Third, the extent of self-conscious polity-building should not be underestimated: the fundamental measures for the construction of an EU area of freedom, security and justice were planned and implemented at the high point of institutional confidence in the early 1990s, revealing not only authority claims but also identity claims.

With the Maastricht Treaty (1993), cooperation among the police forces of the Member States became part of the EU's 'third pillar', retaining, however, its intergovernmental characteristics even after the Amsterdam Treaty (1999). Criticism underlining deficiencies in democratic accountability therefore continued, although the Amsterdam Treaty did transfer certain topics to the first pillar. The remaining third pillar issues, in particular police cooperation, were recognized as legitimate EU policy objectives; but with a Council on Justice and Home Affairs required to decide unanimously, a reduced role of the Commission, the European Parliament confined to a consultative role, and the uncertain ability of the European Court of Justice to fulfil a controlling function, effective power in this policy area rests with the individual Member States.[2]

Justice and home affairs remained a critical area also because most of the measures entered EU legislation as an *acquis*, that is, via the incorporation of decisions taken by groups like TREVI or Schengen into the EU framework. Concerning this body of measures, 'there was virtually no meaningful parliamentary scrutiny, let alone the chance for civil society to have any say or influence' (Bunyan 2002). The full *acquis* (over 700 measures) must be adopted by applicant countries *in toto*, without the possibility of any changes whatsoever. Moreover, the existing institutional structure opens up the possibility for Member States to jump scale, proposing measures at the European level that would face parliamentary scrutiny at the national level and realizing their objectives with soft law instruments, thus eluding national and European parliamentary scrutiny (De Hert 2004).

The objective of EU policy in constructing the 'area of freedom, security and justice' is defined in Article 29 of the Amsterdam Treaty as 'to provide citizens with a high level of safety'; the dominance of the security aspect in this regard has been repeatedly underlined (Twomey 1999). Articles 29 and 30 (on police cooperation) do not specifically mention public order. In fact, as underlined by Commissioner Vitorino and the representative of the European Council during the European Parliament debate (5 September 2001) on the events at the 2001 Genoa G8 summit, the maintenance of public order is the responsibility of the individual Member States, although a (not better defined) European dimension does exist. Article 30 of the Amsterdam Treaty does, however, mention that common action shall include the collection, storage, processing, analysis and exchange of relevant information, that is, characteristic instruments of transnational policing, dominated by 'knowledge work' (Sheptycki 2002).[3]

---

2   Cf. Peers 2000, Denza 2002, Walker 2003b, 2004. On the role of the national parliaments and the European parliament, see Jurgens 2001; Peers 2001.

3   The draft Treaty establishing a Constitution for Europe, which aims to replace all the existing treaties with a single text, in Article III-275 allows for European laws or framework

The case of the EU, where we witness the shift of traditional competences of the national state to the supranational level, is not the only pattern in transnational policing. The case of the US, in fact, is characterized by the internationalization of American law enforcement activity, which saw a sharp rise after 11 September but in its importance had already been underlined (Nadelmann 1993).[4] Finally, a more general transcendence of traditional forms of polity-based 'security sovereignty' – state or supranational – has been observed in the case of the privatization of transnational policing (Walker 2003a, 131).

For all forms of transnational policing, evident problems of individual and institutional accountability emerge. The internationalization of US law enforcement activities affects groups increasingly distinct from the sovereign US citizenry who, at least formally, possess the constitutional capacity to hold US policing to democratic account. As far as transnational private policing is concerned, there is no available forum of public accountability. In the European case, the primarily national forms of control seem inadequate for increasingly supranational arrangements (Walker 2003a, 131f.).

For the emerging EU approach to public order policing, we can speak of a process of formalizing informal practices of international police cooperation and 'unionizing' pre-existing intergovernmental arrangements – a process that is unaccompanied by the establishment of a system of controls, checks and balances comparable to the ones existing on the national level (imperfect as they may be), or even for other EU policy areas. It has been repeatedly noted that justice and home affairs is one of the areas where Member States disagree on the extent to which integration should be pursued. It has also been asserted that little integration has been accomplished in this field, by the late 1990s the busiest area of policy making, according to indices such as Council meetings held and measures proposed (Den Boer and Wallace 2000, 503). As Steve Peers (2000, 2) noted, this misunderstands the nature of justice and home affairs cooperation: 'JHA integration does not depend as much upon drawing up legislative texts as does the "traditional" economic and social integration pursued by the EC. Rather, it weighted far more towards the exchange of information and joint or coordinated operations of national administration.'

The development of an EU approach to public order policing

Research on 'Europrotest' has underlined that the new opportunities created by growing European integration seem to have been used timidly by European citizens so far. Various practical obstacles have been described as hindering international protests: lack of resources for protest organizations (for example, unions);

---

laws establishing measures concerning the collection, storage, processing, analysis and exchange of relevant information.

4   An extensive cooperation agreement between the EU and the US was signed in Copenhagen in 2002, and US officials are participating in Europol and in Eurojust. In the following we will not discuss this particular aspect.

geographical distance; psychological barriers (lack of individual attachment to the EU, lack of a transnational European public sphere, lack of personal interaction between activists); and political opportunities less favourable at the European level than on most national levels. Although transnational protest did exist before Seattle – for example, the European marches against unemployment, precarious employment, and exclusion held since 1997 (Chabanet 2002) – only the recent wave of anti-neoliberal globalization protest seems to have at least partially overcome these barriers (Bédoyan, van Aelst and Walgrave 2004; Imig 2004).

Notwithstanding the fact that the number of transnational, EU-related protests in the 1980s and 1990s was surprisingly small (Imig and Tarrow 2002), the EU was already beginning to develop an approach to public order policing in the second half of the 1990s. In part prompted by football hooliganism, this approach was also directed against protests and street demonstrations.[5] Some protest actions (such as blockades of roads or borders) had in fact led to judicial action at the European level, as they had interfered with the free movement of goods (Muylle 1998; Barnard and Hare 1997). The emerging role of transnational European protest policing follows the pattern generally underlined for transnational policing, that is, the virtual absence of directly 'operational' tasks and the almost complete dominance of 'knowledge work' (Sheptycki 2002; 1998, 64). This is not to say, however, that this 'knowledge work' is without very concrete operational consequences. From early on, in fact, the human rights implications on the operational level were pointed out, in particular regarding the closely connected proactive styles of policing; but there were few consequences, as the victims were generally stigmatized groups like drug dealers (Sheptycki 1994) and football hooligans.

Expanding on a 1996 recommendation on football hooliganism (Official Journal 1997 C 193/1), on 26 May 1997 the European Council adopted (without debate) a Joint Action with regard to cooperation on law and order and security. In Article 1, it stipulated: 'Member States shall provide Member States concerned with information, upon request or unsolicited, via central bodies, if sizeable groups which may pose a threat to law and order and security are travelling to another Member State in order to participate in events.' In the preamble, the 'events' were specified as 'sporting events, rock concerts, demonstrations and road-blocking protest campaigns' (Official Journal 1997 L 147/1). The information to be provided was to be supplied in compliance with national law and to include the fullest possible details regarding the group in question, routes to be taken, means of transport, and so on. In addition, the joint action allowed for the posting of liaison officers to other Member States (upon request), with an advice and assistance role. In order to promote cooperation among Member States, the Council also envisaged yearly meetings of heads of the central bodies for law and order and security to discuss matters of common interest.

This Joint Action envisioning case-by-case information exchange should be seen against the background of the Schengen agreement on the gradual abolition of checks

---

5   For an example of the transnational policing of an international football event, see Adang and Cuvelier 2001.

on the common borders of the signing states: the same territory covered by the 1997 Joint Action is in fact covered by the Schengen manual on police cooperation and public order adopted in November 1996. In addition, a fundamental measure of the developing EU public order policing approach consisted of the use of Article 2(2) of the Schengen Convention, which allows for the temporary reintroduction of border controls 'where public policy or national security so require', creating numerous possible conflicts with the individual right of free movement of persons guaranteed since 1964 by a Community Directive. This provision, of a purely intergovernmental nature, fell completely outside the EU institutional framework, explaining the lack of judicial and parliamentary accountability for its use (Apap and Carrera 2003).[6] The Schengen Borders Code agreed upon between the Council and the EU Parliament in June 2005 – since 1 May 2004 the Parliament has enjoyed co-decision powers for measures concerning the crossing of EU external and internal borders – seems to constitute only limited advances in assuring accountability, transparency, proportionality and information for the public.[7]

The Schengen Agreement, signed in 1985, has been effective since 1995 on an intergovernmental basis and was incorporated into the EU legal framework from May 1999 with the Amsterdam Treaty of 1997.[8] As a compensatory measure for abolishing internal border checks, the Schengen Information System (SIS) was introduced as a union-wide database (Mathiesen 2000; Peers 2000, 209ff.). Its purpose as stated in Article 93 of the Schengen Convention ('to maintain public order and security, including State security') appears very broad and comprehensive. Article 46 of the Convention provides, in fact, for the exchange of information, also without request, 'to combat future crime and to prevent offences against or threats to public policy

---

6   For a table on the frequent use of Art. 2(2), in particular on the occasion of transnational protest events, by country and event from January 2000 to December 2002, see Apap and Carrera 2003, 4–5.

7   The text of the borders code is available at http://www.statewatch.org/news/2005/jun/9630.05.pdf; an analysis by Steve Peers is available at http://www.statewatch.org/news/2005/jul/eu-border-code-final.pdf (accessed March 2006). Member States retain the right to reintroduce internal border controls (see Articles 20–6) 'when there is a serious threat to public policy or internal security'. In cases requiring urgent action they may do so immediately. The notification and consultation procedure established for foreseeable events (to organize cooperation and examine proportionality) involves only the Member State reintroducing border controls, the Council, and the Commission. The European Parliament shall be informed 'as soon as possible', but the Member State shall report to Parliament, if requested, only after the third consecutive prolongation of the measure. Only after the lifting of controls is a report presented to the European Parliament, the Council and the Commission, outlining, in particular, the operation of the checks and the effectiveness of reintroducing border control.

8   The original signing states in 1985 were the Federal Republic of Germany, France, Belgium, Luxembourg and the Netherlands; by 1995, Spain, Portugal, Italy, Greece, Austria, Denmark, Finland and Sweden had joined. In 1996, an agreement with the non-EU members of the Nordic Passport Union (Norway and Iceland) was signed. For the Nordic countries, Schengen came into force in 2001. The United Kingdom and Ireland did not sign the Schengen agreement, but participate in certain aspects, in particular police cooperation.

and public security'. Concern has been raised in particular with reference to Article 99(3) of the convention allegedly allowing for discreet surveillance of political behaviour, also at the request of secret services. SIS (which stores fairly limited and standardized items of information) and the connected SIRENE system (which contains far-reaching, non-standardized information or 'soft' data) are undergoing continual expansion, and the tendency towards convergence and integration among the various registration and surveillance systems in Europe has been underlined. In connection with the development of a more advanced SIS II, civil rights organizations and the European parliament have pointed out the changed characteristics of SIS, which has developed from a compensatory measure for abolishing border checks into a general police cooperation measure.

A fundamental criticism of EU police cooperation in general and of the Schengen mechanism in particular concerns data protection. The 1995 EU directive on data protection does not cover the third pillar; several draft resolutions in this area were circulated between August 2000 and April 2001, but they never materialized further. Under a reorganization of the Council's working parties from July 2001 (reducing them from 26 to 15), the working party on data protection was abolished without explanation. As far as Schengen is concerned, the defence of individual rights is entrusted to the national and joint supervisory authorities. In its Second Annual Report (1997–8), however, the Schengen Joint Supervisory Authority specified that it had been banned from inspecting the central SIS computer system on conditions it could accept (Peers 2000, 218). In specific papers and reports, for instance concerning the control of football hooliganism, often no indication is given that any data protection rules were being applied, and only vague references are made to national and international data protection rules (Peers 2000, 208f.). The danger has been underlined that, in the absence of any standard or minimum level of EU privacy protection, international human rights treaties serve as 'minimum standards' justifying further negative legal integration. Where these minimum standards fall below the level of protection in the national laws of some Member States, those States will be unable to guarantee a continued high level of protection once they supply the data to a European database.[9]

While the imperfect Schengen rules are preferable to the vague (or non-existent) protection applying to the measures governing case-by-case exchanges for information, they give maximum discretion to law enforcement authorities with no indication of the circumstances under which information must or may be released to an individual (Peers 2000, 218). However, the right to have inaccurate information deleted or corrected depends on an individual knowing what information about him

---

9   Peers (2000, 219). See Peers (2000, 5 passim) on the effects of positive (via new European law) and negative (via abolition of national law) integration in the field of justice and home affairs, where the second type is dominant (e.g. in the objective of free movement of prosecution), but largely unaccompanied by the first type, establishing union-wide standards (e.g. for defendants' rights). These mechanisms therefore enforce state power and weaken citizens' rights.

or her is held on a database. In the case of two Welsh football fans detained and deported by the Belgian police on the basis of erroneous information supplied by British authorities (who in turn had received their names from Luxembourg), it took a six-year campaign (with the help of Liberty, a British NGO) lobbying a dozen national and international bureaucracies to get their names removed from Belgian, British and Schengen records (Peers 2000, 188). This 1992 experience was not an isolated event, limited to football hooligans. Stephanie Mills, a Greenpeace activist from New Zealand, was denied access to the entire Schengen area on 25 June 1998 because the French government had entered her name into the SIS system – as indeed it had previously entered those of a number of other Greenpeace staff (Peers 2000, 224). After the Gothenburg incidents, about 400 names are said to have been added to the SIS (Hayes and Bunyan 2004, 260).

Images of protesters: Conceptions of public order

The weakness of formal controls and rules in transnational policing gives special importance to the images of protesters and the conceptions of public order circulating on the supranational level. Although little is known about this aspect, the indications emerging allow us to formulate two hypotheses: (1) because of the continuing intergovernmental character of EU police cooperation, we can expect that national characteristics will remain prominent, providing the privileged channels for the diffusion of recent policing developments; and (2) the secluded character of the fora of experts, not exposed to public scrutiny and political debate, will tend to 'technical' and restricted images and conceptions, giving little consideration to political aspects, in particular citizens' rights.

An example of these mechanisms is provided by a paper prepared for an experts' meeting in Brussels on 15 April 1998, following the Joint Action of 26 May 1997.[10] Presented by the British delegation, it does reflect UK trends and terminology, but also general developments common to Western democracies towards the end of the millennium: human rights standards are presented as acquired and undisputed, with reference to international agreements, but remain largely unreflected as to their bearing on the matters discussed; high importance is attributed to managerial accountability, whereas the problem of democratic accountability of policing is neglected.[11] This seems particularly problematic at the transnational level where controls, checks and balances are notoriously lacking, as is public debate. In proposing increased EU police cooperation, the paper in fact does not mention the human rights implications of transnational policing, nor the transnational quality of EU citizens' rights.

---

10 Available at http://www.statewatch.org/news/2001/aug/7386-98.htm (accessed January 2006).

11 For the narrowing of the discussion about accountability in Great Britain to focus on questions of fiscal and managerial accountability and customer satisfaction, see McLaughlin 1992, 478.

Entitled 'Conflict Management', the paper underlines the need to improve the exchange of information and intelligence and to facilitate a rapid flow of data on all types of crime and disorder, beyond the event-driven practice concerning international football events. Disorder and crime are understood as just different aspects of conflict, which is defined as 'any act that is contrary to the general public's perception of normality or which adversely affects their quality of life'. It is further affirmed that conflict has 'the potential adversely to affect the status quo' and is 'almost always a predictor of future crime and more serious disorder'. A reference to the recent successful use of conflict management in the case of farmers' disputes in the UK indicates that protest is understood as a form of 'conflict'. The absence of a distinction between crime, disorder and protest leads to the attempt to give a common response to all acts 'contrary to the general public's perception of normality or which adversely affects their quality of life', regardless of whether they are perpetrated by criminal intent or are the consequence of the exercise of democratic rights.

The new terminology of 'conflict management' in fact reveals the persistence of a traditional concept of 'public order'. In the Italy of the 1950s, for instance, public order was understood as 'the regular course and the good order of civil life' (*il regolare andamento ed il buon assetto del vivere civile*) (Virga 1954, 53), with the police's task being, in the case of breaches, to restore the status quo ante. In the tension between the regular flow of life, public peace and quiet, and the disruption inevitably caused by street demonstrations, the freedom of expression and assembly would be routinely sacrificed. Similarly, the paper prepared for the 1998 Brussels meeting defines conflict management as the process of identifying tensions in society, outside the norm, and deploying appropriate resources to stop the problem escalating, with the aim of returning 'a community to its former normality'. The objective for the proposed permanent European information system is seen as the capacity for 'pre-empting conflict and informing police tactics to prevent such activity materializing'. From the outset, therefore, there is a visible tendency to minimize the consequences of protest, if not to prevent the protest – that is, an attitude unfriendly towards protest, if unbalanced by specific reflections on the need to guarantee demonstration rights. Similarly negative and above all undifferentiated are the underlying images of the perpetrators of disorder, centred on hooligans connected on the one hand to crime and on the other to political protest.[12]

Alongside these traditional concepts and images draped in new terminology, we find references to a modern conception of police power. The differences between conflict management and a pure law enforcement style are in fact specifically stressed; police are assigned the role to seek to establish, through mediation, what is to be considered as acceptable and unacceptable behaviour throughout a potential conflict

---

12 As the Brussels paper (see note 10 above) states: 'Hooligans often have criminal records that include offences of violence, damage and dishonesty: moreover they are sometimes associated with political demonstrations and direct action groups that have no sporting connections whatsoever. Accordingly, conflict has impacted on all types of organized events, including music festivals, environmental protests and public holiday celebrations.'

event. However, also in this context, the paper speaks of a status quo to be 'regained' and underlines the need to investigate the circumstances that gave rise to the event in order to ensure that 'the opportunity for a recurrence is prevented or minimized'.

The paper reveals no awareness of the potential tension between the professed aims of police action to 'regain a status quo' (or a 'former normality') or even to 'pre-empt conflict' (the definition of conflict including protest), on the one hand, and the freedom of expression and assembly, that is, to protest, by definition a 'disruptive' activity, on the other. References to this issue are limited to the generic affirmation that communities must be allowed to enjoy the freedoms and rights articulated in the European Convention on Human Rights. In addition, four simple 'ethics' are presented as guidance for police officers, deemed necessary because of the high level of discretion that conflict management allows: to 'Secure and Protect', using 'Minimum Force', being 'Fair and Reasonable' whilst 'Searching for the Truth with the Truth'. To 'Secure and Protect', that is, 'the safety of the public from disorder and crime', is defined as 'the primary ethic and the reason for being of the police'. The four ethics are said to have stood the test of time, and it is affirmed that, providing each member of the police force adheres to them, 'the public need not be suspicious about police activity'.

It is doubtful that this conviction would be shared by civil rights organizations or movement activists. The paper for the 1998 Brussels meeting, in fact, makes no specific reference to the role of the police in the protection of freedom of expression and of assembly, that is, the right to protest. The conception of demonstrations (and demonstrators) that is emerging seems to foreshadow the one we have seen applied to transnational protest in the case studies presented in this volume, variously defined as 'managed control' (Vitale 2005), 'selective incapacitation' (Noakes and Gillham, in this volume) or 'exclusionary fortress-oriented policing' (King and Waddington, in this volume).

The EU policing of GJM protests

Characteristics of the GJM and the EU-opportunity structure

The evolution of an EU approach to protest policing saw a sharp acceleration with the emergence of the GJM. This is certainly not a coincidence: research on the history of the maintenance of public order has consistently pointed out that protest policing evolves as a reaction to the transformations of social conflict (Fillieule and della Porta 2006; Fillieule 1997; Tilly 1986) – thus, the establishment of bodies of knowledge and practices in policing as well as the legal framework of crowd control were for the most part implemented in reaction to changes in the nature of protest. This fact suggests that looking at characteristics specific to the GJM will help us to understand the impact of transnational protest at the level of supranational governance. Relevant factors are the nature of the demands voiced, the characteristics of the protesters, the preferred action repertoires, and the targets of protest.

Recent research has pointed out that the GJM, although critical of existing EU institutions, cannot be described as opposing European integration (della Porta 2006). To the contrary, movement organizations and activists converge on the necessity to build 'another Europe', advancing demands for social justice and 'democracy from below'. Since 2002, attention to the construction of 'another Europe' has developed at the European Social Forums, with the presentation of demands for democratization of European institutions and for a charter of social rights. Surveys of activists have confirmed strong criticism of the existing European institutions, but also indicate a high affective identification with Europe and a medium level of support for a European level of governance.[13] These activists therefore represent a 'social capital' of committed citizens that might provide an important source for the building of a European citizenship. As Thomas Risse (2003, 6) has pointed out, contestation is a crucial pre-condition for the emergence of a European public sphere, and a contested public sphere is the only path towards the creation of a supranational democracy. In this sense, the reaction of European institutions – which (in varying degrees as far as the Parliament, the Commission or the Council are concerned) show many of the aspects of closure typical for supranational institutions – is of crucial importance for the development of a democratic EU.

At the national level, the heterogeneity of the GJM has been pointed out as a particularly delicate point for protest policing. The mainstream press (but also police reports) have drawn a picture of structured organizations outnumbered by unorganized, barely politicized and anomic elements, joined by micro-movements seeking violence for the sake of violence. Yet, surveys conducted through questionnaires in the course of anti-G8 demonstrations as well as social forums have challenged such views of the anomic and unorganized nature of the GJM: participants have very varied past and present organizational experiences.[14] On the other hand, the organizational heterogeneity of the GJM is in fact a specific feature whose implications in terms of public order have been repeatedly stressed in the contributions to this volume. In particular, for transnational protest policing – consisting, as underlined above, in 'knowledge work' – the difficulties in the elaboration, exchange and use of information on a new, emerging movement are further increased by unfamiliarity, not only with the specific national political context, but also with the *modus operandi* of the agency supplying the information.

---

13 This type of survey has been used increasingly in recent years, especially following an initial study carried out in France in 1994 that set out the methodological rules (see Favre, Fillieule and Mayer 1997). Della Porta was the first to carry out a survey of this kind on the GJM during the counter-summit in Genoa and during the European Social Forum (ESF) in Florence, followed by Fillieule et al. (2004) on anti-G8 demonstrations in Evian and Agrikoliansky and Sommier (2005), on the Paris Saint-Denis ESF.

14 See, for example, Andretta et al. 2002, and della Porta et al. 2006, on the Florence European Social Forum and the anti-G8 demonstrations in Genoa, Fillieule et al. 2004, on the anti-G8 event in Evian, and Fillieule and Blanchard 2005, on the Paris European Social Forum.

In the case of GJM protests, we are confronted with collective transnationalism (Imig 2004) – that is, the apparently growing phenomenon of protests organized across borders against common supranational targets, involving demonstrators from various countries. In the case of the 2001 demonstrations against the EU Summit in Brussels, roughly 40 per cent of the participants were non-Belgians (Bédoyan, van Aelst and Walgrave 2004, 46). However, the practical, psychological and political barriers that foreigners have to overcome in order to participate seem to have a measurable impact on their profile. These protesters are young, organized, and radical compared to their domestic counterparts (Bédoyan, van Aelst and Walgrave 2004, 46ff.). If these characteristics should not pose insurmountable barriers for a policing of protest respectful of demonstration rights, they do all tie in with police images of 'bad demonstrators' (see della Porta and Reiter, in this volume).

The characteristics of the GJM activists acquire additional importance in connection with the action repertoires of the movement. As surveys in Genoa, Florence and Evian have shown, the GJM has a predominantly nonviolent action repertoire that is, however, variegated and shows a significant propensity for direct action (see della Porta et al. 2006; Fillieule et al. 2004). As the most visible protest form, counter-summits are of particular importance at the transnational (including the European) level. As one of the few occasions when supranational governance is discussed in the media, counter-summits have the potential to arouse public opinion. At the same time, the summit sites become the terrain of direct interaction with police forces, in part because of the declared intention to prevent the smooth operation of the official summit (the objective to prevent the holding of such meetings is far less pronounced in the case of the EU than in the case of the G8) – in part because of the specific problem of the presence of domestic and especially foreign dignitaries (Ericson and Doyle 1999).

In the case of European summits, the host nation-state's need to assert its monopoly of force on its own territory before international public opinion is accompanied by similar mechanisms on the part of European institutions, especially since the creation of an 'area of freedom, security and justice' became an official EU policy objective. This is true in particular for the European Council, simultaneously the sole EU depository of competences for police cooperation and the main target of the protest. The Council became the prime target not only because of its decisive role in EU decision making, but because in its structure the democratic deficit of the EU is particularly apparent. In fact, of the EU institutions, the European Council most reflects an intergovernmental character. In the singular position of being at the same time an executive and a legislative body of the EU, it has shown a tendency for secrecy, shielding its decision making from scrutiny by parliament and civic society also when acting as a legislative body.[15]

---

15 In a recent report (available at http://www.euro-ombudsman.eu.int/special/pdf/en/03295.pdf, accessed March 2006) the EU Ombudsman criticized the Council's continued practice of excluding the public when meeting in its legislative role.

If the heterogeneity of the GJM, the variety in its action repertoires, and the tensions connected with counter-summits do raise particular problems for protest policing at the transnational level, the challenge constituted by the movement is above all a test of European institutions' openness to participation from below. However, the reaction of the European Council, consisting of measures intended to protect its meetings and 'other comparable events', does not point in that direction. In these measures, in fact, the Council puts itself squarely in a purely intergovernmental context: the 'other comparable events' do not refer to meetings of other EU institutions like the Commission or the Parliament, but to meetings of the G8 or of senior politicians from two or more Member States.[16]

EU protest policing measures after Gothenburg and Genoa

The EU institutions, in particular the Council, perceived the GJM as a direct threat: for the first time, the emergence of a movement led to specific measures of European institutions directed against it. Centred on information exchange and geared towards proactive policing, these measures reveal the problems in transparency and democratic accountability, but also in efficiency, connected with the transnational and intergovernmental character of EU police cooperation.

The challenge posed by the violent incidents surrounding the EU Summit in Gothenburg led to swift action by the European Council. At a meeting of the Council for Justice and Home Affairs on 13 July 2001, conclusions on security at meetings of the European Council and other comparable events were adopted, largely centred on greater collaboration among the various national police forces to ensure the peaceful holding of the summits.[17] The targets of the Council measure are defined as extraneous bodies, without a political agenda, using violence for violence's sake, as 'those who abuse these democratic rights by initiating, planning and carrying out acts of violence to coincide with public demonstrations'; as elements who exploit or abuse legitimate demonstrations 'for the sole purpose of committing acts of collective or individual violence'; or simply as 'violent troublemakers'. In no part of the conclusions is reference made to the dynamics of interaction between protesters and police, or to possible errors by the latter.

The conclusions underline the right of citizens to express their opinions freely and to assemble in a peaceful manner, and they recall the importance of a constructive dialogue between the organizers of public demonstrations and the authorities. The aim of the dialogue, however, is not clarified, except in the need to involve 'the

---

16 According to the answer of the British government to the request of the House of Lords Select Committee on European Union for clarification of 'other comparable events', see House of Lords, 'Select Committee on European Union Twentieth Report. Security at EU Council Meetings', available at http://www.publications.parliament.uk/pa/ld200304/ldselect/ldeucom/119/119.pdf, accessed January 2006.

17 Available at: http:// register.consilium.eu.int/pdf/en/01/st10/10916en1.pdf, accessed January 2006; see also Griebenow and Busch (2001, 64ff).

organizer of an event in internal security measures', and to ensure that legitimate demonstrations are not exploited by groups with a violent agenda. Dialogue, therefore, seems unilaterally driven by security objectives, and the objective to guarantee the freedom of opinion and assembly by acting in a 'demonstration friendly way' (as the German constitutional court had put it in its Brokdorf decision) is not mentioned.[18] In fact, the conclusions concentrate on measures designed to keep activists presumed to be a danger to public order and security away from the country hosting the summit.

Expanding on the recommendations contained in the Joint Action of 1997, the conclusions solicit the activation of national contact points for the collection, analysis and exchange of relevant information; the use of 'spotters', that is, police or intelligence officers able to identify persons or groups from their countries likely to pose a threat to public order and security; and the permanent monitoring of operational procedures by the senior officials working party referred to in Article 3 of the Joint Action. This working group was to meet at the request of the host Member State as a Police Chiefs' Task Force in order to advise and monitor, contributing to effective EU police cooperation in support of the Member State hosting the event. In addition, the Task Force was to prepare a joint analysis of violent disturbances, offences and groups and to organize targeted training by the European Police College.[19] Finally, the Council foresaw an examination of the possibility of increasing the powers of Europol in this area.

Concerning information exchange among law enforcement agencies, direct reference is made to the Joint Action of 1997 and to Article 46 of the Schengen Convention (see above). Following the pattern already mentioned, although the respect of the right to the protection of personal data is explicitly underlined, the only concrete reference is to 'compliance with national law'. The extensiveness of the information exchange foreseen is demonstrated by the call for 'the use of all the legal and technical possibilities for stepping up and promoting rapid, more structured exchanges of data on violent troublemakers on the basis of national files'. The exchange of information is closely connected with the application ('if it proves essential') of Article 2(2) of the Schengen Convention, that is, its temporary suspension. In the same context, implementation of expulsion measures and cooperation in the repatriation of expelled demonstrators were discussed. Finally,

---

18 The *Brokdorf Urteil* (1985) defines freedom of speech as the noblest human right, fundamental for a democratic order, and characterizes the freedom of assembly as the collective form of freedom of speech, understood as the expression of popular sovereignty and as the right of the citizen to participate actively in the political process. According to this decision, the constitutional protection of the freedom of assembly extends to spontaneous demonstrations and also to peaceful participants in demonstrations for which violent behaviour on the part of individuals or of a minority is foreseen. In addition, the German constitutional court obligated public authorities to act in a 'demonstration-friendly' way and to actively seek out the cooperation of the organizers of public demonstrations (Winter 1998a, 203s; 1998b, 59ss., 281ss.).

19 In 2002 and in 2003, courses on public order and crowd control were conducted by the European Police College (CEPOL) (see the respective annual reports, www.cepol.net).

direct cooperation between judicial authorities was to be facilitated, with the aim of prosecuting and trying 'violent troublemakers … without undue delay and in conditions guaranteeing a fair trial'.

The Council also took into consideration the proposal of the German interior minister, Schily, to 'unionize' and apply to 'violent troublemakers' a German practice developed to oppose football hooligans and later neo-Nazis, consisting of the *Ausreiseverbot*, a ban on leaving the country.[20] Schily's proposal – providing for the creation of a European database of the 'violent' and the introduction of the *Ausreiseverbot* into all EU countries – met the resistance of the majority of the Council (eight to seven). However, the conclusions contained the recommendation to use 'all the legal possibilities available in the Member States for preventing individuals who have a record of law and order offences from going to the country hosting the event if there are serious reasons to believe that such persons are travelling with the intention of organizing, provoking or participating in serious disturbances of public law and order'.

After Genoa, the difficulties and shortcomings of the EU approach to transnational public order policing became apparent. According to the hearings of the Italian parliamentary investigative commission, problems ranged from difficulties in establishing adequate contacts with police forces in other EU members states to differences in national laws concerning data protection and information exchange.[21] Subsequently, a report of the Belgian delegation to the Police Cooperation Working Party on the actions of European police forces at the EU Summit in Laeken (14 and 15 December 2002) confirmed the difficulties of cooperation.[22] According to this report, many countries did not provide any information; for others it varied from very limited to full and detailed. In addition, there were sometimes problems in interpreting the data because there was no indication of the method of information gathering used. The liaison officers sent by 11 countries had little or no operational information before the event and the liaison function materialized only during the summit. It was also underlined that the various judicial and police frameworks within

---

20 After the clashes during the 1998 World Cup football matches, German passport law was changed to allow hooligans to be barred from leaving the country. Use of this sanction against neo-Nazis was accepted by the constitutional court, even without final sentences, in the case of offences committed during trips abroad resulting in severe damage to the State. Before the G8, the German police issued injunctions to 79 activists against participation in tumult and violence, and barred another 81 from leaving the country, with an obligation to turn up and sign daily (*Der Spiegel* 31/2001, 24). In some cases these measures were confirmed by the administrative magistracy. After Genoa, this practice and the criteria employed to identify and register violent activists or those presumed to be so (in some cases on the basis of a mere document check during a demonstration), were subject to growing criticism (cf. *Der Spiegel* 31/2001; *Die Zeit* 37/2001, 4ff.; Griebenow and Busch 2001).

21 Italian Parliament, 'Commissione d'indagine conoscitiva sui fatti di Genova', Hearing 28 August 2001, 135ff. (available at www.camera.it).

22 Available at http://www.statewatch.org/news/2003/jul/prot09029en2.pdf (accessed January 2006); see also Busch 2002.

which the liaison officers operated did not facilitate the circulation of information. Coming from a variety of police departments and intelligence units, they had access to different types of information, often less than strategic. For spotting 'anti-globalisation troublemakers' (sic), as for other purposes, various police departments sent their own officers, who used techniques not always in line with public order policing as practised in Belgium. Finally, there was no structured international follow-up to the operation, and therefore no joint analysis of violent disturbances.

Apart from its lack of efficiency, the EU approach to transnational public order policing came under particular attack after Genoa for its lack of respect for civil liberties and individual rights. Unresolved, in fact, remained the problems connected with data protection and the individual quality of the right of free movement within the EU. Above all, the purely intergovernmental character of EU police cooperation greatly complicated the citizens' ability to single out those politically and juridically responsible for restrictive measures and to find redress. In fact, however imperfect, information exchange and transnational 'knowledge work' did have direct consequences for protesters, especially foreign ones, EU citizens or not. On the occasion of the Genoa G8 Summit, for instance, more than 2,000 people were refused entry at the borders, in certain cases on a questionable basis (see della Porta and Reiter, in this volume). In particular, refusal also included whole groups, violating the individual quality of the right of free movement within the EU. Similar instances had already been alleged in occasion of the Gothenburg EU Summit (*Tageszeitung*, 18 June 2001). Arrests seem to have affected foreign protesters disproportionately, including in cases where there were no violent incidents.[23]

Some of the civil rights concerns were subsequently taken up by the European Parliament, which showed, as was to be expected, a higher degree of openness than other European institutions. Based on the Watson Report of the European Parliament committee on civil rights and freedoms, justice and home affairs, the Parliament's recommendation to the Council voted by the plenum on 12 December 2001 stressed 'not a few shortcomings' in Member States' responses to the Nice, Gothenburg and Genoa demonstrations.[24] It recommended *inter alia* against blocking frontiers or denying entrance to individuals or groups seeking to take part peacefully in legitimate demonstrations; against any new type of 'blacklist'; against the use of firearms; and against the disproportionate use of force, with national police forces instead instructed to keep violence under control and safeguard individual rights even in cases of mass confusion where violent criminals mingle with peaceful, law-abiding citizens. Other recommendations – to adopt a joint definition of a 'dangerous individual' and dangerous conduct that might justify preventive measures (which particularly in Genoa struck at people even for legitimate behaviour); to avoid

---

23 In Laeken, for instance, 45 Belgians and 118 foreigners were arrested (109 EU citizens). See the report of the Belgian delegation (footnote 22).

24 The Watson Report is available at http://www.europarl.eu.int/omk/sipade3?PUBREF=-//EP//TEXT+REPORT+A5-2001-0396+0+DOC+XML+V0//EN&L=EN&LEVEL=0&NAV=S&LSTDOC=Y (accessed January 2006).

any sort of discrimination between nationals and European citizens in the event of arrest or legal proceedings, guaranteeing defence by an advocate of one's choice even in the event of summary proceedings – bring out the fact that the existence of comparable internal standards is not regarded as sufficient to guarantee the new quality of exercise of the citizens' right to demonstrate and protest Europe-wide.

In this context, however, the limited ability of European institutions to assure democratic accountability in the field of transnational protest policing must be underlined. As already stressed, the maintenance of public order falls under the exclusive competence of the individual Member State. The European Parliament's 2001 annual report on civil rights in the EU deplored 'the violations of fundamental rights such as freedom of expression and movement, the right of due process and the right to physical integrity that have occurred during public demonstrations, particularly at the time of the G8 meeting in Genoa'.[25] The opinion of the committee on petitions on this report, with direct reference to the case of the 'aggressive and violent policing of the anti-WTO [sic.] demonstrations in Genoa', stresses that 'the European Parliament largely lacks the means to do something immediately and effectively when such violations occur, beyond the political condemnation that a resolution allows'.[26]

This weakness is also evident at EU level. The European Parliament's recommendations, in fact, seem not to have been given any great consideration by the Council. The 'Security Handbook for the Use of Police Authorities and Services at International Events Such as Meetings of the European Council' of 12 November 2002 – called for by the Council conclusions of 13 July 2001 – was produced by the Police Cooperation Working Party without reference to the European Parliament recommendations, which had also suggested such a document.[27] The handbook, approved by the Council at its meeting on 28 and 29 November 2002, suggests that future revisions be discussed only by the Police Chiefs Task Force and the committee of experts foreseen in Article 3 of the Joint Action of 1997 and approved by the Article 36 Committee (a coordinating committee of senior officials in the field of police cooperation and judicial cooperation in criminal matters). In this context, it must be underlined that the legal and constitutional status of the Police Chiefs Task Force,

---

25 Committee on Citizens' Freedoms and Rights, Justice and Home Affairs. 'Report on the Human Rights Situation in the European Union 2001', December 2002, 12. Available at   http://www.europarl.eu.int/omk/sipade2?PUBREF=-//EP//NONSGML+REPORT+A5-2002-0451+0+DOC+PDF+V0//EN&L=EN&LEVEL=3&NAV=S&LSTDOC=Y   (accessed January 2006).

26 Ibid., 92. The reply of the committee on petitions itself on 6 October 2003 to a petition from a citizens' group on Genoa confines itself to asserting that no further action was possible (Thomas Meyer-Falk, 'Genua 2001 und das EU Parlament', October 2003, available at http://de.indymedia.org/2003/10/63175.shtml). Considering Art. III-377 of the Treaty establishing a Constitution for Europe, the powers of the Court of Justice of the EU in this field will also remain limited.

27 Available at http://www.statewatch.org/news/2003/jul/prothand12637-r3.pdf (accessed January 2006).

established at the Tampere Summit in October 1999, was never resolved. When the civil rights organization Statewatch applied for access to minutes of their meetings, it was told that the PCTF did not come under the Council of the EU and therefore the documents could not be supplied. As to the control and accountability of this and other new agencies in the field of security and intelligence that can be traced to the EU, there is no mechanism in place in any parliament.[28] A known priority of the Task Force is 'defining strategic and operational actions in the field of maintaining public order whenever events occur that are likely to threaten it'.[29]

The 'Security Handbook' is more precise and exhaustive than the Council conclusions from July 2001 in recalling the basic principles of Western European public order policing: proportionality and moderation; preference for a deescalating police approach 'when possible'; actively pursuing dialogue and cooperation with demonstrators and activists; and seeking to ensure respect for the right to freely express opinions and to assemble in a peaceful manner in accordance with the European Convention on Human Rights. As mentioned above, however, European institutions have no competence regarding the translation of these principles into practice. The handbook underlines, in fact, that maintaining law and order and providing security within the territory of a Member State is a national responsibility and prerogative. During the European parliament debate on the Genoa G8 Summit (5 September 2001), members close to the Italian government coalition had stigmatized any criticism of the operational practice of the police forces as an interference in Italian internal affairs.[30] In the sections dedicated to the policy on law enforcement, the handbook therefore limits itself to the phrasing that 'overall policies *can* include policies such as' (emphasis added): respect of the right to demonstrate and to free speech; proportionality of police actions; dialogue and assistance for the organization of demonstrations as characteristics of police action; 'the police should, *at its discretion and when appropriate* [emphasis added], demonstrate a low level of police visibility and a high level of tolerance regarding peaceful demonstrations'; and so on.

---

28 See Bunyan 2002, who concludes: 'The emerging EU state is indeed different to the national state, not just because it exercises cross-border powers, but rather because even traditional, and often ineffective, liberal democratic means of control, scrutiny and accountability of state agencies and practices are not in place nor is there any political will to introduce them.' For the Police Chiefs Task Force's own conception of their role, see 'Conclusions of the 10th meeting of the Police Chiefs Task Force', 11 and 12 October 2004, available at http://register.consilium.int/pdf/en/04/st14/st14094.en04.pdf (accessed January 2006). In general, see Bunyan 2006.

29 http://www.statewatch.org/news/2001/jun/publicorder.htm.

30 See http://www.europarl.eu.int/omk/sipade3?PUBREF=-//EP//TEXT+CRE+200109 05+ITEM-006+DOC+XML+V0//EN&LEVEL=3&NAV=S&L=EN. MEP Tajani, from Prime Minister Berlusconi's party, Forza Italia, spoke of an exploitation of the incidents also in the European Parliament. 'Parliament must not become the scene of debates on major national issues; it must not become the forum of national debates.'

Another part of the 'Security Handbook' contains a series of recommendations for ensuring collaboration among Member States, in particular in the exchange of information in the tradition of the 1997 Joint Action and the 2001 Council conclusions. Permanent national contact points are supposed to 'provide a permanent risk analysis on known potential demonstrators and other groupings expected to travel to the event and deemed to pose a potential threat to the maintenance of public law and order'. The analysis is to be forwarded at the earliest possible time prior to the international event, and to be updated on a regular basis as the event approaches (at least monthly for the last three months, if necessary weekly or, immediately before the event, daily). This permanent information exchange has to be seen in connection with the recommendation of the handbook to 'utilise the available and appropriate legislative measures to prevent individuals or groups considered to be a threat to the maintenance of public order from travelling to the location of the event. For parties to the Schengen Convention, article 2 (2) of the Schengen Convention can be a useful instrument.'[31]

The model for risk analysis provided in Annex A of the 'Security Handbook' illustrates the broad manner in which the recommendations on information exchange are to be interpreted. Reference is made therein to protesters in general, thus opening the door to surveillance, as a preventive measure, of all demonstrators.[32] Listing the information to be transmitted on the basis of this 'Risk analysis of potential demonstrators and other groupings', the EU Network of Independent Experts in Fundamental Rights (CFR–CDF) in its 'Report on the Situation of Fundamental Rights in the European Union in 2003' comments:

> this enumeration of items already gives an indication as to the risks of discrimination and of chilling the exercise of democratic rights to protest such exchange of information may entail. It would be clearly unacceptable if the exercise of freedom of expression or of peaceful assembly led to the prohibition to travel to other countries of the Schengen zone where European summits are held. (EU Network 2004, 67 note 195)

The reference of the handbook to 'strict compliance with national and international law applicable in each case' with regard to the exchange of information (including personal data) in fact does not seem to resolve the problems of data protection mentioned above. Also unresolved (and not discussed) remains the possible tension

---

31 Other parts of the handbook cover operational planning and cooperation (by supplying liaison officers, observers and operational support), training (among others at CEPOL), the media strategy to be followed (to be geared towards openness and transparency, but also providing 'a single point of contact ... for the media to ensure a coordinated media coverage'), evaluation and monitoring, logistics, criminal investigation and prosecution (with no mention of assuring defendants' rights as called for by the European Parliament).

32 A checklist regarding possible measures on the occasion of European Councils and other comparable events explicitly states that the risk analysis 'pertains to groups of peaceful demonstrators as well as to groups of potential troublemakers'. Available at http://www.statewatch.org/news/2003/jul/prot11572en1.pdf (accessed January 2006).

between the application of Article 2(2) of the Schengen Convention and the individual quality of the right to free movement within the EU. As far as the latter is concerned, an Italian initiative led to a Council resolution passed on 29 April 2004, aimed at 'limiting inconveniences' in the application of Article 2(2) and at assuring more effective, better coordinated cooperation at European level.[33] It called, among other things, for targeted information exchange, making possible intelligence-led checks on suspects. The Member States are invited to supply:

> the Member State hosting a European Council meeting or another comparable event with any information available to them on movements, in order to be present at that event, by individuals or groups in respect of whom there are substantial grounds for believing that they intend to enter the Member State with the aim of disrupting public order and security at the event or committing offences relating to the event.

This Council resolution apparently shows closer attention than previous resolutions to the individual quality of the right to free movement within the EU: with obvious reference to the 1964 Directive, it underlines that the mere existence of criminal convictions should not automatically justify the adoption of measures concerning public order and security. In addition, there seems to be an attempt to go beyond the mere reference to relevant legislation with the formulation (however dubious in its efficacy): 'Nothing in this Resolution should be interpreted as departing from the principle that the exchange of personal data shall comply with the relevant national and international legislation.' However, the resolution further specifies that personal data should be used and kept only until the end of the event for which they were supplied and only for the purposes laid down in the Resolution, 'unless agreed otherwise with the Member State which supplied the data'.

The resolution does not eliminate data protection concerns, nor the basic problem inherent in similar measures, that is, the lack of a definition accepted by all EU Member States of 'public order and security' or 'substantial grounds'. This concern emerges, for instance, from the Twentieth Report of the House of Lords Select Committee on the European Union.[34] When it was clarified that the events (comparable to European Council meetings) to which the resolution applied included meetings of the G8 or of senior politicians from two or more Member States, the Committee underlined that the scope of the measure was very wide and the potential implications for the free movement of persons within the Union and for the handling of personal data correspondingly large. In response, the British government referred to the 1998 Data Protection Act. The Committee then argued that the level of protection offered by national legislation, already alleged to be insufficient in the domestic state security context, remained unclear for transnational information exchange. In this context,

---

33   Available at http:// register.consilium.eu.int/pdf/en/03/st13/st13915.en03.pdf (accessed January 2006).

34   Available at http://www.publications.parliament.uk/pa/ld200304/ldselect/ldeucom/119/119.pdf (accessed January 2006).

it recalled that the individual concerned may not know who is holding his or her personal information and to what use it is being put.

As already mentioned, the Council resolution had apparently assured compatibility with the 1964 Directive on free movement. This Directive makes clear that measures like expulsion on the grounds of public policy, public security or public health must be based exclusively on the personal conduct of the individuals concerned. Previous criminal convictions do not qualify in themselves. The Council resolution had, however, specified that information should be exchanged where 'substantial grounds' existed for believing that individuals intended to enter a Member State with the aim of disrupting public order and security at an international event or committing offences related to that event. When the House of Lords Committee asked for clarification of 'substantial grounds', the government answered that information should be passed 'where there is clear evidence that an individual or a group is intent on causing disruption'. Pressed further on what amounted to 'clear evidence', the government replied: 'Whilst it would not be possible to give a definitive criterion of clear evidence, a recent conviction involving violence, incitement or conspiracy at a similar event may show intention to enter with the aim of causing violence once more.' This response was judged 'not very helpful' by the Committee; pressed again, the minister conceded that something more than a recent conviction would be needed in order to establish 'substantial grounds'. This exchange between two British institutions testifies to the difficulties that already exist in a domestic context in defining public order threats connected with public demonstrations.[35]

Data protection concerns are expressed even more forcefully by the EU Network of Independent Experts in Fundamental Rights (CFR–CDF) in its 'Report on the Situation of Fundamental Rights in the European Union in 2003'. Commenting on the draft of the Council resolution, the network argues that it 'provides a striking illustration of the links between the development of a proactive approach to security and the risks that such an approach entails for the protection of privacy, and more particularly the protection of personal data' (EU Network 2004, 66). It further underlines that the information to be shared between national law enforcement authorities may comprise records of criminal conviction, but is not limited to that sensitive information: relevant information may also consist of the identity of individuals 'with a record of having caused disturbances in similar circumstances'.

---

35 These difficulties, which are political and not 'technical', are certainly not resolved by internal police rules. Initially the government had referred to a nine-point risk assessment plan for the UK police to ensure that the sending of the information is necessary to prevent or detect crime or to enforce the rights or freedoms of others; this plan was also to be enacted when clear evidence of intention to cause disruption existed (see Appendix 3 of the Committee's report). The Committee pointed out that the risk assessment did not address the issue of what amounted to 'substantial grounds' or 'clear evidence' and appeared to be concerned with the balancing of competing interests rather than the criteria for identifying the nature or weight of the evidence on one side of the balance. In a letter of 11 March 2004, the government agreed with this evaluation.

This may result in severely restricting the freedom of movement of protesters, wishing to voice their concerns at the international summits where they have the best chances of being heard. Such a restriction to the freedom of movement chills or impedes the exercise of a democratic right to peaceful assembly and demonstration, which is a component of freedom of expression. And the exchange of personal data, in the circumstances envisaged by the Draft Resolution, appears incompatible with the requirement that any interference with the right to respect for private life should be circumscribed by legal rules of a sufficient quality. (EU Network 2004, 67)

In conclusion, the network argues for the adoption of an instrument seeking to reinforce the protection of the individual vis-à-vis the processing of personal data for police cooperation and the other activities of the third pillar, excluded (as mentioned above) from the EU data protection directive. Initially, in fact, the House of Lords Select Committee on European Union in its Twentieth Report had expressed the concern 'that the resolution might be misunderstood as an attempt by the Union and its institutions to shield themselves from public comment and dissent'. In this context, it may be also recalled that the European Court of Human Rights recognizes that:

> to preserve national security, Member States … undeniably need laws that enable the competent domestic authorities to collect and memorise in secret files information on persons…. Nevertheless … the existence of adequate and sufficient guarantees against abuses [are necessary], for a secret surveillance system intended to protect national security creates the risk of undermining, and even destroying, democracy on the grounds of defending it.[36]

The impact of 9/11 on EU justice and home affairs

To a large extent, the EU approach to protest policing developed in a political situation dramatically changed by the terrorist attacks of 9/11. The emergence of terrorism restricted the room for civil rights advocates on two fronts: the defence of transnational protest rights as well as the demands for greater transparency and democratic accountability as far as EU decisions in the area of justice and home affairs. It also reinforced the security rationale of the EU's 'area of freedom, security and justice'.[37]

It has been observed that, as far as the third pillar of the EU is concerned, we have been going round in circles since the attacks on the Twin Towers: when the TREVI group was created in the mid-1970s, anti-terrorism had in fact been the first and primary concern (Den Boer and Monar 2002). This development seems to have had repercussions for authorities' image of protesters: if in the immediate aftermath of Gothenburg violent incidents at street demonstrations continued to be

---

36 CEDH, 26 March 1987, *Leander*, A, vol. 116, p. 6, §59 and §60.

37 For an account of the risks the response to international terrorism may present for civil rights (repeatedly emphasized also in the European Parliament's reports on human rights in the EU), see EU Network 2003b.

connected with football hooliganism and with common crime, after 9/11 civil rights advocates denounced attempts to associate the GJM or at least its radical fringes with subversion.[38] Commenting on the climate at the time of the drafting of the EU Council Framework Decision on combating terrorism, 'Statewatch' editor Tony Bunyan (2002) underlined the difficulty of raising any criticism: 'However, we also knew that events in Gothenburg and Genoa ... were still fresh in the minds of Ministers and officials. Whatever the eventual wording we knew that the majority of EU governments viewed protest at least as "quasi-terrorist".'

The draft of the framework decision drawn up by the European Commission was in fact criticized for a definition of terrorist offences said to be too large and imprecise, allowing the inclusion of methods of action not uncommon to mass movements (like 'unlawful seizure' of 'places of public use' or 'state or government facilities'), previously subject only to light penalties.[39] The difficulties of defining terrorist offences remain visible in the (considerably amended) final Council Framework Decision: its tenth recital affirms the respect for human rights and fundamental freedoms and specifies that:

> nothing in this Framework Decision may be interpreted as being intended to reduce or restrict fundamental rights or freedoms such as the right to strike, freedom of assembly, of association or of expression, including the right of everyone to form and to join trade unions with others for the protection of his or her interests and the related right to demonstrate.[40]

Commenting in particular on the declaration attached to the Council decision, which mentions the case of those who worked to maintain or re-establish democratic values during World War II, the EU Network of Independent Experts in Fundamental Rights commented: 'A reference to a subjective assessment at a moment when the regulation endeavoured to define the offence objectively, illustrates the difficulties encountered in defining the offence of terrorism, in order to apply special treatment to the said offence which differs from those applied to common law offences' (EU Network 2003b, 11).[41]

---

38 At a meeting of specialized prosecutors and members of Pro Eurojust, convened within the framework of the meeting of the European Judicial Network in Stockholm from 18 to 20 June 2001, it was proposed to compare the lists of potential hooligans that the police had exchanged prior to the European football championship in 2000 with the current lists from Gothenburg. In addition, it was affirmed that in most cases criminal organizations were behind such events, as they were so well organized. See Council of the EU, Note General Secretariat, Brussels, 3 July 2001 (10525/01 LIMITE COPEN 34 ENFOPOL 70), available at http://www.statewatch.org/new/2001/aug/10525.pdf (accessed January 2006).

39 Available at http://europa.eu.int/eur-lex/lex/LexUriServ/site/en/com/2001/com2001_0521en01.pdf (accessed January 2006).

40 Available at http://europa.eu.int/eur-lex/pri/en/oj/dat/2002/l_164/l_16420020622en00030007.pdf (accessed January 2006).

41 In general, for the debate surrounding the drafting of the Council Framework Decision, see Mathiesen 2002.

In corroboration of their concerns, civil rights advocates could point to a Spanish initiative that in early 2002 made a direct link between incidents at mass demonstrations and terrorist offences as defined in the Framework Decision on combating terrorism. The draft Council Decision presented by the Spanish presidency proposed the introduction of a standard form for exchanging information on incidents caused by violent radical groups with terrorist links. The Working Party on Terrorism had 'noticed a gradual increase, at various EU summits and other events, in violence and criminal damage orchestrated by radical extremist groups, clearly terrorizing society, to which the Union has reacted by including such acts in Article 1 of the Framework Decision on combating terrorism, where the offence is defined'.[42] The perpetrators of these acts are described as a loose network of groups 'taking advantage of their lawful status to aid and abet the achievement of the aims of terrorist organisations recognized as such within the European Union'. The information gathered was to be used for prevention and, where appropriate, for the prosecution of 'violent urban youthful radicalism increasingly used by terrorist organisations to achieve their criminal aims, at summits and other events arranged by various Community and international organisations'. The proposal met the opposition of other Member States arguing that the incidents at counter-summits should not be confused with terrorism. The Spanish initiative therefore led only to a non-binding resolution in November 2002, which did allow governments wishing to do so to exchange information on movement activists in the name of the fight against terrorism. As a simple recommendation, it was not necessary to consult the European Parliament or the national parliaments.[43]

In addition to provoking concern about a possible erosion of protest rights, the EU response to terrorism led observers to wonder whether to some extent the clock had been turned back regarding democratic and judicial scrutiny of justice and home affairs business (Den Boer and Monar 2002, 19). The EU Network of Independent Experts in Fundamental Rights, in its thematic comment on the Union's response to terrorism (EU Network 2003b, 9), commented: 'In the European Union, the risk to fundamental rights posed by the adoption of measures to fight terrorism are all the greater since democratic and juridical controls are still very inadequate in the current institutional balance.' The lack of democratic legitimacy was judged all the greater since a large part of the measures consisted of implementations of international commitments and positions decided within the UN, further reducing the option of parliamentary control over intergovernmental options. In addition, according to the experts, the deliberate choice of instruments for an important part of the Union's response deprived 'parliamentary institution of all sources of information and possibility of action'.

---

42 Available at http://register.consilium.eu.int/pdf/fr/02/st05/05712-r1f2.pdf (accessed January 2006).

43 Hayes and Bunyan 2004, 263. The adopted text referred to the 'risk that terrorist organizations will use larger international events for carrying out terrorist offences as defined in Article 1 of the Frameworks Decision on combating terrorism'.

In fact, a report of the European Parliament's Committee on Civil Liberties, Justice and Home Affairs (29 September 2004; Final A6-0010/2004) sharply criticized shortcomings in democratic legitimacy and legal certainty in the 'area of freedom, security and justice', underlining a series of problems connected not only with the EU institutional framework, but also more generally with the international character of the response to terrorism. In particular, the report pointed out that the EU intervened in ways which, while formally compatible with the letter of the European treaties, would be considered unlawful in each of the Member States under their own legal systems: adopting legislative acts affecting personal freedom 'without the full involvement of the European Parliament, under derisively restrictive time constraints and without reliable, accurate and complete information'; concluding 'international agreements on extradition and cooperation in criminal matters ... without any form of ratification by the European Parliament or by national parliaments'; taking measures without their being monitored by the European Court of Justice nor at the national level; adopting administrative acts falling within the executive powers of the Commission, effectively bypassing the national legislation of the 25 Member States, for example in the area of data protection.[44]

Looking more generally at the impact of the terrorist emergency on EU justice and home affairs policies, the predominance of the security rationale traditionally present has clearly been reinforced (Den Boer and Monar 2002, 26). In its above-mentioned report, the European Parliament's Committee on Civil Liberties, Justice and Home Affairs had asked not simply to respect fundamental rights, but to promote them, developing a culture of fundamental rights common to the EU institutions and Member States. A similar perspective seems missing from the 'Hague Programme' on freedom, security and justice adopted at the EU Summit on 4–5 November 2004: the section on 'Strengthening Freedom' is devoted almost exclusively to themes like asylum and the control of migration flows, with security-driven restrictive objectives.

As far as information exchange is concerned, the European Council in September 2001, in the repeatedly mentioned absence of clear data protection rules for the third pillar, committed itself to a particular effort to strike a balance between the protection of personal data and law enforcement authorities' need to gain access to data for criminal investigation purposes (Den Boer and Monar 2002, 27). In fact, the Hague Programme embraces the approach of the 'principle of availability', stating that 'The mere fact that information crosses borders should no longer be relevant.' An unpublished overview report on this principle states that EU citizens want 'freedom, security and justice' and that 'It is not relevant to them [citizens] how the competencies are divided (and information distributed) between the different

---

44 Available at http://www.europarl.eu.int/omk/sipade3?PUBREF=-//EP//NONSGML+ REPORT+A6-2004-0010+0+DOC+PDF+V0//EN&L=EN&LEVEL=2&NAV=S&LSTDOC =Y (accessed January 2006).

authorities to achieve that result'.[45] This overview report suggests that not only should all EU law enforcement agencies have access to personal data regarding law and order, but they should also have access to the national administrative systems of all Member States (for example, registrations including legal persons, vehicles, firearms, identity documents and drivers licences as well as aviation and maritime records). This scenario makes even more pressing the need for a specific set of EU data protection rules for police and intelligence authorities.[46] Recently the Commission has presented a proposal for a Council framework decision on the protection of personal data processed in the framework of police and judicial cooperation in criminal matters, the final outcome, however, is still uncertain.[47]

Concluding, it has been underlined that the EU should probably worry more about the longer-term implications of 11 September, in particular about the risk of a complete domination of EU justice and home affairs by an all-encompassing security rationale.

> If left unchecked, this tendency could ultimately reduce one of the most ambitious political projects of the EU of recent years, the 'area of freedom, security and justice', to that of a mere integrated law enforcement zone. This would leave rather little for European citizens to identify with and add to the Union's 'fortress' character towards the outside world. (Den Boer and Monar 2002, 27)

The above-mentioned Hague Programme seems to show little awareness of these risks, devoting attention to the need for building mutual trust and confidence among the various national law enforcement agencies, but not, as far as justice and home affairs are concerned, between EU institutions and agencies and EU citizens.

---

45 'Statewatch Bulletin', March–April 2005 15(2), available at http://www.statewatch.org/news/2005/jul/06eu-data-prot.htm (accessed March 2006).

46 According to the Opinion of the Europol, Eurojust, Schengen and Customs Joint Supervisory Authorities (presented in September 2004 to the House of Lords Select Committee on the European Union Sub-Committee F for their inquiry into EU counter-terrorism activities), a 'new legal framework for the Third Pillar, as advocated by the Commission, could provide for this but only if that legal framework provides for a tailor-made set of rules applicable to law enforcement activities. Simply reaffirming general principles of data protection shall not be sufficient.' Available at http//www.cbpwebnl/downloads_overig/okt2004_opinies_gcas.pdf (accessed January 2006).

47 The text of the proposal is available at http://eur-lex.europa.eu/LexUriServ/site/en/com/2005/com2005_0476en01.pdf (accessed July 2006). For the critical observations of the European Parliament committee on civil rights and freedoms, justice and home affairs see its report dates 18 May 2006, available at www.europarl.eu/omk/sipade3?PUBREF=/EP/NONSGML+REPORT+A6-2006-0192+0+DOC+PDF+V0//EN&L=EN&LEVEL=0&NAV=S&OSTDOC=Y (accessed July 2006).

Conclusion

The turn taken by the policing of GJM demonstrations seems to challenge the overly smooth image of the evolution of political protest that has been portrayed by public order policing studies in recent years. However, one should not too quickly conclude that policing has entered a new era. In fact, many studies had already stressed that notwithstanding a general trend toward pacification, the possibility of reversals, of political radicalization or increased repression, had hardly disappeared (Fillieule and Jobard 1998; Fillieule 1997; D. Waddington 1992).

As a matter of fact, everything indicates that protest, from the decision to engage in it to the forms that it may take in practice, is influenced by factors that do not show a clear trend of institutionalization or routinization. Moreover, the literature has constantly stressed the *selectivity* of protest policing, with different policing styles being implemented in different situations and towards different actors (Fillieule and della Porta 2006; della Porta and Reiter 1998a; Fillieule 1997; P.A.J. Waddington 1994). The recent return of more militarized styles of policing with a growing use of escalated force, especially in the control of demonstrations by the GJM, can be considered as just one more piece of evidence of this selectivity. Still, things seem to have changed at least in one respect. The analysis we conducted here of the practice of EU police cooperation shows that at this level, more than the gap between recognized legal norms and actual practice noted in the area of law enforcement elsewhere (Fillieule 1997; Favre 1993), it is the vagueness or absence of norms, checks and balances that enables the restriction of protester rights.

Leading European police officers see the EU approach to protest policing as increasingly successful and public order policing as one of the key fields for the furthering of EU police cooperation. In his opening address at the tenth meeting of the PCTF (11–12 October 2004), the chairman in fact underlined that organized crime and terrorism were increasingly being fought jointly and that the joint approach was also used 'increasingly and successfully at sports events and demonstrations of anti-globalists'.[48]

The numerous problematic aspects of transnational protest policing, however, possibly infringing upon protesters' rights, remain largely unresolved. In part, these consist in the technical, legal and conceptual problems that the police themselves have to overcome and which can cause faulty input or elaboration of information. The principal problems that we have underlined in our analysis, however, are connected with the lack of transparency and democratic accountability in EU justice and home affairs, evident, for example, in the very existence and institutional position of a group like the PCTF. To all evidence, these problems are even more pronounced for forms and arenas of transnational policing other than the EU.

The problems of transparency and democratic accountability are not alleviated by the fact that the EU protest policing measures we discussed concentrate on

---

48 Available at http://register.consilium.eu.int/pdf/en/04st14/st14094.en04.pdf (accessed March 2006).

information exchange: as underlined above, 'knowledge work' also has concrete and direct operational consequences, especially when connected with proactive policing approaches geared more at 'pre-empting conflict' than at protecting the exercise of the right to peaceful assembly and demonstration.

In addition, the future development of an operational level in EU protest policing seems likely. Already after the incidents in Genoa, German Interior Minister Schily, together with his Italian colleague Scajola, had called for European riot police units. The 2004 Hague Programme refers to Article III-261 of the draft treaty establishing a Constitution for Europe, which sets out the need to 'ensure that operational co-operation on internal security is promoted and strengthened within the Union'. Article III-275 of the same treaty opens the possibility for European laws or framework laws establishing measures concerning operational cooperation.[49]

For the development of a democratic EU, it seems of fundamental importance to overcome the limits in transparency and democratic accountability in justice and home affairs, in particular concerning police cooperation, facilitating public debate and establishing clear rules for full parliamentary and judiciary oversight on all levels. Closely connected is the need to assure respect for transnational protest rights. Recent developments indicate that these processes will probably be long and difficult. The Schengen Borders Code, the first legal instrument in this policy area fully involving the European Parliament in the decision making process, constituted only limited and not substantial progress (see note 7). Also in the future, integration in justice and home affairs will in all probability continue to be driven by the formalizing of informal arrangements and the 'unionizing' of intergovernmental agreements: in May 2005, seven Member States signed the Prüm Treaty, soon re-baptized Schengen III, agreeing to a broadening of cross-border police cooperation, including information exchange and assistance (also through the sending of agents, specialists and advisors) in the case of large events with a cross-border significance, particularly sports events or meetings of the European Council.[50] Considering the institutional structure of the EU and the weakness of the European public sphere, the risk seems high that the shaping of the concrete form of transnational protest rights will be both state and executive driven.

---

49 Some of the practical problems connected with operational transnational police cooperation became evident at the Evian G8, when (on the basis of an intergovernmental agreement) German police units were deployed in Geneva. See 'Rapport de la Commission d'enquête extraparlementaire/G8', available at http://www.etat-ge.ch/grandconseil/data/texte/RD00532.pdf (accessed March 2006).

50 See http://www.statewatch.org/news/2005/jul/17schengen-III.htm (accessed March 2006). The full text of the convention signed (see in particular Articles 13-15, 26) is available at http://www.statewatch.otg/news/2005/aug/Pr%FCm-Convention.pdf (accessed March 2006).

Chapter 8

The Policing of Transnational Protest: A Conclusion

Donatella della Porta and Herbert Reiter

Introduction

Seattle represented a turning point in many ways. Afterward, criticism of neoliberalist forms of globalization and demands for 'another globalization' entered the public debate – as the American weekly *Newsweek* wrote (13 December 1999, 36), 'one of the most important lessons of Seattle is that there are now two visions of globalization on offer, one led by commerce, one by social activism'. The *Financial Times* (31 August 1999) spoke of a sudden shift 'from the triumph of global capitalism to its crisis in less than a decade'. Protest on the issue of globalization has continued around the world, gaining increasing media visibility. From Seattle onwards, almost every international summit of any importance has been accompanied by counter-summits and protest demonstrations that have often received wider press coverage than the official agenda.

As we have described in this book, Seattle also started an escalation in the policing of transnational protest events in Europe and North America, with the development of new techniques and practices for police control.[1] Attention to the policing of demonstrations has also re-emerged in the social sciences, focused on the policing of transnational protest. This research has opened a new debate regarding the style of protest policing in contemporary Western democracies, reflecting upon innovations vis-à-vis the de-escalating, negotiated model that seemed to dominate in the 1980s and well into the 1990s. In particular, tolerance of minor violations of the law, selective police intervention oriented towards protecting the demonstration rights of peaceful protesters, demilitarization of police intervention and reliance upon bargaining and self-policing do not seem to characterize protest policing in the new wave of transnational forms of protest.

---

1 The (largely unexplored) policing of transnational protest in developing countries seems conditioned by a somewhat different set of problems, for instance, low or non-existent democratic standards or the different positions of these countries in the globalization process (which may lead to situations where the police of underdeveloped countries defend First World business interests against their own populations). See Manning 2000, 185; Sheptycki 2005.

In the first part of our concluding remarks, we will discuss whether these new techniques and practices signify the emergence of a new style of protest policing, supplanting the negotiated management style (variously called 'de-escalation', 'policing by consent', or, in the Italian case, 'the prevention model') dominant in western democracies during the 1980s and 90s. In the second section, we will ask whether the explanatory model developed about a decade ago with reference to the policing of protest in democratic countries (della Porta and Reiter 1998b) is still valid for the analysis of the policing of transnational protest.

A new style of protest policing?

Negotiated management signified a considerable departure from the protest policing style dominant in Western democracies prior to the 1960s and 1970s. The traditional escalated force strategy was, in fact, based on a presumption of irrational crowd behaviour (Schweingruber 2000; Le Bon 1895) and rooted in intolerance of direct forms of political participation. Highly suspicious of any gathering, its adherents gave low priority to demonstration rights and foresaw the massive use of force to suppress even small violations of laws and ordinances. During the '1968' protest cycle, attempts to stop unauthorized demonstrations and a law-and-order attitude toward the 'limited-rule-breaking' tactics that spread from the US civil rights movement to the European student movement (McAdam and Rucht 1993) and then to new social movements in general repeatedly manoeuvred the police into 'no-win' situations. The prevailing police strategy after the 1980s was instead designed to avoid coercive interventions as much as possible. Lawbreaking, implicit in nonviolent, civil disobedient forms of protest, tended to be more or less tolerated by the police, with peacekeeping considered more important than law enforcement.

We can review the new elements of the policing of transnational protest presented in the contributions to this volume along three main types of police strategy (see della Porta and Reiter's chapter):

- *coercive strategies*, as the use of coercive force and/or arms to control or disperse a demonstration;
- *persuasive strategies*, as all attempts to control protest through contacts with activists and organisers;
- *information strategies*, as the diffuse gathering of information as a preventive element in the control of protest, as well as the targeted gathering of information (including the use of audio-visual technology), in order to identify those who break the law without having to intervene directly.

We can, first, observe that at recent transnational protest events *coercive strategies* returned as a prominent aspect of protest policing, apparently recalling the 'escalated force' style, although with adaptations to new protest repertoires, police frames and technologies (Table 8.1).[2] A massive police presence, usually with high visibility, has been observed at numerous transnational protest events in North America and Europe. In most of the cases we considered, police officers donned heavy anti-riot gear and, above all, special units were deployed for coercive intervention against 'troublemakers'. Various types of 'less-lethal' arms were often used against demonstrators, from those traditionally deployed by police public order units, such as tear gas and/or water cannons, to newer developments like hand-held irritating sprays and rubber and plastic bullets, which leave the responsibility for their use largely to individual police officers.[3] Live ammunition was used in Gothenburg (three demonstrators wounded) and in Genoa (one demonstrator killed). In Seattle, Windsor and Gothenburg, groups of demonstrators were encircled by police and kept penned in for long periods.[4] Mass arrests, sometimes far from the demonstration venue, were observed in Seattle, Washington, Prague, Quebec City, Gothenburg and Genoa. Most of these arrests were not confirmed by judicial authorities.

These developments emerge as significant departures from the protest policing styles dominant in the 1980s and 1990s. However, it should be recalled that the advent of negotiated management did not signify the disappearance of coercive intervention. Research has frequently stressed the selectivity of police intervention and the survival of harsh modes of protest policing in the 1980s and 1990s (della Porta 1998; Fillieule and Jobard 1998). However, antagonistic interventions with a 'show of force' attitude and a massive, highly visible police presence were generally reserved for small extremist groups – in this period of demobilization not connected with a broader movement – or for a universally stigmatized phenomenon like football hooliganism. In the case of transnational protest events organized by the global justice movement, these features have been observed in conjunction with mass demonstrations of tens of thousands, if not hundreds of thousands of participants. Massive use of force as a strategy for maintaining public order, however, was effective only with a favourable police–demonstrator ratio (as in Canada or Copenhagen; for New York City see Vitale 2005). In cases of massive demonstrations, with large numbers of peaceful demonstrators and small (but highly mobile) groups of the black bloc, shows of force and indiscriminate intervention produced escalation: police brutality against nonviolent participants has been denounced in numerous

---

2   This table and Tables 8.2 and 8.3 are based on reconstructions of police intervention at the transnational protest events presented in this volume and on interviews with experts conducted in the course of the conference 'Policing Political Protest after Seattle', Fiskebäckskil (Sweden), 1–5 May 2004.

3   All components of the mobile divisions deployed at Genoa had been authorized to use handheld spray cans with irritant CS gas to immobilize possible 'antagonists' at close quarters (Hearing 5 September 2001, 75).

4   This technique was also used during the London May Day protests in 2001, when demonstrators were kept penned in for up to seven hours (Atkinson 2001). In Germany, the illegality of this police technique has been repeatedly affirmed by administrative courts, on the basis of a constitutional court decision (see http://www.dortmunder-polizeikessel.de).

Table 8.1   Coercive strategies in the policing of selected transnational protest events

	Seattle December 1999	Washington April 2000	Windsor June 2000	Prague November 2000	Quebec April 2001	Gothenburg June 2001	Genoa July 2001	Calgary/Ottawa June 2002	ESF-Florence November 2002	Copenhagen December 2002	Evian June 2003
Massive police presence	Yes	Yes	Yes	Yes	Yes	Yes	Yes	Yes	Yes	Yes	Yes
High visibility of police	Yes	Yes	Yes	Yes	Yes	Yes*	Yes	No	No	Yes	Yes
Plainclothes policemen	Yes	Yes	Yes	Yes	Yes	Yes	Yes	Yes	Yes	Yes	Yes
Anti-riot gear	Yes	Yes	Yes	Yes	Yes	Yes	Yes	No	No	Yes	Yes
Special police units	Yes	Yes	Yes	–	Yes	Yes	Yes	Yes	No	No	Yes
Units from more than one police force	Yes	Yes	Yes	–	Yes	Yes	Yes	Yes	Yes	Yes	Yes
Police with visible identification	Yes	Yes	No	–	No	Yes	No	No	No	No	No
Mass arrests	Yes	Yes	No	Yes	Yes	Yes	Yes	No	No	No	Yes
Unconfirmed arrests	No	Yes	Yes	Yes	Yes	Yes	Yes	No	No	No	Yes
Encircling/penning in of demonstrators	Yes	No	Yes	–	No	Yes	Yes	No	No	No	Yes
Excessive use of force	Yes	No	Yes	Yes	Yes	Yes	Yes	Yes	No	No	Yes
Water cannons	No	Yes	No	Yes	No	No	Yes	No	No	No	Yes
Tear gas	Yes	Yes	Yes	Yes	Yes	No	Yes	No	No	No	Yes
Handheld spray cans with irritants	Yes	Yes	Yes	No	Yes	No	Yes	No	No	No	–
Rubber bullets	Yes	Yes	Yes	No	Yes	No	Yes	No	No	No	No
Live ammunition	No	No	No	No	No	Yes	Yes	No	No	No	No

*   Police highly visible, but not in conjunction with authorized demonstrations.

transnational protest events, and, as in Gothenburg and Genoa, police charges have triggered violent reactions even by previously peaceful groups of protesters.

What seems to emerge as a particularly new element in the coercive strategies employed is that the use of force in the control of demonstrations does not appear as a last resort. To a certain extent, we witness the further evolution of tendencies already apparent in the 1980s and 1990s. Confronted in the 1980s with an early version of a black bloc acting at the margins of large demonstrations, some European police forces (for instance in Germany) developed specialized teams within public order units, with the task *inter alia* of intervening selectively against violent fringes at demonstrations. They were fundamental to the strategy of *de-escalating force*, combining commitment to dialogue with targeted action against militant factions, to isolate and arrest them without involving peaceful demonstrators. Without returning to the extremes of escalated force, the rationale for the use of coercive strategies in recent years seems to have been a more general control of the forms and of the time and place of protests. If the policing of some transnational protest events, like the EU counter-summit in Copenhagen, can be interpreted as adhering to a similar strategy, overall the instances of unilateral use of force by the police, unprovoked by any violent or illicit behaviour on the part of protesters, indicate that in the tension between 'policing by consent' and 'policing by coercion' the latter philosophy clearly dominated.

This trend is confirmed if we look at the *persuasive strategies* that perhaps best characterize the different protest policing styles. Negotiations (as well as other direct interactions between police and demonstrators) begin prior to protest events: unaltered by interactions 'in the streets', they show most clearly the attitude of the police towards demonstration rights in general and towards targeted groups in particular. Within the escalated force style, persuasive strategies had habitually taken the form of intimidation: the open threat of active use of police power in order to discourage protest. Bargaining between the police and organizers was restricted to the discussion of logistics and left little room for manoeuvring. For the model developing after the protest cycle of the 1960s, the ideal instead was *cooperation*, with police officers and protest organizers collaborating for the common objective of the peaceful development of a demonstration.

What is striking in the cases of transnational protest policing presented in this volume is the strong deterrent – if not intimidating – elements that characterize the *persuasive* strategies employed (see Table 8.2). In the case of counter-summits, there was a much stronger emphasis on isolating political leaders and dignitaries from the risks of contact with demonstrators than on negotiating with organizers to define spaces and limits of protest. In some cases (Gothenburg, Genoa) serious negotiations started late and were more or less haphazard. While negotiations did precede all the protest events covered, with the exception of Copenhagen and then Florence no particular care seems to have been taken in assuring open communication lines during demonstrations, one of the cardinal points of negotiated management; in fact, contacts between authorities and organizers were often interrupted, at Seattle, Prague, Quebec City, Gothenburg and Genoa, among others. Before 9/11, authorities (for instance in Genoa) were already devoting considerable time and energy to discouraging protests during official summits; but after the terrorist attack on the Twin Towers, summits were more often moved to inaccessible areas (for example, the G8 at Kananaskis) or 'no-go' areas for protesters extended even further (up to ten miles for the G8 in the US in June 2004).

Above all, preparations for the 'fortification' of summit sites and, in general, police measures aimed at its protection constituted public messages difficult to reconcile with a negotiating strategy. In fact, deterrence of demonstrators – both in general and in specific areas – was a main strategic element in the policing of transnational protest events. Fences were built in Seattle and (increasingly sophisticated and impenetrable) in Windsor, Washington, Prague, Quebec City, Gothenburg and Genoa. Special trains transporting activists to Prague were blocked at the borders. As far as the European Union is concerned, border controls were routinely reintroduced during international demonstrations within the Schengen area, and numerous potential participants (also EU citizens) were refused entrance, often on a questionable legal basis. In Quebec City as well as in Genoa, checkpoints were set up at the city borders, and railway stations were closed and/or heavily patrolled.

During the prelude to the summit meetings, the police forces in various countries also employed coercive measures not aimed at protecting the official summit, but offensively directed against movement activists and movement strategies. In Genoa, in Copenhagen, and elsewhere, the police were accused of harassing young people who looked like movement activists, employing continuous identity checks and body searches during the days and nights prior to the protest events. Preventive arrests targeted against specific protest actions and accompanied by the confiscation of propaganda material like puppets or banners were denounced in Seattle and afterwards. Police were reported to have entered and searched demonstrators' headquarters, independent media centres, and legal assistance offices (including those located in premises offered by the local authorities) in Washington, Prague, Gothenburg and (with the most dramatic consequences) in Genoa.

As far as the *information strategies* are concerned (see Table 8.3), the literature on transnational policing has underlined the significance of technical innovation and the influence of advanced surveillance, information processing and communications technologies on the way policing is organized.[5] New terms such as 'strategic', 'pro-active', and 'intelligence-led' policing imply approaches for targeting suspect populations and individuals in a highly systematic way. The trend towards intelligence-led policing, first established in the US with the 'war on drugs', is highly evident in transnational protest policing, both in North America and in Europe. The examples provided in the contributions to this volume, however, seem to indicate that the various police forces' capacity for monitoring the 'suspect population' of the 'no global' protesters was not sufficient to allow them to intervene efficiently in a strategic and pro-active way. The massive amount of information collected on single activists and groups and the political (and not criminal) character of the phenomenon of transnational protest seem to have overstretched their analytical capacities.[6]

---

5   Cfr. Sheptycki 2002, 138ff.; see also Sheptycki 2002, 142, on the British example for economic decisions laying the foundation for intelligence-led policing and the adoption of neoliberal approaches to delivering public police services evident elsewhere in the Commonwealth and globally.

6   These misjudgements seem to consist not only of faulty evaluations of the political positions of certain protest groups, but of miscalculations about the effects of intelligence-led and proactive interventions against certain groups in the global justice movement as a whole.

Table 8.2   Persuasive strategies in the policing of selected transnational protest events

	Seattle December 1999	*Washington April 2000*	*Windsor June 2000*	*Prague November 2000*	*Quebec April 2001*	*Gothenburg June 2001*	*Genoa July 2001*	*Calgary/Ottawa June 2002*	*ESF-Florence November 2002*	*Copenhagen December 2002*	*Evian June 2003*
Negotiation (pre)	Yes	Yes	Yes	Yes	Yes	late	late	Yes	Yes	Yes	Yes
Negotiation (during)	Yes	No	No	No	No	Yes	No	Yes	Yes	Yes	Yes
Barriers	Yes	Yes	weak	Yes	Yes	Yes	Yes	No	No	Yes	Yes
Control at the borders	No	weak	No	Yes	No	Yes	Yes	Yes	Yes	Yes	Yes
Denial of entrance at the borders	No	No	Yes	Yes	No	Yes	Yes	Some	Yes	Yes	Yes
Blocking access to protest areas	limited	No	No	Yes	Yes	No	Yes	Yes	No	No	Yes
Preventive arrests	Yes	Yes	Yes	–	Yes	Yes	Yes	Yes	No	Yes	No
Harassment	No	Yes	Yes	Yes	–	Yes	No	some	No	Yes	–
Entering and search of protesters' offices	No	Yes	No	Yes	No	Yes	Yes	No	No	No	Yes (Indymedia)

The phenomenon of transnational policing, with the massive use of databanks and exchange of information among national police forces in order to prevent individuals deemed dangerous from participating in transnational demonstrations, surfaced especially in the European cases, within the institutional framework of the EU. These practices, which often followed the informal rules developed for the control of football hooligans, emerged as opaque in terms of the protection of citizens' rights. Apart from these new problems of democratic accountability, additional shortcomings (re)emerged that had already marred the information strategies employed during previous protest cycles. In Genoa (as, before, in Washington), widespread alarmist use has been made of information later declared unreliable by the same authorities, recalling (among others) the case of the Chicago Congress of the Democratic Party in 1968 (Donner 1990, 116–17). While this alarmism did not discourage participation at the counter-summits, it favoured the spreading, especially among rank-and-file

Table 8.3   Information strategies in the policing of selected transnational protest events

	Seattle December 1999	Windsor June 2000	Washington April 2000	Prague November 2000	Quebec April 2001	Gothenburg June 2001	Genoa July 2001	Calgary/Ottawa June 2002	ESF-Florence Novemer 2002	Copenhagen December 2002	Evian June 2003
Massive collection of information	Yes	No	Yes	–	Yes	-No	Yes	Yes	Yes	Yes	Yes
Use of alarmist information	Some	–	Yes	–	No	No	Yes	No	Some	Some	No
International exchange of information	No	No	No	Yes	No	Some	Yes	Yes	Yes	Yes	Yes
Plainclothes policemen (infiltration and/or agent provocateur)	Yes	Yes	Yes	Yes	Yes	Yes	Yes	Yes	No	Yes	Yes

police officers, of an image of demonstrators as dangerously violent, or even as terrorists (or infiltrated by terrorists). The deployment of plainclothes police, for instance in Copenhagen, was denounced by movement activists for infiltration attempts and what was seen as *agent provocateur* behaviour.[7]

Based on the evidence of our cases, it might be rash to conclude that the negotiated management model has been replaced by a new protest policing style. In addition, it should be recalled that the former had been singled out not as the only, but as the dominant protest policing style of the decades following the 1968 protest cycle. However, at transnational protest events, significant shifts in the control of protest were observed, some of which we synthesize in Table 8.4. There was indeed a return to the massive use of force, especially oriented toward temporary incapacitation, with protesters forced to the margins. Negotiations took place, but trust between negotiators remained low, also because of the uncompromising messages sent by the police with other interventions aimed at protection and prevention during the period leading up to the demonstrations. Finally, there were clear attempts at 'intelligence-led' policing, with much emphasis given to massive collection and frequent exchange of information that does not seem to translate into 'intelligence' or knowledge of the differentiated protest field.

These characteristics certainly constitute a departure from the negotiated management style, with its 'demonstration-friendly' philosophy. In our cases of

---

7   Two of the plainclothes policemen in service at the anti-EU summit demonstrations of 2002 were found guilty of bearing a mask and were fined.

Table 8.4   Styles of protest policing

Type of strategy	Escalated force	Negotiated management	Policing of transnational protest
Coercive strategies	Massive use of force to deter even minor violations	Coercive intervention as a last resort; tolerance of minor breaches	Massive use of force oriented toward temporary incapacitation
Persuasive strategies	Intimidating use of relations with organizers	Partnership aimed at ensuring the right to demonstrate	Deterrence of demonstrators; low trust in negotiation
Information strategies	Generalized and indiscriminate information gathering	Information gathering focused on punishing offences	Massive collection and transnational exchange of information; alarmist use of information

transnational protest policing, if protest was accepted, police strategies tended to make it invisible or un-influential, negating its significance (what King and Waddington call 'exclusionary fortress-oriented policing' and Noakes and Gillham 'selective incapacitation'). Similar developments seem to emerge at the national level: the American Civil Liberties Union brought legal charges against US authorities for the systematic practice of allowing pro-Bush demonstrators high visibility, while containing anti-Bush protesters far from the eyes and ears of the mass media. The right to demonstrate seems to be recognized selectively in more than one way: poorly protected for foreigners, and with the exclusion of direct action protest repertoires defined as illegal and/or violent. In ultimate analysis, the protest policing strategies applied tend to negate the rights of citizens to determine or to co-determine where, when, and how to express their political opinions, instead allocating to the police the power to 'shape' the protest arena by unilateral, if need be preventive and coercive, intervention – not due to a concrete and imminently dangerous situation, but on the basis of a risk analysis that clearly strains the analytical capacities of the police as well as giving insufficient attention to citizens rights' not only to protest, but to do so visibly and audibly.

However, the attempts of the police to 'shape' the protest arena unilaterally, apart from being problematic as far as democratic rights are concerned, did not achieve the objectives in the case of big mass demonstrations and contributed to an escalation of the conflict. Even from within police forces themselves, the use of brutal force at transnational demonstrations has not been perceived as a successful strategy. On the contrary, most strikingly in Genoa, the image of police riots spread even by the mainstream press – with brutal repression of peaceful demonstrators – was perceived as damaging. After Genoa, in Italy as elsewhere, successful attempts were often made to return to a more negotiated approach, if not to the pure form of the negotiated management strategy. Already in Copenhagen, coercive interventions against mass demonstrations were being avoided, in part due to a large investment in negotiations before and during the events (see Wahlström and Oskarsson's as well as Peterson's chapters). The policing of the first European Social Forum (ESF) in Florence and of the mass demonstration against the war in Iraq (about 500,000 participants according to police) that closed it confirmed that negotiations based upon the common aim of promoting the peaceful development of protest could be successful even in delicate situations with large numbers of heterogeneous demonstrators, a virulent, alarmist campaign against the event and little initial trust between police authorities and movement organizers.

The example of the Florence ESF shows some of the conditions necessary for a successful negotiated management strategy, in this case also aided by learning processes (on both sides) after the Genoa disaster (della Porta and Reiter 2004; for the case of Copenhagen see the chapter by Wahlström and Oskarsson in this volume). Negotiations started months in advance and were conducted with a set interlocutor, reducing mutual mistrust. Despite the movement's heterogeneity and a climate of high tension fed by many centre-right public figures and sections of the press, as well as a virulent campaign against the event, both authorities and movement spokespersons saw the dialogue as positive. Indeed, negotiators from both sides stressed that 'we both had a lot at stake, and we knew it'. Even in tense situations, an operational trust, based upon the shared aim of a peaceful protest event, developed on the basis of a series of tests passed by both sides, as well as a common understanding that both managed important resources not only for the maintenance of public order but also for the logistics of the demonstration. The prefect held political responsibility for the deployment of the police, as well as the task of coordinating public authorities for the accommodation of participants in the ESF and the locations of the various events. On their side, movement organizers had the relevant information on the number and characteristics of the demonstrators. The open question of the representativeness of both agents vis-à-vis their principals (the government and the demonstrators), particularly delicate in protest events involving various police bodies as well as heterogeneous movement organizations, was openly addressed by the two parties, with manoeuvring space left for the local police forces as well as local movement organizers.

If the Florence ESF seems to testify to a (possible) return to negotiated management, the examples of Seattle, Gothenburg and Genoa do not represent mere incidents. In the United States, the use of less-lethal arms also became widespread in the control of non-political public disorders (such as campus beer riots; see McCarthy, Martin, and McPhail 2004), while a strategy of encirclement and isolation of demonstrators also extended to domestic demonstrations (see Vitale 2005). In Europe, protest deterrence through the definition of no-go areas spread, together with a growing emphasis on the exchange of intelligence among national police forces. Moreover, tolerance of minor violations was undermined by a bipartisan agreement between right-wing and centre-left parties to label any form of direct action (such as occupations or roadblocks) or even symbolic actions of civil disobedience (such as paying only half-price for public services or books) as violent. With the exception of the Scandinavian countries, discussions within police unions and police in general with regard to changes in the strategies for addressing public order have not been encouraged. Finally, an image of 'no-global' activists as troublemakers is widespread in all of the cases covered in this anthology.

In fact, while there have been visible attempts at avoiding the brutality that characterized the policing of the anti-G8 protest in Genoa, most elements of the strategy we have seen employed at transnational protest events have since been repeated. In June 2002, the anti-G8 demonstrations in Ottawa and Calgary remained peaceful, with a police strategy relying upon negotiations and low police visibility; however, protests were allowed only far from the summit site, the well-protected and isolated mountain resort of Kananaskis. In addition, police did not renounce border controls or the massive collection of information. No public disorders disturbed the EU Summit in Copenhagen in December 2002, where police chief Kai Vittrup on the one hand invested considerable energy in negotiations (beginning one year before the event), but on the other followed a policy of excluding direct actions, even if nonviolent, together with the use of the 'show of force' tactic.[8] The Danish police leadership stressed an aggressive strategy moving from the static control of space (as in Gothenburg) to proactive control of potentially disorderly situations (Peterson, in this volume). At the anti-G8 protests in Evian, the police – with the support of units from various European countries – were present *en masse* and highly visible. Overall, we can discern the widespread employment of the show of force as a tactic of intimidation.

Thus, while on the one hand the strategies employed by American and European police forces in the case of transnational protest events are largely inconsistent with the negotiated management style, on the other hand they do not seem to form a coherent new style of protest policing. Whereas in the US 'selective incapacitation' seems to emerge as dominant, developments in Canada seem more consistent with the traditional model; in Europe, the picture seems more varied and fluid, oscillating in the same country (Italy) between the re-emergence of elements of the escalated force style and an (at least periodic) return to negotiated management, or (as in Denmark) combining a commitment to negotiation with zero tolerance towards all forms of direct action in a 'negotiated force' protest policing style.

This variation and fluidity in the strategies concretely applied 'in the streets', however, seems to hide considerable consistency in the underlying 'police knowledge' – that is, the police's attitude towards demonstrations and definition of their role in a protest situation. Researchers have reminded us that even 'policing by consent' is a police strategy for the *control* of protest events, although it presupposes the accommodation (as far as possible) of organizers' objectives as to the where, when, and how of a demonstration. This attitude has also found legal expression, for

---

8   The Danish police tactic of surprising activists with preventive arrests and the confiscation of propaganda material seems problematic not only from a political and legal point of view, but also from a purely technical one: it seems in fact hardly applicable in the case of big mass demonstrations (see, in this volume, Peterson, and Wahlström and Oskarsson).

instance in a landmark decision by the German constitutional court.[9] In our cases of the policing of transnational protest, the one common element applied in America and in Europe seems to be that police intervene unilaterally (and often proactively), sometimes in a coercive way, in order to determine the where, when and how of demonstrations. On numerous occasions (not only at transnational protest events, but also at national gatherings), police have been accused of intervening not on the basis of security risks, but in order to make the protest invisible, by distancing it physically from the target (and the press) and by preventing spectacular and therefore media-effective protest actions. This budding new protest policing style is therefore less 'demonstration friendly' than negotiated management, not only in its interventions 'in the streets', but also in its very conception of the right to demonstrate: it concedes the freedom of expression, but tends to negate the accompanying right to be heard.

How to explain (changes in) the policing of protest?

If we are witnessing a general and not-yet concluded (re)negotiation of demonstration rights and accepted or tolerated protest repertoires – a phenomenon that accompanies the current protest cycle as it had accompanied previous ones – we do have to underline that this (re)negotiation did not take as a starting point the 'post-1968 standard'. The research presented in this volume confirms the presence of new trends, especially in the policing of transnational protest events, that shake the (naive?) hopes for an evolution of policing towards more tolerance for political challenges. The question of which factors determined this development allows us also to discuss the extent to which the explanatory model presented in *Policing Protest* (della Porta and Reiter 1998b) needs to be updated.

In our introduction to that volume, we suggested explaining the policing of protest based on characteristics both internal and external to the police, with both types of characteristics filtered through *police knowledge* – that is, the cognitive appreciation by the police of their role in society as well as of external demands and challenges (see Figure 8.1). The research presented in this volume indicates that most of these variables are still relevant for explaining differences in police strategies. As for internal factors, national strategies are visible in the styles developed to address the new wave of protest. As Peterson's chapter suggests, in Gothenburg

---

9   The *Brokdorf Urteil* (1985) defines freedom of speech as the noblest human right, fundamental for a democratic order, and characterizes the freedom of assembly as the collective form of freedom of speech, understood as the expression of popular sovereignty and as the right of the citizen to actively participate in the political process. According to this decision, the constitutional protection of the freedom of assembly extends to spontaneous demonstrations and also to peaceful participants in demonstrations for which violent behavior on the part of individuals or of a minority is foreseen. In addition, the German constitutional court obligated public authorities to act in a 'demonstration-friendly' way and actively to seek the cooperation of the organizers of public demonstrations (Winter 1998a, 203s; 1998b, 59ss., 281ss.).

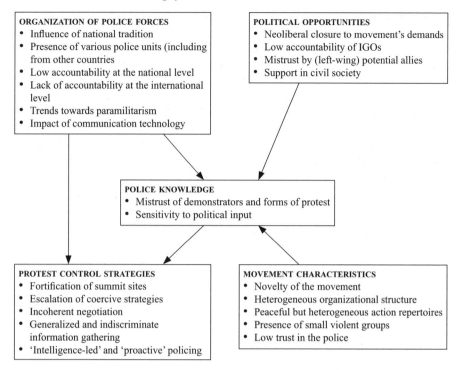

Figure 8.1   Explanations of control strategies of transnational protest

the Swedish police were constrained by their traditional approach to controlling space, unable to adapt to 'deterritorialized' protest strategies. In Genoa, the Italian police tradition of brutal intervention resurfaced and negative consequences of low levels of professionalization and accountability emerged, particularly dramatically in such episodes as the storming of the Diaz school and the mishandling of arrested demonstrators in the Bolzaneto barracks. Differences in police juridical powers can help to explain the capacity of the Danish police to implement preventive controls. The nature of the Canadian public order policing ethos seems in contrast with that of the US (see King and Waddington's chapter).

External factors also remain relevant in explaining police behaviour. Political opportunities have been more or less closed for transnational protest both at home and abroad. At the national level, the global justice movement challenges neoliberal policies that have been popular not only on the right, but also on the left of the parliamentary political spectrum. The movement emerged as particularly strong in the case of centre-right governments, but it also proved very critical of the parliamentary left, perceived not only as domesticated on substantial issues (the labour market, social justice, global distributive justice, etc.), but also more and more elitist in its conception of politics as an activity for professionals. The institutionalization and moderation of social movements in the 1980s and 1990s and their integration into increasingly institutionalized forms of politics contributed – also with a glorified but moderated vision of the '1968' past – to an image of the emerging global justice movement as particularly violent in its action repertoires and particularly poor in its political capacity. The isolation of protestors in the institutional sphere of politics seems to have pushed the police towards harsher strategies, adapted from those applied in preceding decades against weak (politically unprotected) groups and generally stigmatized phenomena like football hooliganism. Some characteristics of the emerging movement – not only its novelty, but also its heterogeneity, loose organizational structures, and use of direct action strategies, as well as widespread distrust of police (see Wahlström and Oskarsson's chapter) – have facilitated police framing of transnational protestors as 'bad demonstrators' (or troublemakers).

For our original model, designed to explain national protest policing styles, to remain useful as an explanatory tool, it must be adapted to the transnational level. In terms of internal factors, we have to add the organizational structures of international policing, its (weak) formal competences and especially the unaccountable culture of informal cooperation (see Reiter and Fillieule's chapter). The international normative system developed in connection with perceived emergencies such as football hooliganism, terrorism and organized crime is now associated with the policing of transnational protest. Little or no protection is given at the international level to the protection of civil liberties, among them demonstration rights. The policing of transnational protest often sees the convergence of different police forces and secret services, as well as the military (see King and Waddington's chapter). Moreover, cross-national exchanges among national police forces have intensified, with international debriefing of police operations and joint preparations as well as co-ordinated interventions.

As for the external variables, transnational protest often targets inter-governmental organizations that offer few channels of access. Notwithstanding the slow development of a transnational public sphere where global problems could be discussed, transnational protests were able to find support from a growing number of international non-governmental organizations and other civil society associations. The main form of transnational protest – counter-summits – presents a specific challenge to police forces obliged to balance respect for demonstration rights with the maintenance of public order and the protection of domestic and especially foreign dignitaries (Ericson and Doyle 1999).

Beyond the adaptation to the transnational dimension, the research collected in this volume also converges in stressing a dynamic that, although mentioned in our explanatory model as part of police knowledge, had remained underspecified: the effect of more general conceptions of policing on protest policing. 'Zero-tolerance' is mentioned in conjunction with the policing of the Kananaskis summit (King and Waddington's chapter; see also Vitale 2005 on the New York City police). As Noakes and Gillham stress in their contribution, the strategic incapacitation approach to the policing of transnational protest in the US reflects the 'new penology' approach, that challenged the previous hopes to intervene on the social causes of crime and focuses instead on the protection of potential victims by the selective incapacitation of those considered as potentially most dangerous. Fundamental in this context is also the impact of the revolution in communications technology on general policing strategies as well as the emergence of a trend towards 'intelligence-led' and 'proactive' policing. The militarization of public order control reflects the augmentation of paramilitary units, used for instance in the intervention against drug dealers, as well as the growth of a military culture exemplified by police training, armament, uniforms and more (on the US, see Kraska and Kaeppler 1997; Kraska 1996). Less-lethal arms have been tested in non-political public order policing (for instance, in response to beer riots on US campuses; see McCarthy, Martin and McPhail 2004). In particular, the struggle against international terrorism is often cited to justify 'zero tolerance' against protesters.

Finally, this volume also points at another macro dimension that intervenes in determining police control of protest: the broader trends in the relationship between states and societies. Research in the 1970s and 1980s had stressed the institutionalization of social movement organizations and the normalization of protest, considered as progressively better accepted in more and more democratic states. The repressive turn in the 1990s and early 2000s reflects the crisis of the welfare state, with its mid-century compromise between a capitalist economy and state intervention oriented to reduce social inequalities (Crouch 2004) and to integrate divergent interests. The toughening of protest policing resonates with a neoliberal approach that restricts the function of the state to guaranteeing (external and internal) security and the free play of market forces.

Bibliography

Adang, Otto, and Christine Cuvelier (2001), *Policing Euro 2000. International Police Cooperation, Information Management and Police Deployment*, Beek: Tandem-Felix.

Adelaide, David (2002), 'G-8 Security Operation – The Stifling and Criminalizing of Dissent', http://www.wsws.org/articles/2002/jun2002/g8-j27.shtml.

Alexander, Lexi R. and Julia L. Klare (1995–96), 'Nonlethal Weapons: New Tools for Peace; Today's Peacekeeping and Humanitarian Missions Often Call for the Use of Force That Will Not Result in Death or Destruction', *Issues in Science and Technology* 12: 67–74.

Allen, S. (2003), 'Velvet Gloves and Iron Fist: Taking the Violence Out of Major International Protests', *The Police Chief* 70(2): 50–5.

American Friends Service Committee (1971), *Struggle for Justice: A Report on Crime and Punishment in America*, New York: Hill & Wang.

Anderson, Malcolm, Monica den Boer, Peter Cullen, William Gilmore, Charles Raab and Neil Walker (1995), *Policing the European Union*, Oxford: Clarendon Press.

Anderson, S. (2001), 'Revelry in Quebec', *Progressive* 65(6): 24–7.

Andretta, Massimiliano, Donatella della Porta, Lorenzo Mosca and Herbert Reiter (2002), *Global, noglobal, new global: La protesta contro il G8 a Genova*, Bari–Rome: Laterza.

Apap, Joanna, and Sergio Carrera (2003), 'Maintaining Security within Borders: Towards a Permanent State of Emergency in the EU?', Centre for European Policy Studies, Policy Brief No. 41.

Ashley, Laura, and B. Olsen (1998), 'Constructing Reality: Print Media's Framing of the Women's Movement, 1966–1986', *Journalism and Mass Communication Quarterly* 75(2): 263–77.

Atkinson, Ian (2001), 'May Day 2001 in the UK, the News Media and Public Order', *Environmental Politics* 10(3): 145–50.

Auerhahn, Kathleen (1999), 'Selective Incapacitation and the Problem of Prediction', *Criminology* 37(4): 703–34.

Barkan, Steven E. (1984), 'Legal Control of the Southern Civil Rights Movement', *American Sociological Review* 49: 552–65.

Barnard, Catherine, and Ivan Hare (1997), 'The Right to Protest and the Right to Export: Police Discretion and the Free Movement of Goods', *Modern Law Review* 60(3): 394–411.

Bauman, Zygmunt (2002), *Society Under Siege*, Cambridge: Polity Press.

Bayley, David (1994), *Police for the Future*, New York and Oxford: Oxford University Press.

Beasley, Norman, Thomas Graham and Carl Holmberg (2000), 'Justice Department Civil Disorder Initiatives Addresses Police Training Gap', *The Police Chief* 67(10): 113–22.

Bédoyan, Isabelle, Peter Van Aelst and Stefaan Walgrave (2004), 'Limitations and Possibilities of Transnational Mobilization. The Case of the EU Summit Protesters in Brussels, 2001', *Mobilization* 9(1): 39–54.

Bendix, Reinhard (1964), *Nation Building and Citizenship. Studies of Our Changing Social Order*, New York: Wiley & Son.

Benford, Robert, and David Snow (2000), 'Framing Processes and Social Movements: An Overview and Assessment', *Annual Review of Sociology* 26: 611–39.

Berger, Peter L., and Thomas Luckmann (1967), *The Social Construction of Reality: A Treatise in the Sociology of Knowledge*, Garden City, New York: Doubleday.

Bergman, B. (2002a), 'Wilderness Worries', *Maclean's* 115(17), 29 April.

Bergman, B. (2002b), 'Ready for the G8', *Maclean's* 115(24), 17 June.

Betänkande av Göteborgskommittén (2002), SOU 2002:122, Stockholm: Fritzes Offentliga Publikationer.

Betz, Katrina (2000), 'General Investigation Report. Pennsylvania State Police. Incident No. K1–009948', 1 August.

Beveridge, Dirk (1999), 'Tear Gas Fired on Demonstrators Against World Trade Organization', *Associated Press State and Local Wire*, 30 November.

Bird, J. (2002), 'Dissent Without Tear Gas', http://www.ucobserver.org/archives/sep02_nation.htm.

Bittner, Egon (1967), 'The Police Skid-Row', *American Sociological Review* 32: 699–715.

Björk, Micael (2004), 'Legal Space and the Policing of Protest: Between Frustration and Aggression in Sweden and Denmark, 2001–2002', paper presented at the conference 'Policing Political Protest after Seattle', Fiskebäckskil, Sweden, 5 May 2004.

Björk, Micael, and Abby Peterson (eds) (2002), *Vid politikens yttersta gräns: Perspektiv på EU-toppmötet i Göteborg 2001*, Stockholm: Brutus Östlings Bokförlag Symposion.

Boskey, S. (2001), 'Dangerous Change in Police Tactics', http://goods.perfectvision.ca/FTAA/ViewBrief.cfm?REF=60.

Bourdieu, Pierre (1980), *Le sens pratique*, Paris: Minuit.

Brearley, Nigel, and Mike King (1996), 'Policing Social Protest: Some Indicators of Change', in C. Critcher and D. Waddington (eds), *Policing Public Order: Theoretical and Practical Issues*, Aldershot: Avebury, pp. 101–16.

Bunyan, Tony (2002), 'The "War on Freedom and Democracy". An Analysis of the Effects on Civil Liberties and Democratic Culture in the EU', Statewatch analysis 13, http://www.statewatch.org/news/2002/sep/analy13.pdf.

Bunyan, Tony (2006), 'The EU's Police Chief Task Force (PCTF) and Police Chiefs Committee', Statewatch analysis, http://database.statewatch.org/unprotected/article.asp?aid=26928.

Burgess, John (2000), 'Protesters at WTO Plan D.C. Follow-Up', *Washington Post*, 26 January: E1.

Burgess, Timothy, Carlos de Imus, Bruce Heller, Dorothy Mann, Eric Schnapper and Ruth Schroeder (2000), 'Report to the Seattle City Council WTO Accountability Committee by the Citizens' Panel on WTO Operations', 7 September.

Busch, Heiner (2002), 'Vor neuen Gipfeln. Über die Schwierigkeiten internationaler Demonstrationen', *Bürgerrechte & Polizei/Cilip* 72: 53–7.

Campbell, Duncan (1980), 'Society under Surveillance', in P. Hain (ed.), *Policing the Police 2*, London: Calder, pp. 37–61.

Campbell, D., and M. Shahin (2002), 'Ottawa Police Brace for G8', http://members. rogers.com/citizenspanel/citizen_may_16.html.

Canadian Security Intelligence Service (CSIS) (2000), 'Anti-Globalization – A Spreading Phenomenon', report #2000/08, http://www.csis.gc.ca/en/publications/ perspectives/200008.asp.

Canadian Security Intelligence Service (2002), *Militant Anti-globalization Tactics*, Ottawa: CSIS (Restricted Access).

Caredda, Giorgio (1995), *Governo e opposizione nell'Italia del dopoguerra*, Rome–Bari: Laterza.

CBC News (2000a), 'Protest Peaceful as Oil Meeting Opens in Calgary', 12 June, http://cbc.ca/cgi-bin/templates/view.cgi?/news/2000/06/11/oil_opens000611.

CBC News (2000b), 'Calgary Ready for Worst as Oil Meeting Opens', 14 June, http://cbc.ca/cgi-bin/templates/view.cgi?/news/2000/06/11/oil_opens000611.

CBC News (2001a), 'Security Tight as G-20 Meeting Begins in Ottawa', 16 November, http://cbc.ca/cgi-bin/view.cgi?/news/2001/11/16/ottawa_meet0111176.

CBC News (2001b), 'G-20 Makes Promises, Protesters Make Noise', 18 November, http://cbc.ca/cgi-bin/view?/news/2001/11/17/g20_011117.

CBC News (2002), 'The Activists', 31 March, http://www.cbc.ca/news/features/g8/ activists.html.

Chabanet, Didier (2002), 'Les marches européennes contre le chômage, la précarité et les exclusions', in R. Balme, D. Chabanet and V. Wright (eds), *L'action collective en Europe*, Paris: Presses de Sciences Po, pp. 461–94.

Chang, J., B. Or, E. Tharmendran, E. Tsumara, S. Daniels and D. Leroux (2001), *Resist! A Grassroots Collection of Stories, Poetry, Photos and Analysis from the Québec City FTAA Protests and Beyond*, Halifax: Fernwood.

Chiesa, Giulietto (2001), *G8/Genova*, Turin: Einaudi.

Citizens Panel on Policing and the Community (CPPC) (2002), *Overview Report and Recommendations*, Ottawa: CPPC.

Civil Liberties Association, National Capital Region (CLANCR) (2002), 'Letter from the CLANCR President to the Ottawa Police Service Deputy Chief', 30 September, http://members.rogers.com/witnessgroup/civil_liberties_letter_to_ol ice.html.

Cockburn, Alexander, Jeffrey St. Clair and Allan Sekula (2000), *5 Days That Shook the World*, London: Verso.

Colomba, Gianpiero (2003), 'Polizia e ordine pubblico: Il controllo della protesta e della violenza negli stadi', doctoral thesis, University of Florence, Faculty of Political Science 'Cesare Alfieri'.

Commission for Public Complaints Against the RCMP (CPC) (2000), *Chair's Interim Report With Respect to the Events of May 2 to 4 1997 in the Communities of Saint-Sauveur and Saint-Simon, New Brunswick*, Ottawa: CPC.

Commission for Public Complaints Against the RCMP (CPC) (2001a), *Chair's Final Report With Respect to the Events of May 2 to 4 1997 in the Communities of Saint-Sauveur and Saint-Simon, New Brunswick*, Ottawa: CPC.

Commission for Public Complaints Against the RCMP (CPC) (2001b), *Commission Interim Report Following a Public Hearing into the Complaints Regarding the Events that Took Place in Connection with Demonstrations During the Asia Pacific Economic Cooperation Conference in Vancouver, B.C. in November 1997 at the UBC Campus and Richmond Detachments of the RCMP*, Ottawa: CPC.

Commission for Public Complaints Against the RCMP (CPC) (2002), *Chair's Final Report Following a Public Hearing into the Complaints Relating to RCMP Conduct at Events that Took Place at the UBC Campus and Richmond RCMP Detachment During the Asia Pacific Economic Cooperation Conference in Vancouver, B.C. in November 1997*, Ottawa: CPC.

Commonwealth vs. Kathleen Sorenson (2000), 'Court Transcript, Municipal Courts of Philadelphia', 10 August.

Cook, Joseph W. III, Maura T. McGowan and David P. Fiely (1994/1995), 'Non-Lethal Weapons Technologies, Legalities, and Potential Policies', *USAFA Journal of Legal Studies* 5: 23–43.

Couloumbis, Angela, Maria Pangritis and Diane Marshall (2000), 'With No Warning, Clashes Begin', *Philadelphia Inquirer*, 2 August: AA1.

Crime Control Digest (1992a), 'Detroit, LAPD Looking at the Use of Non-Lethal Weapons', *Crime Control Digest* 26: 9–10 (30 November).

Crime Control Digest (1992b). 'LAPD Uses Rubber Bullets to Quell Disturbance', *Crime Control Digest* 26: 5–6 (21 December).

Critcher, Chas, and David Waddington (eds) (1996), *Policing Public Order: Theoretical and Practical Issues*, Aldershot: Avebury.

Crouch, Colin (2004), *Post Democracy*, Cambridge: Polity.

Cunningham, David (2004), *There's Something Happening Here: The New Left, the Klan and FBI Counterintelligence*, Berkeley: University of California Press.

Curet, Monique, and Helen Kennedy (2000), 'Protesters Fight Cops in the Streets', *New York Daily News*, 24 August.

Czech News Agency (2000), 'Czech Police Bracing Themselves to Avert Another Seattle', *Global News Wire*, 20 September.

Dasgupta, Partha (1988), 'Trust as a Commodity', in D. Gambetta (ed.), *Trust: Making and Breaking Cooperative Relations*, Oxford: Blackwell, pp. 49–72.

Davenport, Christian (1995), 'Multi-dimensional Threat Perception and State Repression: An Inquiry into Why States Apply Negative Sanctions', *American Journal of Political Science* 39: 683–713.

Davenport, Christian (ed.) (2000), *Paths to State Repression: Human Rights Violations and Contentious Politics*, Boulder, CO and New York: Rowman and Littlefield.

Davenport, Christian (2005a), 'Understanding Covert Repressive Action: The Case of the U.S. Government against the Republic of New Africa', *Journal of Conflict Resolution* 49: 120–40.

Davenport, Christian (2005b), 'Introduction. Repression and Mobilization: Insights from Political Science and Sociology', in C. Davenport, H. Johnston and C. Mueller (eds), *Repression and Mobilization*, Minneapolis: University of Minnesota Press, pp. vii–xli.

De Hert, Paul (2004), 'Division of Competencies between National and European Levels with Regard to Justice and Home Affairs', in J. Apap (ed.), *Justice and Home Affairs in the EU. Liberty and Security Issues after Enlargement*, Cheltenham and Northampton, MA: Edward Elgar, pp. 55–99.

Deflem, Mathieu (2002), *Policing World Society: Historical Foundations of International Police Cooperation*, Oxford: Clarendon Press.

della Porta, Donatella (1995), *Social Movements, Political Violence, and the State: A Comparative Analysis of Italy and Germany*, Cambridge: Cambridge University Press.

della Porta, Donatella (1996), 'Socal Movements and the State: Thoughts on the Policing of Protest', in D. McAdam, J. McCarthy and M. Zald (eds), *Comparative Perspectives on Social Movements. Political Opportunities, Mobilizing Structures and Cultural Framings*, Cambridge: Cambridge University Press, pp. 62–92.

della Porta, Donatella (1998), 'Police Knowledge and Protest Policing: Some Reflections on the Italian Case', in D. della Porta and H. Reiter (eds), *Policing Protest: The Control of Mass Demonstrations in Western Democracies*, Minneapolis: University of Minnesota Press, pp. 228–52.

della Porta, Donatella (2004), 'Multiple Belongings, Tolerant Identities and the Construction of Another Politics: Between the European Social Forum and the Local Social Fora', in D. della Porta and S. Tarrow (eds), *Transnational Protest and Global Activism*, Lanham, MD: Rowman and Littlefield, pp. 175–202.

della Porta, Donatella (2006), 'Social Movements and the European Union: Eurosceptics or Critical Europeanists?', Notre Europe Policy Paper 22, July.

della Porta, Donatella, Massimiliano Andretta, Lorenzo Mosca and Herbert Reiter (2006), *Globalization from Below. Transnational Activists and Protest Networks*, Minneapolis and London: University of Minnesota Press.

della Porta, Donatella, and Olivier Fillieule (2004), 'Policing Social Movements', in D. Snow, S. Soule and H. Kriesi (eds), *The Blackwell Companion to Social Movements*, Oxford: Blackwell, pp. 217–41.

della Porta, Donatella, and Herbert Reiter (1997), 'Police du gouvernement ou des citoyens?', *Les Cahiers de la sécurité intérieure* 27: 36–57.

della Porta, Donatella, and Herbert Reiter (eds) (1998a), *Policing Protest: The Control of Mass Demonstrations in Western Democracies*, Minneapolis: University of Minnesota Press.

della Porta, Donatella, and Herbert Reiter (1998b), 'Introduction: The Policing of Protest in Western Democracies', in D. della Porta and H. Reiter .(eds), *Policing Protest: The Control of Mass Demonstrations in Western Democracies*, Minneapolis: University of Minnesota Press, pp. 1–32.

della Porta, Donatella, and Herbert Reiter (2003), *Polizia e protesta. Il controllo dell'ordine pubblico in Italia dalla Liberazione ai 'noglobal'*, Bologna: Il Mulino.

della Porta, Donatella, and Herbert Reiter (2004), *La protesta e il controllo. Movimenti e forze dell'ordine nell'era della globalizzazione*, Milan and Piacenza: Altreconomia and Berti.

Den Boer, Monica (ed.) (1997), *Undercover Policing and Accountability from an International Perspective*, Maastricht: European Institute of Public Administration.

Den Boer, Monica, and Jörg Monar (2002), '11 September and the Challenge of Global Terrorism to the EU as a Security Actor', *Journal of Common Market Studies* 40 (Annual Review): 11–28.

Den Boer, Monica, and William Wallace (2000), 'Justice and Home Affairs', in H. Wallace and W. Wallace (eds), *Policy-making in the European Union*, Oxford: Oxford University Press, pp. 493–530.

Denza, Eileen (2002), *The Intergovernmental Pillars of the European Union*, Oxford: Oxford University Press.

Donner, Frank (1990), *Protectors of Privilege*, Berkeley: University of California Press.

Drake, John, and Gerald Mizejewski (2000), 'D.C. Police Arrest Hundreds, Then Free Many', *Washington Times*, 16 April: C1.

Driller, Ulrich (2001), '"Wir können auch anders" – "Wir aber nicht". Möglichkeiten und Grenzen des polizeilichen Konzepts "Konfliktmanagement" im CASTOR_ Einsatz 2001. Entwicklung, Evalution, Diskussion', *Polizei & Wissenschaft* 3: 29–50.

Duncan, James C. (1998), 'A Primer on the Employment of Non–Lethal Weapons', *Naval Law Review* 45: 1–56.

Dvorak, Petula, and Michael Ruane (2000), 'Police, Protesters Claim Victory', *Washington Post*, 17 April: A1.

Earl, Jennifer (2003), 'Tanks, Tear Gas and Taxes', *Sociological Theory* 21: 44–68.

Earl, Jennifer, Sarah A. Soule and John McCarthy (2003), 'Protest Under Fire? Explaining Protest Policing', *American Sociological Review* 69: 581–606.

Emsley, Clive and Richard Bessel (2000), 'Introduction', in R. Bessel and C. Emsley (eds), *Patterns of Provocation: Police and Public Disorder*, New York and Oxford: Berghahn Books, pp. 1–9.

Ericson, Richard, and Aaron Doyle (1999), 'Globalization and the Policing of Protest: The Case of APEC 1997', *British Journal of Sociology* 50(4): 589–608.

Ericson, Richard, and Kevin Haggerty (1997), *Policing the Risk Society*, Oxford: Clarendon Press.

EU Network of Independent Experts in Fundamental Rights (CFR–CDF) (2003a), 'Report on the situation of fundamental Rights in the European Union and its Member States in 2002', drafted upon request of the European Commission, http://europa.eu.int/comm/justice_home/cfr_cdf/doc/rapport_2002_en.pdf.

EU Network of Independent Experts in Fundamental Rights (CFR–CDF) (2003b), 'The Balance Between Freedom and Security in the Response by the European Union and its Member States to the Terrorist Threats', thematic comment drafted upon request of the European Commission, http://europa.eu.int/comm/justice_home/cfr_cdf/doc/obs_thematique_en.pdf.

EU Network of Independent Experts in Fundamental Rights (CFR–CDF) (2004), 'Report on the Situation of Fundamental Rights in the European Union in 2003', drafted upon request of the European Commission, http://europa.eu.int/comm/justice_home/cfr_cdf/doc/report_eu_2003_en.pdf.

Favre, Pierre (1993), 'La manifestation entre droit et politique', in CURAPP, *Droit et politique*, Paris: PUF, pp. 281–92.

Favre, Pierre, Olivier Fillieule and Nonna Mayer (1997), 'La fin d'une étrange lacune de la sociologie des mobilisations. L'étude par sondage des manifestants: fondements théoriques et solutions techniques', *Revue Française de Science Politique* 1: 3–28.

Fears, Darryl (2000), 'For the Men in Black, Anarchy Makes Sense', *Washington Post*, 17 April: A6.

Feeley, Malcolm, and Jonathan Simon (1992), 'The New Penology: Notes on the Emerging Strategy of Corrections and Its Implications', *Criminology* 30: 449–74.

Fillieule, Olivier (1997), *Stratégies de la rue. Les manifestations en France*, Paris: Presses de Sciences Po.

Fillieule, Olivier, and Philippe Blanchard (2005), 'Carrières militantes et engagements contre la globalisation', in E. Agrikoliansky and I. Sommier (eds), *Radiographie du mouvement altermondialiste: Le second Forum Social Europeén*, Paris: La Dispute, pp. 157–83.

Fillieule, Olivier, Philippe Blanchard, Eric Agrikoliansky, Marko Bandler and Florence Passy (2004), 'L'altermondialisme en réseaux: Trajectoires militantes, multipositionnalité et formes de l'engagement: les participants du contre-sommet du G8 d'Evian (2003)', *Politix* 17(67): 13–48.

Fillieule, Olivier, and Donatella della Porta (eds) (2006), *Policiers et manifestants. Maintien de l'ordre et gestion des conflits collectives*, Paris: Presses de Sciences Po.

Fillieule, Olivier, and Fabien Jobard (1998), 'The Policing of Protest in France. Towards a Model of Protest Policing', in D. della Porta and H. Reiter (eds), *Policing Protest: The Control of Mass Demonstrations in Western Democracies*, Minneapolis: University of Minnesota Press, pp. 70–90.

Finnegan, William (2000), 'After Seattle: Anarchists Get Organized', *New Yorker*, 17 April: 40–51.

Fisher, William V. (2001), Personal interview with Commanding Officer of the Philadelphia Police Department's Civil Affairs Unit, 31 May.

Francisco, Ronald A. (1996), 'Coercion and Protest: An Empirical Test in Two Democratic States', *American Journal of Political Science* 40: 1179–204.

Francisco, Ronald A. (2005), 'The Dictator's Dilemma', in C. Davenport, H. Johnston and C. Mueller (eds), *Repression and Mobilization*, Minneapolis: University of Minnesota Press, pp. 58–83.

Genoa Legal Forum (2002), *Dalla parte del torto. Avvocati di strada a Genova*, Genoa: Fratelli Frilli.

Gainer, Terrance (2001), Personal interview with Executive Assistant Chief of Washington D.C. Metropolitan Police Department, 3 July.

Garland, David (1985), *Punishment and Welfare: A History of Penal Strategies*, Aldershot: Gower.

Garland, David (2001), *The Culture of Control: Crime and Social Order in Contemporary Society*, Chicago: University of Chicago Press.

George, Susan (2001), 'J'étais a Goteborg', *Courriel d'information ATTAC* 246: 1–4.

Gillham, Patrick F. (1999), Activist Field Interviews in Seattle, WA, 27 November–2 December.

Gillham, Patrick F. (2000), Activist Field Interviews in Washington, DC, 16 April.

Gillham, Patrick F. (2003), 'Mobilizing for Global Justice: Social Movement Organization Involvement in Three Contentious Episodes, 1999–2001', Ph.D. dissertation, Department of Sociology, University of Colorado, Boulder, CO.

Gillham, Patrick, and Gary Marx (2000), 'Complexity and Irony in Policing and Protesting: The World Trade Organisation in Seattle', *Social Justice* 27(2): 212–36.

Gitlin, Todd (1980), *The Whole World is Watching*, Berkeley: University of California Press.

Goffman, Erving (1959), *The Presentation of Self in Everyday Life*, London: Penguin Books.

Goffman, Erving (1974), *Frame Analysis. An Essay on the Organization of Experience*, Boston: Northeastern University Press.

Griebenow, Olaf, and Heiner Busch (2001), 'Weder Reisefreiheit noch Demonstrationsrecht in der EU?', *Bürgerrechte & Polizei/Cilip* 69(2): 63–9.

Gubitosa, Carlo (2003), *Genova nome per nome. Le violenze, i responsabili, le ragioni. Inchiesta sui giorni e i fatti del G8*, Milan and Piacenza: Altreconomia and Berti.

Gupta, Dipak K., Harinder Singh and Tom Sprague (1993), 'Government Coercion of Dissidents: Deterrence or Provocation?', *Journal of Conflict Resolution* 37: 301–39.

Gurr, Ted (1986), 'Persisting Patterns of Repression and Rebellion: Foundations for a General Theory of Political Coercion', in Margaret Karms (ed.), *Persistent Patterns and Emergent Structures in a Waning Century*, New York: Praeger, pp. 149–168.

Habermas, Jürgen (1998), *The Inclusion of the Other*, Cambridge, MA: MIT Press.

Habermas, Jürgen (2001), *The Postnational Constellation: Political Essays*, Cambridge: Polity.

Harris, Linda (2000a), 'Push for ERA Inspired Life of Work for Women, Gay Rights and AIDS Issues', *Philadelphia Inquirer*, 13 August: A1.

Harris, Linda (2000b), 'Charges Dropped Against 38 Convention Protesters', *Philadelphia Inquirer*, 28 November: B1.

Harris, Linda, and Craig McCoy (2000), 'Accused Protest Leader is Cleared of All Charges', *Philadelphia Inquirer*, 15 November: A1.

Harris, Linda, and Craig McCoy (2001), 'Protester Convicted of 1 Charge, Acquitted on 3', *Philadelphia Inquirer*, 18 March: E2.

Hayes, Ben, and Tony Bunyan (2004), 'The European Union and the "Internal Threat" of the Alternative World Movement', in F. Polet and CETRI (eds), *Globalizing Resistance. The State of Struggle*, London: Pluto, pp. 258–71.

Hoyle, Charles (1998), *Negotiating Domestic Violence: Police, Criminal Justice and Victims*, Oxford: Oxford University Press.

Ifflander, Henrik (2002), 'Protesthanteringens kulturella inramning – En jämförelse av opinionsbildningens roll i Sverige och Danmark vid utvecklingen av polisens protesthantering', unpublished manuscript, CD essay, Department of Sociology, Gothenburg University.

Imig, Doug (2004), 'Contestation in the Streets: European Protest and the Emerging Euro-politics', in G. Marks and M.R. Steenberger (eds), *European Integration and Political Conflict*, Cambridge: Cambridge University Press, pp. 216–34.

Imig, Doug, and Sidney Tarrow (eds) (2002), *Contentious Europeans. Protest and Politics in an Emerging Polity*, Lanham, MD: Rowman and Littlefield.

Info Shop (2004), 'Black Bloc for Dummies', http://www.infoshop.org/blackbloc/faq.html.

Innes, M. (2000), 'Professionalising the Role of the Police Informant: The British Experience', *Policing and Society* 9(4): 357–84.

Jaffe, Mark (2000), 'A Disobedience School for Would-Be Protesters', *Philadelphia Inquirer*, 10 April: A1.

Jaime-Jimenez, Oscar, and Fernando Reinares (1998), 'The Policing of Mass Demonstrations in Spain: From Dictatorship to Democracy', in D. della Porta and H. Reiter (eds), *Policing Protest: The Control of Mass Demonstrations in Western Democracies*, Minneapolis: University of Minnesota Press, pp. 166–87.

Jefferson, Tony (1990), *The Case Against Paramilitary Policing*, Milton Keynes: Open University Press.

Jenkins, J. Craig, and Charles Perrow (1977), 'The Insurgency of the Powerless: Farm Worker Movements (1946–1972)', *American Sociological Review* 42: 249–68.

Jett, Monty B. (1997), 'Pepper Spray: Training for Safety', *FBI Law Enforcement Bulletin* 66: 17–23.

Jurgens, Erik (2001), 'National Parliamentary Control on Justice and Home Affairs Policy Making', *Integrated Security in Europe. A Democratic Perspective*, special edition of *Collegium, News of the College of Europe* 22: 84–9.

Kahn, Joseph (2000), 'Prague Journal: Protesters Assemble, Hoping for Rerun of Seattle's Show', *New York Times,* 22 September: A4.

Karpantschof, Rene, and Flemming Mikkelsen (2002), 'Fra slumstormere til autonome – husbesættelse, ungdom og social protest i Danmark 1965–2001', in F. Mikkelsen (ed.), *Bevægelser i demokrati. Foreninger og kollektive aktioner i Danmark*, Aarhus: Aarhus Universitetsforlag, pp. 99–129.

Kaufman, L.A. (2002), 'A Short History of Radical Renewal', in Benjamin Shepard and Ronald Hayduk (eds), *From Act Up to the WTO*, New York: Verso, pp. 35–41.

Keary, Jim, and Clarence Williams (2000), 'Hundreds Arrested as IMF Meets; Police Make Deal With Protesters', *Washington Times*, 18 April: A1.

Kenny, John M. (2000), 'What's So Special About Non-Lethal Weapons, Human Effects – Everything', *Marine Corps Gazette* 84: 28–9 (June).

Kerner, Otto (1968), *Report on the National Advisory Commission on Civil Disorders*, New York: Dutton.

Kerr, J. (2002), 'Turning the Page on Public Order Events: Community Relations Group Breaks Down the Barriers', *Pony Express: The RCMP's National Magazine* (June): 6–8.

Killam, D. (2001), 'The Royal Canadian Mounted Police and Public Order: An Evaluation', unpublished masters project, Kingston: Queen's University.

King, Mike (1997), 'Policing and Public Order Issues in Canada: Trends for Change', *Policing & Society* 8(1): 47–76.

King, Mike and Nigel Brearley (1996), *Public Order Policing: Contemporary Perspectives on Strategy and Tactics*, Leicester: Perpetuity Press.

King, Mike and David Waddington (2004), '"Coping with Disorder"? The Changing Relationship between Police Public Order Strategy and Practice – A Critical Analysis of the Burnley Riot', *Policing and Society* 14(2): 118–37.

Kinney, Monica Yant (2000), 'Beginning in High School, His Causes Included Hunger, Poverty and Prison', *Philadelphia Inquirer*, 13 August: A1.

Kinney, Monica Yant, and Angela Couloumbis (2000), 'Catalyst for Chaos, or Singled out Unfairly?' *Philadelphia Inquirer*, 4 August: A17.

Klein, Naomi (2000) *No Logo*, New York: Picador.

Klein, Naomi (2001), 'The Police Kidnapping of Jaggi Singh', http://organicconsumers,org/corp/quebecreports.cfm.

Klein, Naomi (2002), *Fences and Windows. Dispatches from the Front of the Globalization Debate*, London: Flamingo.

Kraska, Peter B. (1996), 'Enjoying Militarism: Political/Personal Dilemmas in Studying U.S. Paramilitary Units', *Justice Quarterly* 13: 405–29.

Kraska, Peter B. and Victor E. Kaeppler (1997), 'Militarizing American Police: The Rise and Normalization of Paramilitary Units', *Social Problems* 44(1): 1–18.

Kriesi, Hanspeter, Ruud Koopmans, Jan Willem Duyvendak and Mario Giugni (1995), *New Social Movements in Western Europe: A Comparative Analysis*, Minneapolis: University of Minnesota Press.

Le Bon, Gustave (1895), *La psychologie des foules*, Paris: PUF (in English as *The Crowd. A Study of the Popular Mind*, 1897).

Levy, Marc (2000), 'In Ruling, Free Speech Prevails Over Security', *Philadelphia Inquirer*, 30 July: A23.

Lewer, Nick (1995), 'Non-lethal weapons', *Medicine and War* 11: 78–90.

Lichbach, Mark Irving (1987), 'Deterrence or Escalation? The Puzzle of Aggregate Studies of Repression and Dissent', *Journal of Conflict Resolution* 31: 266–97.

Lipsky, Michael (1980), *Street-Level Bureaucracy. Dilemmas of the Individual in Public Services*, New York: Sage.

Lyon, David (2003), *Surveillance after September 11*, Cambridge: Polity Press.

Mahoney, J. (2000), 'Protesters at World Petroleum Meeting Meet High Fences, Lots of Police', *Toronto Globe & Mail*, 12 June.

Makhoul, A. (2002), 'Reaching Past the Barricades: Conflict Resolution at International Summit Events', *Community Stories* (February), Ottawa: Caledonian Institute of Social Policy, www.caledoninst.org.

Manning, Peter K. (2000), 'Policing New Social Spaces', in J.W.E. Sheptycki (ed.), *Issues in Transnational Policing*, London and New York: Routledge, pp. 177–200.

Marantz, Steve (2000), '3 Philly Officers Injured Battling Violent Protests', *Boston Herald*, 2 August: 6.

Marino, G. Carlo (1995), *La repubblica della forza. Mario Scelba e le passioni del suo tempo*, Milan: Angeli.

Marshall, Thomas Humphrey (1950), 'Citizenship and Social Class', in T.H. Marshall and T. Bottomore (eds), *Citizenship and Social Class*, London: Pluto, pp. 3–51.

Martin, Eamon (2002), 'Anti-capitalists Take Canada's Capital', http://hartford-hwp.com/archives/27d/062.html.

Mathiesen, Thomas (2000), 'On Globalization of Control: Towards an Integrated Surveillance System in Europe', in P. Green and A. Rutherford (eds), *Criminal Policy in Transition*, Oxford and Portland, OR: Hart Publishing, pp. 167–92.

Mathiesen, Thomas (2002), 'Expanding the Concept of Terrorism?', in P. Scraton (ed.), *Beyond September 11. An Anthology of Dissent*, London: Pluto Press, pp. 84–93.

Mawby, Rob (2002), *Policing Images: Policing, Communication and Legitimacy*, Cullompton: Willan.

McAdam, Doug (1982), *Political Process and the Development of the Black Insurgency, 1930–1970*, Chicago: University of Chicago Press.

McAdam, Doug (1983), 'Tactical Innovation and the Pace of Insurgency', *American Sociological Review* 48: 735–48.

McAdam, Doug, and Dieter Rucht (1993), 'The Crossnational Diffusion of Movement Ideas', *Annals of the AAPSS* 529: 56–74.

McCarthy, John, Andrew Martin and Clark McPhail (2004), 'The Policing of U.S. University Campus Community Disturbances, 1985–2001', paper presented at the conference 'Policing Political Protest after Seattle', Fiskebäckskil, Sweden, 1–5 May.

McCarthy, John, Clark McPhail, and Jackie Smith (1996), 'Images of Protest: Dimensions of Selection Bias in Media Coverage of Washington Demonstrations, 1982 and 1991', *American Sociological Review* 61(3): 478–99.

McCoy, Craig, and Linda Harris (2000a), 'City Police Knew of Infiltration', *Philadelphia Inquirer*, 8 September: B1.

McCoy, Craig, and Linda Harris (2000b), 'Protesters Trusted Wrong Volunteer', *Philadelphia Inquirer*, 1 October: B1.

McCutcheon, D. (2002), 'Watching World Leaders', *Canadian Security* 12–14 (October): 16.

McLaughlin, Eugene (1992), 'The Democratic Deficit. European Union and the Accountability of the British Police', *British Journal of Criminology* 32(4): 473–87.

McLeod, D., and J. Hertog (1998), 'Social Control and the Mass Media's Role in the Regulation of Protest Groups; The Communicative Acts Perspective', in D. Demers and K. Viswanath (eds), *Mass Media, Social Control, and Social Change*, Ames: Iowa State University Press.

McNally, D. (2001), 'Mass Protest in Quebec City: From Anti-globalization to Anti-capitalism', *New Politics* 8(3): 76–86.

McPhail, Clark, and John D. McCarthy (2005), 'Protest Mobilization, Protest Repression and their Interaction', in C. Davenport, H. Johnston and C. Mueller (eds), *Repression and Mobilization*, Minneapolis: University of Minnesota Press, pp. 3–32.

McPhail, Clark, David Schweingruber and John McCarthy (1998), 'Policing Protest in the United States: 1960–1995', in D. della Porta and H. Reiter (eds), *Policing Protest: The Control of Mass Demonstrations in Western Democracies*, Minneapolis: University of Minnesota Press, pp. 49–69.

Messinger, K. (1968), *The Crime of Punishment*, New York: Viking.

Metress, Eileen K., and Seamus P. Metress (1987), 'The Anatomy of Plastic Bullet Damage and Crowd Control', *International Journal of Health Services* 17: 333–42.

Meyer, David S., and Sidney Tarrow (1998), 'A Movement Society: Contentious Politics for a New Century', in D.S. Meyer and S. Tarrow (eds), *The Social Movement Society: Contentious Politics for a New Century*, Oxford: Rowman and Littlefield, pp. 1–28.

Miethe, Terance, and Hong Lu (2005), *Punishment: A Comparative Historical Perspective*, New York: Cambridge University Press.

Mikkelsen, Flemming (2002), 'Kollektive aktioner og politiske bevægelser i Danmark efter Anden Verdenskrig', in F. Mikkelsen (ed.), *Bevægelser i demokrati. Foreninger og kollektive aktioner i Danmark*, Aarhus: Aarhus Universitetsforlag, pp. 45–80.

Miller, Gary J. [1992] (1996), *Hierarkins ekonomi. Att styra effektiva organisationer*, Stockholm: SNS Förlag.

Montgomery, David (2000a), 'Protests End With Voluntary Arrests', *Washington Post*, 18 April: A1.

Montgomery, David (2000b), 'Last Protesters leave Jail for $5', *Washington Post*, 22 April: B1.

Montgomery, David, and Arthur Santana (2000), 'After Seattle, Protest Reborn; Demonstrators and Police Prepare for World Bank, IMF Meetings Here', *Washington Post*, 2 April: A1.

Moore, Will H. (1998), 'Repression and Dissent: Substitution, Context and Timing', *American Journal of Political Science* 42: 851–73.

Morgan, Jane (1987), *Conflict and Order. The Police and Labour Disputes in England and Wales (1900–1939)*, Oxford: Clarendon Press.

Morin, Gerald M. (2000), 'Personal Reflections on the Ill-Fated First APEC Inquiry', in W. Pue (ed.), *Pepper in Our Eyes: The APEC Affair*, Vancouver: UBC Press, pp. 159–70.

Morton, Gary (2001), 'Dancing with Teargas in Our Eyes', http://www.nadir.org/nadir/initiativ/agp/a20/gary.htm.

Muir, William Kerr Jr. (1979), *Police: Streetcorner Politicians*, Chicago and London: University of Chicago Press.

Muylle, Koen (1998), 'Angry Farmers and Passive Policemen: Private Conduct and the Free Movement of Goods', *European Law Review* 23: 467–74.

Nadelmann, Ethan A. (1993), *Cops Across Borders. The Internationalization of US Law Enforcement*, University Park: Pennsylvania State University Press.

National Union of Public and General Employees (2000), 'Police Turn on OAS Protesters in Windsor', http://www.nupge.ca/news_2000/News%20June/n05jn00 c.htm.

Neale, Jonathan (2002), *You Are G8, We Are 6 Billion*, London: Vision Paperbacks.

News Tribune (1999), 'Seattle Police Use Tear Gas Against World Trade Organization Protesters', 1 December.

Newton, Christopher (2000), 'Homeless Marchers Block Traffic in GOP Convention Protest', *Associated Press State and Local Wire*, 31 July.

Noakes, John (2001a), 'Beyond Negotiated Management: Selective Incapacitation and the Police Response to Recent Protests in the United States', paper presented at the Annual Meeting of the American Sociological Association, Anaheim, CA.

Noakes, John (2001b), 'From Water Cannons to Rubber Bullets: How the Policing of Protest has Changed and What it Means', *The Long Term View* 5(2): 85–94.

Noakes, John, Brian Klocke and Patrick Gillham (2005), 'Whose Streets? Police and Protesters Struggle over Space in Washington, DC, 29–30 September, 2001', *Policing and Society* 15(3): 235–54.

Noakes, John, and Karin Wilkins (2002), 'Shifting Frames of the Palestinian Movement', *Media, Culture, and Society* 42: 1–23.

Oliver, Pam, and Daniel J. Myers (1999), 'How Events Enter the Public Sphere: Conflict, Location, and Sponsorship in Local Newspaper Coverage of Public Events', *American Journal of Sociology* 105(1): 38–87.

Olson, Mancur (1965), *The Logic of Collective Action. Public Goods and the Theory of Groups*, Cambridge, MA: Harvard University Press.

O'Neill, Kevin Francis (1999), 'Disentangling the Law of Public Protest', *Loyola Law Review* 45: 411–526.

Opp, Karl-Dieter, and Wolfgang Roehl (1990), 'Repression, Micromobilization, and Political Protest', *Social Forces* 69: 521–47.

O'Reilly, Kenneth (1989), *Racial Matters*, New York: The Free Press.

Orpheus (2002), 'Confronting the Global Plunderers', http://rwor.org/a/v24/1151-1160/1156/g8_canada.htm.

Oskarsson, Mikael (2002), Dialog med förbehåll. Polisens kontaktgrupp, demonstrationsnätverken och det tragiska dilemmat i Göteborg', in M. Björk and A. Peterson (eds), *Vid politikens yttersta gräns: Perspektiv på EC-toppmötet i Göteborg 2001*, Stockholm: Brutus Östlings Bokförlag Symposion, pp. 81–113.

Ostrom, Elinor (1990), *Governing the Commons: The Evolution of Institutions for Collective Action*, Cambridge: Cambridge University Press.

Ottawa Police Service (2002a), *G20 Interim Report*, Ottawa: OPS.

Ottawa Police Service (2002b), *An Agenda for Excellence for Major Events: Police and Community Challenges*, Ottawa: OPS.

Ottawa Police Service (2002c), *G8 Summit Conference, Related Demonstrations National Capital Region, Public Order Unit Operational Plan* (draft), Ottawa: OPS (Restricted Access).

Palidda, Salvatore (2001), 'L'Italie saisie par la tentation auteurstaire', *Le Monde Diplomatique* (October): 14–15.

Parsmo, Jonas (2002), 'Representativa representationer? Om utomparlamentariska aktörers närvaro i pressens skildring av Göteborgsmötet', in M. Björk and A. Peterson (eds), *Vid politikens yttersta gräns: Perspektiv på EC-toppmötet I Göteborgg 2001*, Stockholm: Brutus Östlings Bokförlag Symposion.

Peers, Steve (2000), *EU Justice and Home Affairs Law*, London: Longman.

Peers, Steve (2001), 'Democratic Control by the European Parliament in Relation to Control of Justice and Home Affairs', *Collegium* 22 (*Integrated Security in Europe, A Democratic Perspective*, 14–17 November): 78–83.

Pepino, Livio (2001), 'Obiettivo. Genova e il G8: I fatti, le istituzioni, la giustizia', *Quale Giustizia* 5: 881–915.

Peterson, Abby (1997), *Neo-Sectarianism and Rainbow Coalitions. Youth and the Drama of Immigration in Contemporary Sweden*, Aldershot: Ashgate.

Peterson, Abby (2001), *Contemporary Political Protest: Essays on Political Militancy*, Aldershot and Brookfield, VT: Ashgate.

Peterson, Abby (2002) 'Toppmötets regnbågskoalitioner: experiment i demokratiska samtal', in M. Björk and A. Peterson (eds), *Vid politikens yttersta gräns: Perspektiv på EC-toppmötet I Göteborgg 2001*, Stockholm: Brutus Östlings Bokförlag Symposion, pp. 55–80.

Peterson, Abby (2003a), 'Contentious Politics and Transnational Summits: Reconnaissance Battles in the Frontier Land', paper prepared for presentation at the Congress of the European Sociological Association, Murcia, Spain, 23–27 September.

Peterson, Abby (2003b), 'A Textbook Police Campaign: The European Union Summit in Copenhagen December 2002', unpublished manuscript, Department of Sociology, Gothenburg University.

Peterson, Abby, and Mikael Oskarsson (2002), 'Öppenhet och övervakning: Om sammandrabbningar mellan polis och demonstranter under EU-toppmötet i Göteborg 2001', in M. Björk and A. Peterson (eds), *Vid politikens yttersta gräns: Perspektiv på EC-toppmötet I Göteborg 2001*, Stockholm: Brutus Östlings Bokförlag Symposion, pp. 114–43.

Petrella, R. (2001), 'Criminaliser la contestation', *Le monde diplomatique* (August): 8.

Pianta, Mario (2002), 'Parallel Summits: an Update', in H.K. Anheier, M. Glasius and M. Kaldor (eds), *Global Civil Society*, Oxford: Oxford University Press, pp. 371–7.

Poe, Steven C., and C. Neal Tate (1994), 'Repression of Human Rights to Personal Integrity in the 1980s: A Global Analysis', *American Political Science Review* 88: 853–72.

Poe, Steven C., C. Neal Tate and Linda Camp Keith (1999), 'Repression of the Human Rights to Personal Integrity Revised: A Global Cross-national Study Covering the Years 1976–1993', *International Study Quarterly* 43: 291–313.

Pony Express (2002), 'The Summit Revisited', *Pony Express: The RCMP's National Magazine* (September/October): 14–16.

Postman, David, Jack Broom and Warren King (1999), 'Clashes, Protests Wrack WTO', *Seattle Times*, 30 November: A1.

Postman, David, Mark Rahner and Eric Sorenson (1999), 'Peace Settles Over Downtown—Negotiations Calm Protesters; Retailers Await Holiday Shoppers', *Seattle Times*, 3 December: A1.

Powers, Richard Gid (1987), *Secrecy and Power*, New York: Free Press.

President's Commission on Law Enforcement and Administration (1967), *The Challenge of Crime in a Free Society*, Washington, DC: US Government Printing Office.

Rebick, Judy (2000), 'Police Repression in Windsor', http://www.cbc.ca/news/viewpoint/columns/rebick/rebick00060.

Rebick, Judy (2001a), 'Quebec City: Policing the People', http://members.optushome.com.au/thesquiz/qcrebick.htm.

Rebick, Judy (2001b), 'Quebec: Day One', http://www.organicconsumers.org/corp/quebecreports.cfm.

Rebick, Judy (2001c), 'It Won't End in Quebec City', http://www.labournet.net/world/104/quebec6.html.

Reiner, Robert (2000), *The Politics of the Police*, Oxford: Oxford University Press.

Reiter, Herbert (1992), *Politisches Asyl im 19. Jahrhundert. Die deutschen politischen Flüchtlinge des Vormärz und der Revolution von 1848/49 in Europa und den USA*, Berlin: Duncker & Humblot.

Richman, Bradford (2001), Personal interview with Special Assistant to the Philadelphia, Chief of Police, 31 May.

Rikspolisstyrelsens utvärdering av EU-kommenderingen i Göteborg år 2001, RPS.

Risingtide (2000), 'World Petroleum Congress 2000 – Activist Update', http://www.risingtide.nl/greenpepper/climate/wpc.html.

Risse, Thomas (2003), 'An Emerging European Public Sphere? Theoretical Clarifications and Empirical Indicators', paper presented to the Annual Meeting of the European Union Studies Association (EUSA), Nashville, TN, 27–30 March.

Routledge, Paul (1997), 'Swarms and Packs', in S. Pile and M. Keith (eds), *Geographies of Resistance*, London: Routledge, pp. 68–86.

Royal Canadian Mounted Police (2001), *Commissioner's Response to the Interim Report Prepared by the Commission for Public Complaints against the RCMP (CPC)*, Ottawa: RCMP.

Rubinstein, Jonathan (1980), 'Cops' Rules', in R.J. Landman (ed.), *Police Behavior*, New York: Oxford University Press.

Rucht, Dieter (2002), 'The EU as Target of Political Mobilization: Is There a Europeanization of Conflict?', in R. Balme, D. Chabanet and R. Wright (eds), *L'action collective en Europe*, Paris: Presses de Sciences Po, pp. 163–94.

Ruzza, Carlo (2004), *Europe and Civil Society: Movement Coalitions and European Governance*, Manchester: Manchester University Press.

Scher, Abby (2001), 'The Crackdown on Dissent', *The Nation* 272 (5 February): 23–6.

Schweingruber, David (2000), 'Mob Sociology and Escalated Force: Sociology's Contribution to Repressive Police Tactics', *Sociological Quarterly* 41: 371–89.

Scotton, G. (2002), 'WPC Policing Blueprint Sets Tone for G-8 Plans', http://www.geocities.com/ericsquire/articles/calher050652.htm.

Seattle Police Department (2000), 'After Action Report, World Trade Organization Ministerial Conference, 29 November–3 December 1999', www.cityofseattle.net/spd/SPDMainsite/wto/spdwtoaar.htm.

Sheptycki, James W.E. (1994), 'Law Enforcement, Justice and Democracy in the Transnational Arena. Reflections on the War on Drugs', *International Journal of the Sociology of Law* 24(1): 61–75.

Sheptycki, James W.E. (1995), 'Transnational Policing and the Makings of a Postmodern State', *British Journal of Criminology* 35(4): 613–35.

Sheptycki, James W.E. (1998), 'The Global Cop Cometh. Reflections on Transnationalization, Knowledge Work and Policing Subculture', *British Journal of Sociology* 49(1): 57–74.

Sheptycki, James W.E. (2000), 'Surveillance, Closed Circuit Television and Social Control', *Policing and Society* 9(4): 429–34.

Sheptycki, James W.E. (2002), *In Search of Transnational Policing. Towards a Sociology of Global Policing*, Aldershot: Ashgate.

Sheptycki, James W.E. (2005), 'Policing Protest When Politics Go Global. Comparing Public Order Policing in Canada and Bolivia', *Policing and Society* 15(3): 327–52.

Shichor, David (1997), 'Three Strikes as Public Policy: The Convergence of the New Penology and the McDonaldization of Punishment', *Crime and Delinquency* 43: 470–92.

Simon, Jonathan (1993), *Poor Discipline*, Chicago: University of Chicago Press.

Skolnick, Jerome H. (1966), *Justice without Trial: Law Enforcement in Democratic Society*, New York: John Wiley and Sons.

Skolnick, Jerome H. [1969] (2002), *The Politics of Protest: Violent Aspects of Protest and Confrontation. A Staff Report to The National Commission on the Causes and Prevention of Violence*, Honolulu: University Press of the Pacific.

Skolnick, Jerome H. and James Fyfe (1993), *Above the Law: Police and the Excessive Use of Force*, New York: Free Press.

Slobodzian, Joseph (2001), 'Puppet Factory, Pair Suing Phila. in Arrest', *Philadelphia Inquirer*, 23 January: B4.

Smith, Jackie (2001), 'Globalizing Resistance: The Battle of Seattle and the Future of Social Movements', *Mobilization* 6: 1–20.

Stark, Rodney (1972), *Police Riots: Collective Violence and Law Enforcement*, Belmont: University of California Press.

Starr, Barbara (1993), 'Non-Lethal Weapon Puzzle for US Army', *International Defense Review* 26(4): 319–20.

Sturm, Michael and Christoph Ellinghaus (2002), 'Polizeiliche Strategien zwischen Imagepflege und Gewalt', in *Bürgerrechte und Polizei/CILIP* 72: 23–30.

Sund, Steven (2001), Personal interview with Lieutenant in Washington D.C. Metropolitan Police Department's Special Operations Division, 3 July.

Sztompka, Piotr (1999), *Trust: A Sociological Theory*, Cambridge: Cambridge University Press.

Tarrow, Sidney (1998), *Power in Movement: Social Movements, Collective Action and Politics*, New York: Cambridge University Press.

Thomas, Janet (2000), *The Battle in Seattle: The Story Behind the WTO Demonstrations*, Golden, CO: Fulcrum Publishers.

Tilly, Charles (1986), *The Contentious French*, Cambridge, MA: Belknap Press of Harvard University Press.

Tilly, Charles (2000), 'Spaces of Contention', *Mobilization* 5(2): 135–59.

Torrance, Judy (1986), *Public Violence in Canada, 1867–1982*, Montreal: McGill-Queen's University Press.

Twomey, Patrick (1999), 'Constructing a Secure Space: The Area of Freedom, Security and Justice', in D. O'Keefe and P. Twomey (eds), *Legal Issues of the Amsterdam Treaty*, Oxford and Portland, OR: Hart Publishing, pp. 351–74.

Uysal, Ayshen (2005), 'Organisation du maintien de l'ordre et répression policière en Turquie', in D. della Porta and O. Fillieule (eds), *Maintien de l'ordre et police des foules*, Paris: Presses de Sciences Po, pp. 257–79.

Virga, Pietro (1954), *La potestà di polizia*, Milan: Giuffrè.

Vitale, Alex (2005), 'From Negotiated Management to Command and Control: How the New York City Police Department Polices Protest', *Policing and Society* 15(3): 283–304.

Vittrup, Kai (2002a), *Strategi*, Copenhagen: Københavns Politi.

Vittrup, Kai (2002b), *Operation*, Copenhagen: Københavns Politi.

von Hirsch, Andrew (1993), *Censure and Sanctions*, Oxford: Clarendon Press.

Waddington, David (1992), *Contemporary Issues in Public Disorder: A Comparative and Historical Approach*, London: Routledge.

Waddington, David (1996), 'Key Issues and Controversies', in C. Critcher and D. Waddington (eds), *Policing Public Order: Theoretical and Practical Issues*, Aldershot: Avebury.

Waddington, David, and Chas Critcher (2000), 'Policing Pit Closures 1984–1992', in R. Bessel and C. Emsley (eds), *Patterns of Provocation: Police and Public Disorder*, Oxford: Berghahn Books, pp. 99–120.

Waddington, David, Karen Jones and Chas Critcher (1989), *Flashpoints: Studies in Public Disorder*, London: Routledge.

Waddington, P.A.J. (1991), *The Strong Arm of the Law: Armed and Public Order Policing*, Oxford: Oxford University Press.

Waddington, P.A.J. (1994), *Liberty and Order: Public Order Policing in a Capital City*, London: UCL Press.

Waddington, P.A.J. (1998), 'Controlling Protest in Contemporary Historical and Comparative Perspective', in D. della Porta and H. Reiter (eds), *Policing Protest: The Control of Mass Demonstrations in Western Democracies*, Minneapolis: University of Minnesota Press, pp. 117–40.

Waddington, P.A.J. (1999a), 'Armed and Unarmed Policing', in R.I. Mawby (ed.), *Policing Across the World*, London: UCL Press, pp. 151–66.

Waddington, P.A.J. (1999b), *Policing Citizens: Authority and Rights*, London: UCL Press.

Waddington, P.A.J. (2003), 'Policing Public Order and Political Contention', in T. Newburn (ed.), *Handbook of Policing*, Cullompton: Willan, pp. 394–421.

Wagner, Arlo (2000), 'City Drops Charges, IMF Protesters Walk', *Washington Times*, 9 June: C1.

Wahlström, Mattias (2003a), 'Tillit och föreställningar: Kommunikation mellan aktivister och polis, ur ett aktivistperspektiv', unpublished paper, University of Gothenburg, Department of Sociology.

Wahlström, Mattias (2003b), 'Trust and Performance: Communication between Police and Protesters from an Activist Perspective', paper prepared for presentation at the Congress of the European Sociological Association, Murcia, Spain, 23–27 September.

Wahlström, Mattias (2004), 'How to Talk Away Violence: Communication Between Police and Protesters in Copenhagen', *Il Dubbio – rivista transnazionale di analisi politica e sociale*, 5(2): 66–81.

Wahlström, Mattias, and Abby Peterson (2005), 'Between the State and the Market: The Political struggle between the Animal Rights Movement and the Swedish

Fur Industry', in M. Boström, A. Føllesdal, M. Klintman, M. Micheletti and M.P. Sørcnscn (cds), *Political Consumerism: Its Motivations, Power, and Conditions in the Nordic Countries and Elsewhere. Proceedings from the 2nd International Seminar on Political Consumerism, Oslo August 26–29, 2004*, Copenhagen: Nordisk Ministerråd, pp. 225–254, http://www.norden.org/pub/velfaerd/konsument/sk/TN2005517.pdf.

Walker, Neil (2003a), 'The Pattern of Transnational Policing', in T. Newburn (ed.), *Handbook of Policing*, Uffculme: Willan, pp. 111–35.

Walker, Neil (2003b), 'Freedom, Security and Justice', in B. de Witte (ed.), *Ten Reflections on the Constitutional Treaty for Europe*, Fiesole: European University Institute, pp. 163–86.

Walker, Neil (ed.) (2004), *Europe's Area of Freedom, Security, and Justice*, Oxford and New York: Oxford University Press.

Wedge, Dave (2004), 'Tragedy at Fenway', *Boston Herald*, 27 October: 5.

Weibull, L., and L. Nilsson (2002), 'EU-toppmötet i svensk opinion', in M. Björk and A. Peterson (eds), *Vid politikens yttersta gräns*, Stockholm: Symposion, pp. 176–88.

Welch, Michael (1996), 'Critical Criminology, Social Control, and the Alternative View of Corrections', in Jeffrey Ross (ed.), *Cutting the Edge: Current Perspectives in Radical/Critical Criminology and Criminal Justice*, Westport, CT: Preager, pp. 107–21.

Whitman, Bradford (2001), Personal interview with special assistant to the Philadelphia police commissioner, 31 May.

Wilson, James Q. (1975), *Thinking About Crime*, New York: Basic Books.

Winter, Martin (1998a), 'Police Philosophy and Protest Policing in the Federal Republic of Germany (1960–1990)', in D. della Porta and H. Reiter (eds), *Policing Protest: The Control of Mass Demonstrations in Western Democracies*, Minneapolis: University of Minnesota Press, pp. 188–212.

Winter, Martin (1998b), *Politikum Polizei. Macht und Funktion der Polizei in der Bundesrepublik Deutschland*, Münster: LIT.

Wisler, Dominique, and Hanspeter Kriesi (1998), 'Public Order, Protest Cycles, and Political Process: Two Swiss Cities Compared', in D. della Porta and H. Reiter (eds), *Policing Protest: The Control of Mass Demonstrations in Western Democracies*, Minneapolis: University of Minnesota Press, pp. 91–116.

Wisler, Dominique, and Marco Tackenberg (2000), 'The Role of the Police: Image or Reality?', in R. Bessel and C. Emsley (eds), *Patterns of Provocation: Police and Public Disorder*, Oxford: Berghahn, pp. 121–42.

Witness Group (2002), *Report and Recommendations on the Policing of G-8 Events in Ottawa*, Ottawa: Witness Group.

Wright, Alan (2002), *Policing: An Introduction to Concepts and Practice*, Cullompton: Willan.

Yeates, Nicola (2001), *Globalization and Social Policy*, London: Sage.

Zinola, Marcello (2003), *Ripensare la polizia: ci siamo scoperti diversi da come pensavamo di essere*, Genoa: Frilli.

Zollman, Ted M., Robert M. Bragg and Devin Harrison (2000), 'Clinical Effects of Oleoresin Capsicum (Pepper Spray) on the Human Cornea and Conjunctiva', *Ophthalmology* 107(12): 2186–9.

Index